A New Earth

"Awake! Awake Jerusalem! O lovely Emanation of Albion"
Plate 97 from Blake's *Jerusalem*; reproduced by Courtesy of the
Trustees of the British Museum.

A New Earth

The Labor of Language in *Pearl*,
Herbert's *Temple*, and
Blake's *Jerusalem*

Douglas Thorpe

The Catholic University of America Press
Washington, D.C.

Copyright © 1991
The Catholic University of America Press
All rights reserved
Printed in the United States of America

The paper used in this publication meets the minimum requirements
of American National Standards for Information Science—Permanence of Paper
for Printed Library materials, ANSI Z39.48-1984.
∞

Library of Congress Cataloging-in-Publication Data
Thorpe, Douglas, 1953–
  A new earth : the labor of language in *Pearl*, Herbert's *Temple*,
and Blake's *Jerusalem* / by Douglas Thorpe.
    p. cm.
  Includes bibliographical references.
    1. Christian poetry, English—History and criticism. 2. Blake,
William, 1757–1827. Jerusalem. 3. Herbert, George, 1593–1633.
Temple. 4. Pearl (Middle English poem) 5. Figures of speech.
6. Metaphor. 1. Title.
PR508.C65T48 1990
821.009'382—dc29
ISBN 0-8132-0728-2 (alk. paper)
90-31201

And I saw a new heaven and a new earth: for the first heaven and the first earth were passed away; and there was no more sea.

And I John saw the holy city, New Jerusalem, coming down from God out of heaven, prepared as a bride adorned for her husband.

And I heard a great voice out of heaven saying, Behold, the tabernacle of God is with men, and he will dwell with them, and they shall be his people, and God himself shall be with them, and be their God.

Rev. 21:1–3

Contents

Preface   ix

1. Introduction   1

2. *Pearl*
   Lessons in Interpretive Construction   27

3. "Delight into Sacrifice"
   Resting in George Herbert's *Temple*   73

4. Razing *Jerusalem*
   Blake's Word as World   123

5. Conclusion
   Toward the End of the Image   177

6. Epilogue   201

   Bibliography   205
   Index   215

Preface

This is a work whose title has changed a number of times over the past six years as it went from dissertation to book, changes reflected in content—and, frankly, in me. Yet the book remains at its core what it always was: a study of the language of three of England's greatest religious poets, seen from the perspective of both theological and linguistic concerns. What has changed is the way I have viewed those overlapping concerns, a change most clearly reflected in the opening and closing chapters and reflected in the title. I now see this issue of language, and of metaphor in particular, as closely woven into larger concerns of our culture, and especially our ongoing dualism (body-spirit), and the related question of human laboring on the planet. These "bookend" chapters can be read independently of the three central chapters and will, I hope, be of interest to a variety of readers regardless of their knowledge of, or interest in, these poets. The conclusion in particular carries my argument beyond poetry and into these other matters.

It is also true, however, that these end pieces provide support and confirmation (I hope) of my analysis of the poets. The book is meant to be of a piece, and the argument should be clearly set forth in each chapter, however much the poets may differ from each other.

A glance through the Bibliography should give the reader a notion as to where my intellectual debts lie. Particular and more personal thanks must go to Hazard Adams and Miceal Vaughan at the University of Washington for work on the original version. Equal thanks go to more recent readers of the manuscript—James Dougherty, Thomas J. J. Altizer, Jon A. Quitslund, and Stephen Happel—and to David J. McGonagle, director at The

Catholic University of America Press. The staffs at St. Mary's College (Notre Dame) and at Seattle Pacific University (especially Lisa Harlow and Elizabeth Lopez) persevered and produced. Encouragement and patience were unfailing from family and from friends, especially (at St. Mary's) Max Westler, Tom Bonnell, and Paula Carlson, and (at Seattle Pacific), Rob Snyder and Tom Trzyna.

Thanks, too, to the Association for Religion and Intellectual Life, and to Nancy Malone and Denise Levertov in particular, for the Coolidge Fellowship in Cambridge, Massachusetts. Here indeed spirit found flesh, community.

A final word of appreciation to the family at the Honey Bear Bakery, where revisions were talked through and chewed over.

A portion of Chapter 2 originally appeared in *Studies in English Literature* and a part of the Conclusion in *Parabola*.

The book is dedicated to Judy: "And though their love was hangin' on a limb / She taught him how to dance. . . ."

A New Earth

"Thus wept they in Beulah over the Four Regions of Albion"
Plate 25 from Blake's *Jerusalem*; reproduced by Courtesy of the Trustees of the British Museum.

I
Introduction

For we are labourers together with God: ye are God's husbandry, ye are God's building. According to the Grace of God which is given unto me, as a wise master-builder, I have laid the foundation, and another buildeth thereon. But let every man take heed how he buildeth thereon.

1 Cor. 3:9–10

I

"Split asunder since birth," Octavio Paz writes, man "is reconciled with himself when he becomes an image, when he becomes another."[1] But it is not just the image that makes this possible, Paz concludes, but image working in metaphor, the basis for this analysis of three of the greatest religious poets in English literature. These three begin with the same hypothesis, that we are indeed "split asunder"; each, in his way, finds in the image, and more particularly in metaphor (pearl, temple, city), the means to reconcile us with ourselves, to lead us out in order to bring us home. Each finds in image "the bridge that desire places between man and reality." In metaphor, each reveals how "desire becomes active: it does not compare or show similarities but it reveals—and further, it causes—the ultimate identity of objects that seemed irreducible to us." Thus, Paz claims, "stars, shoes, tears . . . trees . . . is all an immense family, all is in mutual communication and is unceasingly transformed."[2] Or, as Blake similarly concludes, in metaphor we see "All Human Forms identified even Tree Metal Earth & Stone. . . ."[3]

1. In *The Bow and the Lyre*, trans. Ruth L. C. Simms (Austin: University of Texas Press, 1973), p. 97.
2. Paz, *Bow and the Lyre*, p. 98.
3. *The Complete Poetry and Prose of William Blake*, rev. ed., ed. David V. Erd-

In this study of these three—the *Pearl*-Poet, Herbert, and Blake—I wish to show how each grounds his own poetics in an understanding of figurative language drawn from the New Testament parables: the language of Jesus, who brought to fruition a radically new understanding of "building the Kingdom."[4] I hope to show both a continuity and a development in this poetics, as each poet wrestles with universal concerns of salvation in the midst of different historical circumstances.

I hope, however, that this study does more than provide some insights into these three religious poets, as valuable as that in itself might be. Instead, I want to use these writers as a means of exploring the relationship between language and the world, between body and spirit, and, as a related issue, the nature of what we call labor. Like Blake, who sees his own work as a building enterprise, both the *Pearl*-Poet and Herbert are profoundly conscious of poetry as a visible, even tangible object; of the poem as its own singular entity, containing its own formal

---

man (Berkeley and Los Angeles: University of California Press, 1982), p. 258. This edition is hereafter cited in the text as E.

4. Throughout this text I shall be using the term *metaphorical language* along with the term *symbol* in order to point to different, yet closely associated aspects of figurative language. Thus, the phrase "kingdom of heaven" is metaphorical, wherein, as Paul Ricoeur comments, the literal interpretation (kingdom) "self-destructs in a significant contradiction." *Interpretation Theory: Discourse and the Surplus of Meaning* (Fort Worth: Texas Christian Press, 1976), p. 50. Yet, it is also symbolic (as "kingdom") whether one claims that such a word or phrase simply "points to" an otherwise unknowable referent, as in the Augustinian conception of "sign," or one claims that it either partly or wholly "embodies" that referent, as in many variations in the English and German Romantics; or finally, whether one claims that there is no referent for it to embody or to point to (as Paul de Man asserts in his argument against the symbol). For more detailed studies of the complex history of the literary symbol, see Tzvetan Todorov, *Theories of the Symbol* (Ithaca, N.Y.: Cornell University Press, 1982), and Hazard Adams, *Philosophy of the Literary Symbolic* (Tallahassee: University Presses of Florida, 1983). De Man's well known argument concerning allegory and symbol is perhaps still best represented in his essay "The Rhetoric of Temporality," in *Blindness and Insight*, rev. ed. (Minneapolis: University of Minnesota Press, 1983), pp. 187–228. For a contemporary religious (Roman Catholic) interpretation of symbol as the "expression" or the "self-realization of a being in the other" (as Jesus, for example, is the "symbol" of God), see Karl Rahner, "The Theology of the Symbol," and "Poetry and the Christian," in *Theological Investigations IV: More Recent Writings* (New York: Seabury Press, 1974, 1976), pp. 221–52, 357–67.

Introduction 3

structure. And yet each as a religious poet is well aware that the body is both more and less than meets the eye. As such, each of these poets struggles with the meaning embodied within the physical form, not just in a book or a poem but beyond that in the concrete world.

I am also claiming that this concern has its underpinnings in the language and vision of Jesus, as these have come down to us in the Gospels, and in particular in the parables, a vision that actually subverts what we have come to think of as the vision and language of Christianity, which has tended to affirm a spirit-mind-body split, which roughly corresponds to political and economic hierarchies: church-state-individual. Just as spirit and mind dominate over the body in traditional Christian thought, church and state dominate over the individual, who is, not coincidentally, often the woman or man at the economic bottom left to do the physical labor.

In Susan Handelman's study of Rabbinic methods of interpretation, she notes that unlike Hebrew, in which *davar* means both "word" and "thing," affirming the essential reality of language, in both Plato and Aristotle "the realm of words is not the realm of meaning and truth. . . . Like Plato, Aristotle considers the central act of knowing a movement *beyond* discourse, beyond talking."[5] Handelman traces the Christian borrowing of Greek thought, in particular this severing of Being (*ousia*) from language, letter from spirit, through Philo, Origen, and especially Augustine, who ridicules the Jews' adherence to signs and their apparent interpretive failure to see through signs. Handelman notes, however, "Jews adhere to signs not because they take the sign for the thing as *res* in the Greek philosophical sense, but because there is no primal division between word and thing in Jewish thought" (117).

Handelman claims that recently theorists have attempted to overcome this tendency toward dualism, primarily through a re-

---

5. Susan Handelman, *The Slayers of Moses: The Emergence of Rabbinic Interpretation in Modern Literary Theory* (Albany: State University of New York Press, 1982), p. 8.

turn to metaphor, citing in particular Ricoeur, Gadamer, and Derrida. She concludes that metaphor does not discard the particular, the letter, on the way to the universal; instead, "[i]n metaphor, to see the similar is to appreciate the 'same' within and in spite of 'difference'. . . . Metaphor exists within the tension of identity and difference, and metaphorical resemblance is at bottom a unity of identity and difference."[6]

Language itself is a body, a world. I want, through this analysis, to look at how such poets explore the nature of language even as they struggle to extricate themselves from this political, theological, and psychological dualism, or fall, into which they and we were born. The primary tool in their labor is metaphor, a poetic device made possible only because of our consciousness of our separation from others but also affirming the imaginative overcoming of this split—an "apocalypse," I would further suggest, rooted firmly in the interrelationship between body and mind. If our understanding of rationality since Descartes, if not since Plato, reinforces the split between mind, body and spirit, metaphor should remind us that meaning is primordially rooted in the body.[7] At the same time, although dismissed as "fictive" or illogical by the same rationalists who dismiss the bodily, metaphor is the imaginative tool that lifts the individual out of a particular perspective, making possible the recognition of a unity between apparently disparate entities. Metaphor, then, affirms the body and yet simultaneously redefines it by imaginatively connecting separate entities into a single unified whole. Metaphor creates a world where men and women are roses and cities, where

---

6. Handelman, *Slayers of Moses*, p. 23. Later Handelman will qualify these comments, claiming that metaphor is a "Christian" mode of figuring (unlike metonomy, which she associates with Judaism).

7. See especially Mark Johnson's *The Body in the Mind: The Bodily Basis of Meaning, Imagination and Reason* (Chicago: University of Chicago Press, 1987), p. xxxvi–xxxvii: "My epigram for this undertaking is 'putting the body back into the mind.' Imaginative projection is a principle means by which the body (i.e. physical experience and its structures) works its way up into the mind (i.e. mental operations)." From a different perspective, see Morris Berman's *Coming To Our Senses: Body and Spirit in the Hidden History of the West* (New York: Simon and Schuster, 1989).

Introduction 5

wine is blood and bread is body. Metaphor, the poet's spice, is the secret ingredient transforming food for the body into food for the soul—which is another name for the body of Christ.

If religious poets have traditionally been understood to seek to express the inexpressible, I would suggest here by way of preface that these poets reveal that whatever we know of the "ineffable" is known precisely in our own labor, which is inevitably rooted in a concrete here and now. Further, our true labor, these works indicate paradoxically, is a giving up, a letting go, a dying to oneself. All that we call work should be a metaphor for this ongoing, eternal labor of sacrificial love, modeled on the labor of Christ. It is, then, perhaps "a voyage into the interior, but it is a voyage which culminates in a loss of our interior, a loss reversing every manifest or established center of our interior to make possible the advent of a wholly new but totally immediate world."[8] It becomes "total" through revelatory labor, of which art is a paradigm, itself based on the ultimate Christian paradigm of sacrificial action, the Eucharist. Fundamental to this act is a "radically new integration of mind and matter, of body and soul, as body or matter finally becomes indistinguishable from the center and the depths of mind and consciousness." Altizer continues, following the path laid down by D. G. Leahy's study of the Mass:

> Accordingly, a real presence that once was real in the moment of consecration and thereafter now becomes real in a cosmic and universal epiphany. That epiphany heralds the termination of history itself, thereby inaugurating a new world, a world realizing the "eucharistic essence of existence itself."[9]

Existence is eucharist: the perpetual action of creation, which we repeat in our labors, is simultaneously thanksgiving and sacrifice. These are eternally one, the light and dark, receiving and giving up.

---

8. Thomas J. J. Altizer, *Total Presence: The Language of Jesus and the Language of Today* (New York: Seabury Press, 1980), p. 106.
9. *History as Apocalypse* (Albany: State University of New York Press, 1985), pp. 245–46.

Leahy concludes: "What is in fact happening in essence is the transcendental repetition of the creation itself. . . . Everything now comes to exist actually in the form of the body itself."

* * *

In the beginning, the story goes, was the Fall, known to us now as a creation of self-consciousness in which humans are apparently the only strangers in the world. With this creation comes the necessity of painful labor for both woman and man: "I will greatly multiply thy sorrow and thy conception; in sorrow thou shalt bring forth children . . . cursed is the ground for thy sake; in sorrow shalt thou eat of it all the days of thy life. . . . In the sweat of thy face shalt thou eat bread . . ." (Genesis 3:16–19). Yet with the necessity of labor comes the possibility of salvation, for by means of labor we continually re-conceive the world. Labor forges our historical links to this world and makes possible our subsequent perception that the transformed world is not other at all but us.

The myth of Babel represents the parody of such labor: all of the attempts to climb out of this world into another through our own building fail because that other world will always and invariably be a version of this world, only somehow more precious because of its materials (streets of gold, gates of pearl). How, after all, do we conceive heaven except through image? The building of Babel is an interpretive failure, a misunderstanding of figure, and so, finally, of the point of human labor and life. Babel suggests that what we have on earth is not enough, but it does so because it misunderstands what it is we have. And it misunderstands because it fails to grasp the point of metaphor, which teaches that labor itself is truly, as Blake said, imaginative creation. The builders of Babel project a kingdom somewhere far above; the builders in metaphor (these poets at least) locate kingdom nowhere but in the sacrificial activity of labor itself: work founded on the way and love of the cross.

Labor's function, the poets suggest, is truly to build this kingdom, the "new earth," recognizing that this means, paradoxically, to build what is already here but appears absent—the presence of God—by destroying what appears to be here but is not: our sense of separateness, our inherent loneliness in these bodies. This is what we offer up, as though upon an altar.

Our work, then, is not to make God immanent, but to open ourselves to what already is. Labor is both the way and the end of building, just as "building" carries within itself both verb and noun. The point of building is the "radical reversal" of consciousness that Altizer describes: "it is not that the old creation must literally cease to be if the new creation is to be real, but rather that everything which is manifest and actual as world must perish if a truly and fully new actuality of the world is to be realized. . . . To evoke apocalyptically the presence of the new is to shatter and reverse the presence and manifestation of the old."[10]

Once realized, nothing at all stands between self and God. Work goes on as world goes on, but who is it now that works—and on what? The artist reveals that there is finally no distinction between dancer and dance, between weaver and cloth, between farmer and land. She is that land in a very real (if metaphorical) sense. What we labor over is our own body writ large: the body of Christ.

* * *

In an essay on the Buddhist conception of beauty, Soetsu Yanagi comments:

> We human beings are accustomed to thinking, "I am now painting a picture" or "I am now weaving cloth." According to Buddhism, however, such phrases express a dualistic relationship from which no true picture or cloth can result. Buddhism says that the root of the dualism is the word "I" and that it must vanish, until the stage where "picture draws picture" or "cloth weaves cloth" is reached. . . . Instead of man turning to Buddha or Buddha to man, Buddha turns to Buddha, all distinction or opposition between Buddha and man having disappeared.

---

10. Thomas J. J. Altizer, *Descent into Hell: A Study of the Radical Reversal of the Christian Consciousness* (New York: Seabury Press, 1979), p. 85.

Yanagi concludes: "We speak of 'offering prayers to God'—but true prayers are not those offered by man to God, they are, so to speak, God's voice whispered to God himself."[11]

As out of a desert, work done in time leads us out of time; this is one reason Blake says, "Eternity is in love with the productions of time." Such production is the goal of labor for both male and female: what might feel like a giving up is instead a giving birth into a larger world, a larger body. And for these poets the work itself, the book, embodies this new conception, as well as being a description of this conception. At labor's end we find before us, as within us, a revelation of what it is to be human, to labor in the vineyard. It is as Thomas Merton describes liturgical prayer, which, his biographer adds, "does not speak of what is beyond us," but "of what already is, what we already *are*." Merton writes:

> It will tell us over and over again that we are Christ in this world, and that He lives in us, and that what was said of Him has been and is being fulfilled in us: and that the last, most perfect fulfillment of all is now, this moment, by the theological virtue of hope, placed in our hands. Thus the liturgy of earth is necessarily one with the Liturgy of heaven. The Psalms are our Bread of Heaven in the wilderness of our Exodus.[12]

For a poet, of course, this revelation occurs in and through language crafted into beauty. As an artist, the poet also reveals in this way the function of beauty (and all labor is intended to manifest beauty), which is itself intended to reveal the "inner structure of matter,"[13] or the underlying ground that sustains us. Through this creative act, which is the antithesis of Babel, the artist finds himself healed, made whole, and simultaneously

---

11. Soetsu Yanagi, *The Unknown Craftsman: A Japanese Insight into Beauty*, adapted by Bernard Leach (New York: Kodansha International Ltd., 1972), pp. 145–46.
12. *Bread in the Wilderness* (New York: New Directions, 1953), p. 38. Quoted by Michael Mott in *The Seven Mountains of Thomas Merton* (Boston: Houghton Mifflin, 1984), p. 284.
13. See the interview with Seyyed Hossein Nasr, the author of *Islamic Art and Spirituality*, in *Parabola* XIII (Spring 1988), p. 34.

creates an object through which others may find healing for this split, because what is created is in its own self-sacrificing process an embodiment of kingdom. Inside and outside, self and other disappear or are redefined in a death that is simultaneously birth.

Thus the split between the self and the world that consciousness creates is healed in part by our own labor, which restores us to the knowledge that the building we most truly work on in the world is us. This explains the fact that the object created in *The Pearl, The Temple,* and *Jerusalem* is in a figuratively real sense the creator of the object himself. The Dreamer becomes pearl through his own sacrificial labor, which is in great part the creation of his poem; so too does Herbert become temple, and so does Blake build, enter, and become that Jerusalem that lives as the manifestation of the Divine Imagination.

Put differently, "[w]hen the artist reveals the reality concealed in things, he sets it free and, in turn, he liberates and purifies himself."[14]

* * *

"At night he stands up," Rilke writes, "the distant call of birds / already deep inside him":

> He thought of the hour in that other southern garden . . . when the call of a bird did not, so to speak, break off at the edge of his body, but was simultaneously outside and in his innermost being, uniting both into one uninterrupted space in which, mysteriously protected, only one single place of purest, deepest consciousness remained. On that occasion he had closed his eyes, so that he might

---

14. Chang Chung-yuan, *Creativity and Taoism: A Study of Chinese Philosophy, Art and Poetry* (1963; reprint, New York: Harper & Row, 1970), p. 8. Compare the comments by the Benedictine scholar Dom Jean Le Clerc, writing on the twelfth-century Abbot Suger of Saint-Denis, who, according to William Alexander McClung, took "literally St. Paul's architectural metaphors (Ephesians 2:19ff)." Le Clerc "argued that 'edification' was not merely a metaphor but should recall us to its root meaning and that sacred architecture, 'requiring the vision of divine glory for its design but physical labor for its material construction,' was 'the perfect realization of the Benedictine concept of labor as a process of edification.'" McClung concludes, "Architecture assumed an ethical as well as an eschatological function, not only representing Paradise to men but preparing them to enter it." See *The Architecture of Paradise: Survivals of Eden and Jerusalem* (Berkeley: University of California Press, 1983), p. 70.

not be confused . . . by the outline of his body, and the Infinite passed into him from all sides, so intimately that he believed he could feel the stars which had in the meantime appeared, gently reposing within his breast.[15]

2

Recent "new hermeneutic" critics in Germany and America, students of Bultmann and of Heidegger's phenomenology, have focused attention once again on Biblical language, and in particular on Jesus' parables, which critics claim are the closest we come to the language of Jesus himself.[16] These parables, Paul Ricoeur asserts, "can also have the function of reorienting by disassociating."[17] Robert Funk comments:

> the parable evokes a radically new relation to reality in its everydayness. . . . By means of metaphor, the parable "cracks" the shroud of everydayness lying over mundane reality in order to grant a radically new vision of mundane reality.[18]

More recently, David Tracy has summarized this perspective:

> That strategy of disorienting may serve the function of reorienting the reader by disclosing a new religious possibility: a way of being in the world not based on the ethics of justice and merit but of pure gift, pure graciousness, indeed, in Wesley's phrase, of "pure unbounded love."[19]

The very phrase "kingdom of God," Tracy suggests, "performs a similar limit function by serving as a radical qualifier

---

15. The first quote is from Rilke's poem "The Spanish Trilogy" ("Die Spanische Trilogie"), trans. Stephen Mitchell in *The Selected Poetry of Rainer Maria Rilke* (New York: Vintage Books, 1984), p. 121; the second, also translated by Mitchell, is titled "An Experience"; see p. 311 of the same volume.

16. See C. H. Dodd, *The Parables of the Kingdom* (1935; reprint, New York: Charles Scribner's Sons, 1961), p. 1, and Norman Perrin, *Rediscovering the Teaching of Jesus* (New York: Harper & Row, 1967).

17. Paul Ricoeur, "The Specificity of Language," *Semia* 4 (1975), p. 120.

18. Robert Funk, *Language, Hermeneutic and the Word of God: The Problem of Language in the New Testament and Contemporary Theology* (New York: Harper & Row, 1966), pp. 194–95.

19. "Metaphor and Religion," in *On Metaphor*, ed. Sheldon Sacks (Chicago: University of Chicago Press, 1979), p. 98.

upon the whole model (the kingdom of God). That qualifier radicalizes the model. . . ."[20]

To say "kingdom" is to speak, apparently, of the literal: that is, the plain, nonmetaphorical, external object.[21] To modify it with the genitive phrase "of God" is to undermine that literal and thus, in Ricoeur's terms, to "disorient" the listener or reader. The parables then complicate this further by drawing an analogy between this metaphorical kingdom and the world within which we live and work:

> The kingdom of heaven is like a merchant in search of fine pearls, who, on finding one pearl of great value, went and sold all that he had and bought it. (Matt. 13:45–46)

This kingdom is less place and more act. It is a way of being in the world, as we are asked to see as well in Jesus' life. A man sells all he has in order to purchase one pearl, the story tells us; this is what the kingdom is "like." It is giving up all you have (and are) for the sake of something greater, which is who you truly are.

The word of the parable, Jesus explains, is a seed sown not in the ground but in the heart. The text here discloses its own metaphorical underpinning; the movement between outer and inner, between physical and spiritual, is the word's point:

> When any one hears the word of the kingdom and does not understand it, the evil one comes and snatches away what is sown in his heart. (Matt. 13:18)

This same passage between outer and inner (by way of metaphor) is the passage demanded in all of the parables, as well as in such cryptic statements as Jesus' various comments to Nicodemus ("unless one is born both of water and the Spirit, he

---

20. Ibid., p. 98.
21. I shall have more to say about the nature of the literal in Chapter 4, on Blake, for part of Blake's task, I argue, is to dispense with the literal-metaphorical duality, where one inevitably denies the other, in order to see both as "contrary states of mind," or ways of seeing held simultaneously. See also Northrop Frye, *Anatomy of Criticism* (1957; reprint, New York: Atheneum, 1969), pp. 73–82.

cannot enter the kingdom of God"), statements that baffled the literal-minded Pharisee: "Nicodemus said to him, How can a man be reborn when he is old? . . . How can this thing be?" (John 3:4, 9).

It is also the journey suggested in Jesus' statement "Destroy this temple, and in three days I will raise it up" (John 3:19). What appears to be literal (and thus extremely offensive to his Jewish listeners) is metaphorical. We are to understand the temple now to refer not to a physical building but to Jesus' own body, which will be "raised" three days after its destruction. Here again such a statement, especially in light of the repeated emphasis on the physical manifestation of the resurrected Jesus, asks the readers to rethink their own conception of the material world and body. What, even, does it mean to be "raised" in this context?

What must change, Jesus' words imply, is not anything related to the external temple, whether it be the actual rebuilding or simply a closer attention to the laws and rites associated with it; instead it is a change involving mind, spirit, and body, a "turning around," undefinable (and, it is claimed, unavailable) except through this paradoxical Word[22] who teaches the essential unity of these three aspects of life: the same unity that is figured in the Holy Trinity. Jesus as the incarnate Word of God became the symbol of God,[23] embodying in his own death and resurrection the metaphorical truth of life: he who loses his life shall gain it. Sacrifice of self, or self-denial for the sake of another (what Blake calls annihilation of the "Selfhood"), is the meaning, the crucifixion said, of all Jesus' statements and stories. The Last Supper and the subsequent journey to Golgotha together become one metaphor representing this journey that all must endure in order to find the kingdom. This, in fact, is what kingdom means, what kingdom is: it exists in and as the ongoing labor of love.

---

22. On the relationship between Jesus as the Word and the sacraments, see Rahner, "The Word and the Eucharist," in *Theological Investigations IV: More Recent Writings* (New York: Seabury Press, 1974, 1976), pp. 253–86.

23. Rahner, "Theology of the Symbol," p. 236.

Introduction

* * *

This journey toward a metaphorical understanding of kingdom and temple is begun in the Old Testament, as the prophets attempt to persuade their people that to rely on the physical temple and the law as magical talismans, outward guarantees of Jahweh's presence, is to misinterpret the terms of the covenant (a problem that rises again over the sacraments):

> To the Jerusalem of their day, the decadent Davidic kingdom, they announce an antipolitics: put faith in your walls, your alliances, your idols, and you will be destroyed; put faith in God above, and though the city may fall, you will live, and later God will restore it to you. To Babylon . . . they announce the passive subversion of the politically helpless: you have only your walls and your idols to put faith in: they crumble, and you will be destroyed.[24]

Increasingly the notion of city and kingdom is internalized until, as James Dougherty continues, with the completion of Judeo-Christian revelation and the writings of the earliest Church Fathers, the holy city was no longer just a physical place, a magical "center" of the world. The holy city's magic, indeed, had always lain in the dimension of the imagination: in a knowledge of inner shrines and spiritual mysteries perceived by the mind's eye rather than by the body's. He then concludes:

> To render that holy city in words was seldom simply to describe its walls and temples—as they were or even as they should have been. Through the words of scripture, that city became a shrine, or the rival of a hostile city, or a far off cynosure. It symbolized spiritual fulfillment; or the conflict between life centered on self and dedicated to the service of God; or religious life as stabilized and communalized by a completion still remote in time. The words of scripture gave the holy city a manifold symbolic reality.[25]

This transformation of the temple and city in the Christian writings—in John's revelation of the New Jerusalem, for in-

---

24. James Dougherty, *The Five Square City: The City in the Religious Imagination* (Notre Dame, Ind.: University of Notre Dame Press, 1980), p. 8.
25. Dougherty, *Five Square City*, p. 22.

stance, where there is no temple, "for its temple is the Lord God the Almighty and the Lamb"—becomes the foundation on which subsequent writers build. The New Testament gave the Christian poet not just "metaphors for poetry," as did Yeats's instructors, but also the vision that made metaphor—and thus potentially, poetry itself, that most metaphoric of all uses of language—central to the Christian perspective. That vision, after all, is metaphorical, as we have just seen. Poetry then becomes, potentially, a bridge, or a way to this seeing.

Yet the danger now was the possibility of totally dismissing the physical as irrelevant or, worse, as dangerous; as early as John and Paul an antimaterial trend is evident in Christianity.[26] Can then the poet claim that the kingdom is made present in his construction as it was in Jesus' words? For Jesus' words are not just the "way" but are, like Jesus himself, the "truth" and "life" (John 14:6). Our own words, as Augustine taught, are merely signs, like the walls of our cities and temples. They point us to a reality greater than themselves. Like the chalice that holds the wine of the Mass for the "communicant," human words are vessels, or means of voyaging. Of course, as makers ourselves, cast in the image of a creative deity, we are continually tempted to build ourselves a home in and through our own creation, preeminently the city, our greatest artifact.[27] Instead, Augustine tells us, we must use (*uti*) and not simply enjoy (*frui*). His brief, yet haunting allegory in *On Christian Doctrine* remains the best summation of this tension:

> Suppose we were wanderers who could not live in blessedness except at home, miserable in our wandering and desiring to end it and to return to our native country. We would need vehicles for land and sea which could be used to help us to reach our homeland, which is to be enjoyed. But if the amenities of the journey and the

---

26. See L. William Countryman, *Dirt, Greed and Sex: Sexual Ethics in the New Testament and Their Implications for Today* (Philadelphia: Fortress Press, 1988), especially pp. 142, 231–32.

27. See Jacques Ellul, *The Meaning of the City*, trans. Dennis Pardee (Grand Rapids, Mich.: William B. Eerdmans Publishing Company, 1970), pp. 1–9.

motion of the vehicles delighted us, and we were led to enjoy those things that we should use, we should not wish our journey to end quickly, and, entangled in a perverse sweetness, we should be alienated from our country, whose sweetness would make us blessed.[28]

The sweetness that entangles us, as I stress in Chapter 3 (on Herbert), is reflected in art's own sweetness, which also tempts us to linger among its flowers. The task then, as the *Pearl*-Poet and Herbert see it, is to turn (in Herbert's words) "delight into sacrifice" through the aesthetic act itself. And the tool is metaphor, which undermines even as it builds, and builds as it undermines. Through it we can both build and use that building to reveal its own inadequacy. Only through metaphor can we grasp that we cannot grasp "home" or "kingdom," which, these writers claim, remains beyond us, beyond our language. Thus, poem after poem ends with the poet's apparently giving up, finding completion only through this sacrificial gesture. "Building" is only completed (and then only temporarily) by this "unbuilding," a turning completed only with the Eucharistic sacrament; in Herbert, with "Love (III)," the heavenly banquet itself. Thus even in completion the poems point to a beyond, imagined in this life, made temporarily present in the sacrament, but otherwise unknown, ungrasped. It is an expectation, a goal, a prayer.

And yet a tension remains. The poem after all is visible as a physical object, there on the page to be seen and heard; the words of the poem more than most call attention to themselves as words, as things with a beauty and glory in and of themselves. This is particularly true of these three poets, an odd fact, given that these writers also, it appears, are eager for their words to be transparent, read as metaphors. Yet almost more than any other poems

---

28. *On Christian Doctrine*, trans. D. W. Robertson, Jr. (New York: Bobbs-Merrill, 1958), pp. 9–10. John Freccero summarizes: for Augustine, as for Plato and Aristotle, "words point to things, but those things are themselves signs pointing to God, the ultimately signified." See "The Fig Tree and the Laurel: Petrarch's Poetics," in *Diacritics* 5 (1975), p. 36. See also Margaret W. Ferguson, "St. Augustine's Region of Unlikeness: The Crossing of Exile and Language," *Georgia Review* 29 (1975), pp. 842–64.

in the English tradition these find ways of calling attention to their own embodied nature. The *Pearl*'s text is constantly self-referential; in every stanza it reminds us of its own concrete existence simply through its ornate and intricate structure: its repeated words, its circularity. The *Temple* too creates signs that are structures demanding to be seen on the page as objects composed of words. In poems such as "Easter Wings" (discussed in greater detail in Chapter 3), we see the poem first as a physical object, a representation, even before we read the actual words. And *Jerusalem*, when read in the "Illuminated" form Blake created, again invites us to be first a "seer" and secondarily a reader, until we recognize that to be a reader is inevitably to be a seer (in both senses of the word).

Language in these three writers becomes visible, material. As Leon Roudiez has commented, such materiality "does suggest opacity. No longer transparent, the sign would point nowhere but to itself." He quotes Michel Foucault, who has described the "silent, careful placing of a word on the whiteness of a sheet of paper, where it can have neither sonority nor interlocutor, where it has nothing to say but itself, nothing to do but shine in the brightness of its being."[29]

Here we arrive at the point furthest removed from Augustine, where the word finally ceases to be word, a sign of something other than itself. Here word is completely lacking in transparency. However, with the three poets under discussion the tension between opacity and transparency is never resolved; this is also to say that the text, and the words that make up the text, remain

---

29. Leon Roudiez, "Readable/Writable/Visible," in *Visible Language* 12 (1978), p. 232. This issue of the materiality of language has been much discussed in recent years, going back (at least) to the Russian school and the Prague school of formalists. See in particular Jan Mukarovsky, *The Word and Verbal Art*, ed. and trans. John Burbank and Peter Steiner (New Haven: Yale University Press, 1977), pp. 1–9, quoted by Kathleen Henderson Staudt in "The Text as Material and as a Sign: Poetry and Incarnation in William Blake, Arthur Rimbaud, and David Jones," *Modern Language Studies* 14 (1984), p. 13. Mukarovsky comments that in literature language is "a material, like metal and stone in sculpture, like pigment and the material of the pictorial plane in painting." Yet "language in its very essence is already a sign" (p. 9). See also Julia Kristeva's study, *Revolution of Poetic Language* (New York: Columbia University Press, 1977), pp. 5–6, 25–30.

Introduction

caught in the tension that defines metaphor. As Roudiez again suggests, "the concept of metaphor itself could be used as a metaphor of what takes place here."[30] These texts, insofar as they remain opaque, celebrate themselves as objects and invite the reader to celebrate. Yet insofar as we respond to their metaphoricity, the texts suddenly become transparent. Foucault comments, "Metaphor is the metaphysics of the image, in the sense that metaphysics is the destruction of physics. The true poet," he adds, "denies himself the accomplishment of desire in the image."[31] The word *pearl* in the poem of that name must, for both narrator and reader, be grasped as a metaphor: that is, grasped not simply by the hand but by the mind. So too in Herbert and Blake. These poems offer up their own verbal (or book-bound) bodies in a metaphorical reading that reminds us that as humans we are more than body, or that body is more than flesh and bone. They remind us that body, including the body of our own work, is also beauty. Such labor too potentially manifests the divine.[32]

30. Roudiez, "Readable/Writable/Visible," p. 234.
31. Michel Foucault, "Dream, Imagination, and Existence," trans. Forrest Williams, in *Dream and Existence*, a Special Issue from the *Review of Existential Psychology and Psychiatry* 19 (1984–85), p. 72.
32. Compare this to Ernst Becker's comments on the dualism of the body, or finitude, and what he calls the symbolic self. The body knows death, but the self denies death. See *The Denial of Death* (New York: Free Press, 1973), p. 75. Designated as a signifier, the body in these terms points us always to the unseen, unknowable signified, the hidden self. See Ellie Ragland-Sullivan's study of metaphor in Lacan in *Jacques Lacan and the Philosophy of Psychoanalysis* (Urbana: University of Illinois Press, 1986), pp. 233–58. See also Jacques Derrida, "Structure, Sign and Play in the Discourse of the Human Sciences," in *Writing and Difference*, trans. Alan Bass (Chicago: University of Chicago Press, 1978), esp. pp. 278–79, and "White Mythology: Metaphor in the Text of Philosophy," in *Margins of Philosophy*, trans. Alan Bass (Chicago: University of Chicago Press, 1982), pp. 207–71. It is one of the contentions of this study that, contra Derrida, the self is exactly what is made known in metaphor, even if this self remains (like the kingdom) ever allusive, more act than place. My position is closer to Stanley Corngold's in *The Fate of the Self*; see especially "Hölderlin and the Question of Self" (New York: Columbia University Press, 1986), pp. 21–53. The following discussion suggests precisely the same tension that I have been struggling to articulate. He quotes Blanchot, who "describes the destiny of the poet who mediates the sacred. This torn existence is not only a consequence but . . . is the very division of the poet, his obliteration in the embrace of the word which—

The body is apparently opaque, limited, material; the true Self is transparent, unlimited, immaterial. The human, these poets suggest, both is a marriage of these contradictions and lives perpetually within the tension generated by this apparent split. Metaphor, like the incarnate Christ, is the sign of this tension and its resolution. It has two faces: as image, or body, the metaphor is of the physical world, but when seen by the mind as a metaphor (and metaphor only exists in the eye of the beholder) the image ceases to be simply itself and becomes another. Thus, although rooted via image in the world, the metaphor truly springs to life only in the imagination, the kingdom where the splintered worlds are healed and where both body and spirit become redefined as aspects of the same single reality.

The core of the problem for each of our poets is hermeneutical. The language of these poets is apparently descriptive (of "kingdom"), and yet what that language tells us is that "kingdom" cannot be described. Yet kingdom *is*, but to be known as such it must be experienced, lived in the here and now of physical and mental sacrificial labor. Right here is the divine love revealed, and only here.

* * *

This paradox can be fruitfully compared to recent attempts to explain the way the world looks to physicists, a view remarkably similar, I think, to the way Jesus apprehends the world, and the way these poets do. Here again, any attempt simply to describe this world is doomed to failure. David Finkelstein compares this to the use of a language of *mythos* as opposed to a language of logos—the latter being the attempt to find a model outside the experience that will accurately portray that experience—an impossibility, Finkelstein concludes. Instead, a language of mythos,

---

existence having disappeared—alone persists, continues." Corngold, however, argues, "The subject of poetry is . . . not the effacement of the poet but the repetition of the moment of effacement; what survives in the poem is thus the poet's experience, not of self-effacement, but of its impossibility, and hence of the necessity of being a self" (p. 51). I would only add that for a poet such as Herbert the self or body constituted in and by the poem is claimed to be that self known as a member of the Divine Body, or Christ.

Introduction 19

"a language which alludes to experience but does not attempt to replace it or to mold our perception of it is the true language of physics."[33] I would push this further by suggesting that such a language is itself the experience, precisely as it acknowledges its own limitations and failures.

Finkelstein uses the following example:

> If you want to envision the quantum as a dot then you are trapped. You are modelling it with classical logic. The whole point is that there is no classical representation for it. We have to learn to live with the experience.
> Question: How do you communicate the experience?
> Answer: You don't. But by telling how you make quanta and how you measure them, you enable others to have it. (277)

These poems, in a sense, are "how to" guides. This is particularly true in their continual attempt to force us outside a logical (or "classical") pattern of interpretation, where things are always either this or that, never both. Here again the description of the world in modern physics can aid us. For example, a description of a photon: Logic would suggest that at any given moment "a single photon must be polarized one way or the other" (that is, either horizontally or diagonally). But "[p]ure experience is never restricted to merely two possibilities. Our conceptualization of a given situation may create the illusion that each dilemma has only two horns, but this illusion is caused by assuming that experience is bound by the same rules as symbols" (286).

This world of "symbols" that Gary Zukav describes corresponds to classical logic, described as a "set of blinders . . . which not only restricts our field of vision, but distorts it" (277). Here

---

33. Gary Zukav, *The Dancing Wu Li Masters: An Overview of the New Physics* (New York: William Morrow, 1979), p. 277. All subsequent quotations from this book will be cited in the text. In a recent exhibit of new work by American painters, the critic Kay Larson notes, "Artists who turn to science for metaphors have begun to resemble mystics, not rationalists." See *New Work New York* (Lawrence, Kans.: Spencer Museum of Art, 1988), unpaged. Handelman somewhat similarly suggests that "reality" (Torah) is a process, continually altered by our labor within it and upon it. "Thus interpretation is not essentially separate from the text itself—an external act intruded upon it—but rather the *extension* of the text . . . a part of the continuous revelation of the text itself. . . ." (p. 39).

the language approaches that of Blake, a writer who understood well how our vision of the world is based on the language or symbols with which we attempt to describe and understand it. We have lived for centuries as a culture with one way of seeing (call it Newtonian), wherein "our three-dimensional reality is separate from, and moves forward in, a one-dimensional time." But imagine for a moment (as Einstein did) a four-dimensional reality, where the fourth dimension is time. Here's the difference:

> The Newtonian view of space and time is a *dynamic* picture. Events *develop* with the passage of time. Time is one-dimensional and *moves* (forward). . . . The special theory of relativity, however, says that it is preferable, and more useful, to think in terms of a static, nonmoving picture of space and time. . . . If we could view our reality in a four-dimensional way, we would see that everything that now seems to unfold before us with the passing of time, already exists *in toto*. . . . We would see all, the past, the present, and the future with one glance. (171–72)

The world is not what it seems. Matter is not what it seems. Mass is energy and energy is, well, "eternal delight."

One function of art—explicitly for Blake, and, I'm arguing, implicitly for the other two poets—is the reconnection of this body to what Blake calls Imagination. Body, after all, including the body of our work, is itself "a portion of soul discerned by the five Senses" (E 34). Metaphor is the means. The result is not the rejection of the body but the affirmation of it as the manifestation, the act of the mind.[34] Body is what spirit, or idea or energy, becomes without ceasing to be spirit.

By extension, then, the poem invites the reader to see the world in precisely the same way, as the incarnation of the divine mind. The world is Christ's body, God's ongoing labor of love.

* * *

As object, the world, like the poem, is opaque; as sign it is

---

34. See also the comments by the physicist David Bohm, quoted by Zukav: "The ultimate perception does not originate in the brain or any material structure, although a material structure is necessary to manifest it" (*Dancing Wu Li Masters*, p. 327).

transparent, and in its transparency it returns us to its source. All three poets agree with this understanding of metaphor; what separates Blake from the other two is the location of that source. The *Pearl*-Poet and Herbert, I shall argue (with some qualifications), accept Augustine's definition of the human word as sign. The poem as a self-constructed object (as pearl or temple) points or leads the reader; like Dante's Virgil, it functions as a guide on a journey that ends at heaven's gate. Yet it does end there: metaphor is not sacrament to these writers. Instead, it is closer to the definition put forth by Karsten Harries:

> Metaphor speaks of what remains absent. All metaphor that is more than an abbreviation for more proper speech gestures towards what transcends language. Thus metaphor implies lack. God knows neither transcendence nor metaphor—nor would man, if he were truly godlike. The refusal of metaphor is inseparably connected with the project of pride, the dreams of unmediated vision, a vision that is not marred by lack, that does not refer to something beyond itself that would fulfill it.[35]

There are variations on this notion of "lack" in our language in many modern critics, yet most of them (for vastly different reasons) will deny to metaphor (or symbol) any ability to contain or embody. Paul de Man preferred allegory to the symbol precisely because allegory more clearly reveals its own limitations: the fact that our language exists within the void and points, finally, to nothing (nothing that we can know, at least).[36] Paul Ricoeur defines metaphor as a purely human linguistic construct, which again acknowledges its own inability to embody what it points to (for Ricoeur, it points to symbol, which is by definition "prelinguistic").[37] Metaphor both "is" and "is not." "The 'is like'

35. "Metaphor and Transcendence," in *On Metaphor*, p. 82.
36. See de Man, "The Rhetoric of Temporality." For a recent critique of this position, see Hazard Adams's essay "Synecdoche and Method" in *Critical Paths: Blake and the Argument of Method*, ed. Dan Miller, Mark Bracher, and Donald Ault (Durham, N.C.: Duke University Press, 1987), pp. 45–46.
37. See Ricoeur's *Interpretation Theory: Discourse and the Surplus of Meaning* (Fort Worth: Texas Christian Press, 1976), pp. 57–63. For a more extended critique of Ricoeur's theory of metaphor and symbol, see Chapter 4 of this work, and see Hazard Adams, *Philosophy of the Literary Symbolic*, chapter 12.

of the figurative representation of the unconditioned implies an 'is not.' "[38]

Ricoeur borrows Kant's term *grenze* (limit) in order to clarify his own definitions. Limit, he argues,

> implies not only and not even primarily that our knowledge is limited, has boundaries, but that the quest for the unconditioned puts limits on the claim of objective knowledge to become absolute.[39]

We also find in Murray Krieger, who also struggles against the sense of defeat (or imprisonment) in Derrida and de Man, this Kantian qualification of our own metaphorical language. Thus, Krieger's definition of metaphor is not unlike that in both *Pearl* and *The Temple*. The poem, Krieger argues, is a self-contained whole, has "presence,"[40] and thus in some sense embodies (if only embodying itself, as its own being or object); yet what it contains is also "the vision of that incompleteness." It is awake to its own failure to contain reality. Krieger uses Keats's "Ode to a Nightingale" as an example of this self-reflective quality, or what he calls (borrowing from Keats) the "waking dream" that is the poem:

> As in dream, the symbol creates for us a surrogate reality, claiming the completeness of an irreducible domain within its eccentric terms, although it also stimulates a wakefulness that undercuts its metaphoric extravagances and threatens to reduce symbol to allegory.[41]

The poem is on these terms a whole, a completed construction that reveals even in its own completion the fact that it remains a "surrogate reality." The difference between Krieger and these

---

38. Ricoeur, "The Specificity of Language," p. 143.
39. Ibid.
40. For Krieger's theory of "poetic presence and illusion," see his essay, "A Waking Dream," in *Allegory, Myth and Symbol*, ed. Morton Bloomfield (Cambridge, Mass: Harvard University Press, 1982), pp. 1–22. See also his *Poetic Presence and Illusion: Essays in Critical History and Theory* (Baltimore: Johns Hopkins University Press, 1979).
41. Krieger, "Waking Dream," pp. 21–22.

earlier religious poets is that the reality not contained in *Pearl* or *The Temple* is a reality known in Jesus' words and, as the Liturgy has it, "in the breaking of the bread." Not surprisingly, both poems leave us at exactly this point, with the awakened *Pearl* Dreamer's observing Mass from the nave of his cathedral and with Parson Herbert's being served by the Host himself in a heavenly communion. Both poems, then, demonstrate how "delight" becomes "sacrifice," not only for the poem's protagonist, but also for the reader, who (if the poem has done its job) comes out at the poem's end in the same place, like the *Pearl* Dreamer, but newly awakened and ready to sell all he has to become metaphorically what he has read.

For Blake, too, "we become what we behold."[42] But for Blake there is no reality other than the reality the poem contains; there is no symbol that is "pre-" or "supralinguistic," no symbol, in other words, not formed by the human imagination itself. A radical Protestant, Blake saw all creation (and not just Baptism and the Lord's Supper) as a mental, spiritual act, taking place through the imagination. To see this truth is in fact to awaken, Blake argued, and to awaken is to receive the sacrament as a gift: as "Throwing off Error . . . & receiving Truth."[43] To see by way of metaphor is to see as Jesus sees ("what is above is within"), which is to see ourselves as Jesus.

"God becomes as we are, that we may be as he is," Blake commented at the beginning of his "canon" (E 3). For Blake too the incarnation is the central event in human history, which is the story of the Fall of humanity into a vision of creation and labor he does on something outside himself, a world he attempts to impose himself upon in a continual (if futile) attempt to get it back inside. The incarnation is central because it reverses this fallen vision: the created one is Himself still "in" the creator. It is, thus, Blake who comes closest to the vision of the New Tes-

---

42. A frequently used expression in Blake. See *Jerusalem* 30:50 and 32:14.
43. See "A Vision of the Last Judgement," E 562. One dimension to this historical movement from *Pearl* to *Jerusalem* is an evolution from a Roman Catholic vision of sacrament to a Protestant vision.

tament's word witnessed to by recent Biblical critics; it is Blake who affirms that in his work, as in "The Great Code of Art" (the Bible),[44] the word of God is present fully, can be entered fully, known as both divine and human. Metaphor, Blake implies, gives us the truth of our existence as well as the way to that truth: way, truth, and life are one in metaphor as the rider of this imaginative chariot becomes the chariot himself.[45] In reading we become Jerusalem, the holy city and bride of Jesus; not just the place where divine, imaginative activity occurs but that labor itself seen as the pouring forth of its own divine presence, the way the sun's rays emanate from that central star. Reading is part of our labor: just as the poet gives birth to himself in the creation of the poem, so too do we potentially give birth to our larger Self in the reading. We "enter into the image" as Blake asks of us, finding that to do so is both a death—a loss of our old self, a perspective that confined us—and a birth. "A Last Judgement" passes over us, Blake says, and we find ourselves remade, whole, when "no man was himself."[46]

* * *

The point of this work is not to resolve once and for all the issue of metaphor's meaning, to answer definitively, or to judge one poet or another as "right"; nor, I might add, am I making any particular claims for traditions of poetic "buildings" or "cities," although my focus here points obviously enough in the direction of later works, such as *Ulysses* and *Finnegans Wake*, *Paterson*, and even *The Four Gated City*, where again the metaphor

44. So called by Blake in *The Laocoön*, E 274.
45. See David Sten Herrstrom, "Blake's Transformations of Ezekiel's Cherubim Vision in Jerusalem," *Blake: An Illustrated Quarterly* 15 (1981), p. 66. This interpretation is worth comparing to Augustine's (as Stephen Happel reminds me, in correspondence); in Augustine the way and the truth are united only in this single person of Jesus, who is "the only reality we can legitimately enjoy and utilize as instrument." For Blake, Jesus is the living, temporal enactment of the *way* of metaphor, a way that each of us must become.
46. The final quote is from Gonzalo in *The Tempest*. The Blake quotes are both from *A Vision of the Last Judgement*. A contrasting position is taken by Hazard Adams in his essay in *Critical Paths*, pp. 47–71. Adams there views the reader as the critic, who invariably takes a position outside the text and who exists then in an ironic relationship with that text.

of building (and unbuilding) plays a major role in the construction of the work.[47] Instead I am suggesting that by looking carefully at three poets from three distinct epochs, analyzing their metaphorical constructs in the light of Biblical practice (which was their own guide) and in light of various contemporary theories of metaphor, we shall come to understand more clearly a tradition of religious verse linked across four hundred years by its profound sense of metaphor as speaking most clearly the way by which people must see and journey. For all their differences, it is enlightening to see how consistent is this vision of metaphor, as, above all else, a self-sacrificing sign, modeled on the road Jesus took to Golgotha, the building He constructed by means of His own self-emptying.

Does this remain true for our own century, and more particularly for our own time? Is Samuel Beckett the end of the line I have been tracing, the point where all attempts to speak the unspeakable cease? Or is he the start of another? Are the works of the Absurd a means of entering the "cloud of unknowing," or do they simply tell us that nothing—and no one—is there? The line is thin indeed between these two perspectives, between, we might say, the playful metaphorical language of Jewish Midrash and the playful, metaphorical language of a Jacques Derrida.[48]

We shall also see our own recent theories of metaphor and symbol more clearly, I believe, from such a broad perspective. Thus, if I occasionally examine Blake or Herbert or the *Pearl*-

---

47. A recent example that traces in a somewhat similar fashion the development or history of the idea of "temple" or "paradise" is McClung's lovely *The Architecture of Paradise*.

48. Derrida writes: "Whether He is Being or the master of beings, God himself is, and appears as what He is, within difference, that is to say, as difference and within dissimulation." See *Writing and Difference*, trans. Alan Bass (Chicago: University of Chicago Press, 1978), p. 74, quoted by José Faur in "God as a Writer: Omnipresence and the Art of Dissimulation," *Religion & Intellectual Life* 6 (1989), p. 37. See also Faur's *Golden Doves with Silver Dots: Semiotics and Textuality in Rabbinic Tradition* (Bloomington: Indiana University Press, 1986), and Handelman's *Slayers of Moses*. Finally, see Bruce Kawin's "On Not Having the Last Word: Beckett, Wittgenstein, and the Limits of Language," in *Ineffability: Naming the Unnameable From Dante to Beckett*, ed. Peter S. Hawkins and Anne Howland Schotter (New York: AMS, 1984), pp. 189–202.

Poet through the lens of Ricoeur, Krieger, or de Man, it is equally true that I am examining these later thinkers by means of the sharply burning vision of the poets. If we are to understand how metaphor and symbol work on us, and where the figurative takes us (whether that be to the kingdom of heaven or the imagination's own blank), it is best to seek for answers from those who had the most at stake in an answer.

2

Pearl

Lessons in Interpretive Construction

At 5:30, as I was dreaming, in a very quiet hospital, the soft voice of the nurse awoke me gently from my dream—and it was like awakening for the first time from all the dreams of my life—as if the Blessed Virgin herself, as if Wisdom, had awakened me. We do not hear the soft voice, the gentle voice, the feminine voice, the voice of the Mother: yet she speaks everywhere and in everything. Wisdom "cries out in the market place— if anyone is little let him come to me."[1]

Given the evident, if subtle, sense of humor of the poet of *Pearl* and *Sir Gawain and the Green Knight*, it is my suspicion that he would be quietly amused at the stacks of papers, monographs, and books piling up in recent years attempting to set, fix, and define his "wemles" gems. I suspect he would also be amused to learn, if he did not already know, that the root of the word *interpret* apparently means "to traffic in, to sell," fittingly implying that all those who interpret these poems are themselves potentially "joyles jueleres," struggling to spot a lost, precious pearl.[2]

---

1. Quoted from Thomas Merton's Restricted Journals (July 2, 1960), in Michael Mott's *The Seven Mountains of Thomas Merton* (Boston: Houghton Mifflin, 1984), p. 361.
2. *The American Heritage Dictionary*, p. 1543; note that the words *prostitute* and *pornography* come from the same root. For a survey of criticism on the poem, see especially the bibliography provided by Malcolm Andrew and Ronald Waldron in their edition of *The Poems of the Pearl Manuscript* (Berkeley and Los Angeles: University of California Press, 1979), pp. 5–13. Of particular interest should be John Gatta, Jr., "Transformation Symbolism and the Liturgy of the Mass in Pearl," *Modern Philology* 71 (1973–74), pp. 243–56; James Milroy, "*Pearl*: The Verbal Texture and the Linguistic Theme," *Neophilologus* 55 (1971), pp. 195–208; Barbara Nolan, *The Gothic Visionary Perspective* (Princeton, N.J.: Princeton Uni-

It is certainly true that the jeweler himself, through much of the poem, is a poor interpreter indeed, one of those, upbraided by Bonaventura, who read without unction, investigate without wonder, and examine without piety.[3] He is a literalist, as we might expect of a man who spends his days weighing, examining, and evaluating the value of small gems; the real is what is before him, and value lies in what he possesses, what he holds within his hands.[4] He is, in fact, rather like the disciples as we see them following Jesus on his wanderings in the Gospels, listening and so often failing to hear. "But Peter said to him, 'Explain the parable to us.' And he said, 'Are you also still without understanding?'" (Matt. 15:15). Again and again, they struggle valiantly to follow their master's leaps into the figurative—into paradox, as Ricoeur would say—and yet continually they come up short:

> When the disciples reached the other side, they had forgotten to bring any bread. Jesus said to them, "Take heed and beware of the leaven of the Pharisees and Sadducees." And they discussed it among themselves, saying "We brought no bread." But Jesus, aware of this, said "O men of little faith, why do you discuss among yourselves the fact that you have no bread? Do you not yet perceive? Do you not remember the five loaves of the five thousand, and how many baskets you gathered? . . . How is it that you fail to perceive that I did not speak about bread. Beware of the leaven of the Pharisees and Sadducees." Then they understood that he did not tell them to beware of the leaven of bread, but of the teaching of the Pharisees and Sadducees. (Matt. 16:5–12)

---

versity Press, 1977); Cary Nelson, *The Incarnate Word* (Urbana: University of Illinois Press, 1973); Joyce Rogers Emert, "*Pearl* and the Incarnate Word: A Study in the Sacramental Nature of Symbolism" (Ph.D. diss., University of New Mexico, 1969; Dissertation Abstracts 30:4940A–41A); and Anne Howland Schotter, "Vernacular Style and the Word of God: The Incarnational Art of *Pearl*," in *Ineffability: Naming the Unnameable from Dante to Beckett*, ed. Peter S. Hawkins and Anne Howland Schotter (New York: AMS, 1984), pp. 25–31.

3. Saint Bonaventura, *The Mind's Road to God*, trans. George Boas (New York: Bobbs-Merrill, 1953), p. 5.

4. See John Hill, "Middle English Poets and the Word: Notes toward an Appraisal of Linguistic Consciousness," *Criticism* 16 (1974), p. 154.

Interpretive Construction

"Matthew" here kindly interprets this cryptic comment for those among us even slower than the disciples and, in doing so, comes close to stripping this short speech of its power to transform us by forcing us to see: Do you not remember the five loaves . . . ? Stop worrying about bread. Stop worrying about "Who is the greatest in the kingdom of heaven?" (Matt. 18:1) and "Who can be saved?" (Matt. 19:25), for "with God all things are possible" (Matt. 19:26), including granting the same reward to the "last" as He grants to the "first" (Matt. 20:16).

Even more specifically, the Dreamer is like those disciples who walk with the risen Lord on the road to Emmaus, journeying toward a goal that is with them even as they walk but that breaks upon them only at the end. As they walk, they speak to this stranger, discussing the events of the day, their terrible loss, and the strange story brought to them by "some women of our company." Yet, unbeknown to them, it is they who fail to understand the significance of this story and of their loss, and it is the stranger who must interpret the mystery, doing so by making figures of the Old Testament that shadow forth the truth of Jesus' sacrifice. Yet, even this is not enough; they do not see until the sacrament is reenacted before their eyes: "When he was at table with them, he took the bread and blessed, and broke it, and gave it to them. And their eyes were opened and they recognized him, and he vanished out of their sight" (Luke 24:30–31).[5]

Similarly, the Dreamer in the *Pearl* must undergo a journey that is primarily a journey of insight: an education into the ways of seeing. The Maiden's first words to him warn of what is to come: "Sir, ye haf your tale mysetente" (257), that is, misunderstood or distorted.[6] When he immediately hungers to join her on the other side of the river, she again, with a certain amount of

---

5. All Biblical translations, unless otherwise noted, are from the Revised Standard Version. On the separation of the liturgy itself into two parts (Word and Eucharist), see Gatta, "Transformation Symbolism," p. 250.
6. All references to *Pearl* are from *The Poems of the Pearl Manuscript*, ed. Malcolm Andrew and Ronald Waldron (Berkeley: University of California Press, 1979), unless otherwise noted. The Middle English letters "þ" and "3" have been modernized. Translations are my own or from this edition, again unless otherwise noted.

exasperation, says "Why borde [jest] ye men? So madde ye be! / Thre wordez hatz thou spoken at ene: / Unavysed, forsothe, wern alle thre" (290–92). Next, she says quite specifically that the problem is not simply one of speaking without true comprehension; it is also one of seeing without insight, that is, believing only what you see: "I halde that jueler lyttel to prayse / That leuez [believes] wel that he sez wyth yghe . . ." (301–2).

Yet what the Maiden will reveal to the Dreamer in her talks is what Jesus reveals to those disciples at Emmaus: kingdom is known in this world not in talk but in embodied sacramental action. Talk, *sermo*, is preparation for the breaking of bread, where our eyes are truly opened. Here we learn that we too must at last not just speak but be as Christ is: be broken, utterly opened up to God, and thus inevitably wounded, made vulnerable to the world. Thus, although the physical act, the "literal," finds its fullest significance in our receptivity to the figurative meaning embodied within it—not all bread breaking is perceived as sacrament—nonetheless this kingdom we experience in our sacramental labor is fully revealed to us only in and through that physical: the mundane acts of breaking and eating, of drinking the wine. We can distinguish literal and figurative, body and spirit, but to separate them is finally impossible, at least for us who dwell in a physical world. *Pearl* is in part about this danger: it is a poem composed mostly of talk that yet recognizes the fine irony of that fact. What else can the poet do but talk and in that talk attempt to make these distinctions clear, so that the reader can, like the dreamers in both Blake and the *Pearl*-Poet, leap into this river surrounding Jerusalem and awaken.

Yet the awakening does not lead to an abandonment of the embodied life; instead it leads to a correct interpretation and living of that life, a transformation of that life. Instead of attempting to cling and possess, both literally and figuratively, the Dreamer learns that true ownership comes in letting go, which is what the awakened dreamer does at poem's end, knowing that the model is in the act that Jesus performs at the Last Supper, itself a sign of the act to be performed at Golgotha. These acts are figuratively and truly the same and are repeated for those weak-eyed sojourners on the way to Emmaus. Here indeed is the meaning of the embodied life; here is where labor is truly perceived as sacrament, where spiritual and physical marry. Here in this sacrifice is the ongoing Annunciation, the giving of birth to love in the world.

As readers, we also hunger to possess, if only meaning. We are jewelers in danger of interpreting the text as some have interpreted the parables, unwilling or unable to allow the polyvalent and paradoxical to break in upon us. Thus, clinging to our own tiny gems, we miss the pearl of great price, the kingdom, which we become through the Word (Jesus) who shatters "the shroud of everydayness lying over mundane reality in order to grant a radically new vision of mundane reality."[7] As Spearing comments, this is a dilemma facing the actors in each of the works of this poet. I would claim that much that this critic has to say would apply equally to the reader of these texts, the reader, that is, who attempts to contain the uncontainable:

> We find in the Gawain poet's works this central and repeated subject of a confrontation between man and something more than man. That "something more" possesses an all-encompassing power, but one whose implications man is unwilling to admit. He is not willing to accept the role of humility and submission that it should impose on him; he wishes to play the heroic role implied by the traditional alliterative style—to be independent, to choose for himself. He struggles to defeat the power with which he is confronted, to evade or outwit it, but his struggle is necessarily vain, and therefore absurd.[8]

I would only add that a final paradox of the poem, and a sign

---

7. Robert W. Funk, *Language, Hermeneutic and the Word of God* (New York: Harper & Row, 1966), pp. 194–95. See also F. David Martin, *Art and the Religious Experience: The "Language" of the Sacred* (Lewisburg, Pa.: Bucknell University Press, 1972), pp. 42–43.

8. A. C. Spearing, *The Gawain-Poet: A Critical Study* (Cambridge: Cambridge University Press, 1970), p. 30. See also Nelson, *Incarnate Word*, pp. 30–49; W. A. Davenport, *The Art of the Gawain-Poet* (London: University of London/Athlone Press, 1978), p. 34; and Charles Muscatine, *Poetry and Crisis in the Age of Chaucer* (Notre Dame, Ind.: University of Notre Dame Press, 1972), p. 55.

of the humility of the poet, is the recognition that, as at Emmaus, language alone is not sufficient for this breakthrough. The Dreamer listens, but ironically in his desperation to grasp he fails to grasp that there is *nothing at all to grasp*. It is not simply the Pearl Maiden's words that awaken him, although this is surely a part of what allows him at last to resign himself to God. As at Emmaus, it is the physical act that brings the truth home, and in that moment the physical embodiment (Pearl Maiden and city, or Jesus) vanishes, as if no longer necessary, as if now fully realized not as some external reality to be sought after but instead as a reality to be experienced in one's own life. Not I, as Paul said, but Christ in me. This is the moment, I believe, that Herbert also faces in his struggle to give himself over to God and become that temple of the Holy Spirit that Paul also describes; and it is what Blake's Albion faces in his nightmarish vision of a world beyond him that increasingly binds him down the more he attempts to impose economic, militaristic and religious control over it, until it is at last revealed as a figment of his imagination. The enemy, these poets reveal, is not simply out there, because out there is always also in here.

* * *

It has been noted by critics that, given the first-person narrative of the poem, we can assume, as Spearing comments, "two states of consciousness . . . that of the Dreamer who naively experiences the successive phases of his adventure, and that of the narrator who has already learned the lesson of the vision, and who is telling the story with the benefit of that wisdom."[9] Yet further behind this rather simple narrator stands the poet, creating the narrator who recounts the dream. This split is familiar enough to readers of medieval dream visions; "Dante" is the pilgrim who journeys, the narrator who tells of the journey, and the poet who "arranges," who makes the poem. Similarly with *Piers Plowman*, in which "Will" has already journeyed but presents himself as the naive and inexperienced "Will" who first set

---

9. Spearing, *Gawain-Poet*, p. 106.

Interpretive Construction 33

out (and behind each stands the poet, usually identified as Will Langland).

But I am more particularly interested here in arguing that the reader, too, is intended to move through these levels, as journey leads to conversion, a turning around that amounts to a new way of seeing, and thus (for the *Pearl*-Poet, as for Langland) to the sacraments, where the believer is joined ritually to the Body of Christ and becomes himself temple or pearl. The poem from this perspective acts as Virgil did for Dante: It is the guide, the vehicle, but not the goal itself.

John Freccero comments that Dante too hopes for a similar shift to take place within the reader:

> Dante considered his poem to be a relationship between his experience and the experience of his readers, not simply a literary object.... It is Dante's conviction that the poetic record of his conversion will prepare the way for the conversion of others, as Virgil prepared it for him.[10]

Barbara Nolan likewise notes that readers, depending always on God's grace, may learn to share through the agency of poetic form and words the narrator's ecstatic realization of the "isplendor di Dio...."[11]

Yet how exactly this happens has always been a greatly debated question. Nolan clearly shows how for a man like Abbot Suger the cathedral building itself became a model of the divine order, or a figural representation of the kingdom's harmony and glory, which could, when entered into imaginatively, lead one to the true kingdom. Yet always the problem returns: by the fourteenth century, in spite of the repeated reminders that nothing was possible without the grace of God acting within the believer (or beholder), for many people the simple act of entering the building and witnessing the Mass was a magical gate into the

---

10. John Freccero, Introduction, *Dante: A Collection of Critical Essays*, ed. John Freccero (Englewood Cliffs, N.J.: Prentice-Hall, 1965), p. 3.
11. Nolan, *Gothic Visionary*, p. 43. See also *Paradiso* I, 64–72, Emert, "*Pearl* and the Incarnate Word," pp. 36, 129, and William Alexander McClung, *The Architecture of Paradise* (Berkeley: University of California Press, 1983), pp. 69–70.

kingdom. Jungmann comments, "In the late Middle Ages the corporeal was often shown honor that amounted to superstition. . . ." The people felt assured of unfailing results and thus were "lulled into a false security, as though the salvation of souls could be assured by merely hearing Mass."[12] Once again, a Pharisaic mentality develops; it seems possible again to earn—or even buy—one's way to heaven.

The dreamer in *Pearl* is himself guilty of such misinterpretation and is at times almost comical in his desire to grasp what is by nature ungraspable. Yet, it is he who emerges from the dream river at the poem's end with a sigh and some simple wisdom— "Lorde, mad hit arn [they are] that agayn thee stryuen, / Other proferen thee oght agayn thy paye" [against thy pleasure] (1199–1200)—which leads him to more simple wisdom contained in the poem's final stanza: "To pay [please] the Prince other sete saghte [or be reconciled to Him] / Hit is ful ethe [easy] to the god Krystyin" (1201–2). He takes his pearl "for pity" and commits it to God, having apparently learned the lesson[13] taught in the parables about "selling all one has to obtain the pearl of great price": the kingdom of heaven.

Something indeed has been learned here; otherwise, we suspect, the dreamer would never have become the narrator, as Spearing suggests. However, as we return to the poem's opening (as the conclusion invites us to do), we recognize a complexity, a finesse and subtlety, that is belied by the simple dreamer and narrator, even in the poem's conclusion, a complexity evident in every stanza of the poem. We are invited to draw a distinction between this naive dreamer and the creator of this baroque gem. The form is as close as human creator can come to perfection,

---

12. Joseph A. Jungmann, *The Mass of the Roman Rite* (New York: Benziger Brothers, 1951), pp. 128–30. See also Joseph M. Powers, *Eucharistic Theology* (New York: Seabury Press, 1967), p. 31: "'Take and eat' . . . had become 'Gaze on the Host and find your salvation in the gazing.'" A related issue develops in *Sir Gawain and the Green Knight* concerning the significance of, and the relationship between, the Pentangle on Gawain's shield and the girdle given as a "magical gift" by Bercilak's wily wife.
13. Some critics have disagreed; see especially Milroy.

Interpretive Construction 35

with its interlocking stanzas, its link words, its circular structure; yet, within this architectural marvel is the struggling, painful, yet comic imperfection of the man whose experience is being recounted. It is as Muscatine has suggested:

> The awakening, the imperfection of the dreamer's understanding and of his self-control, are essential to the meaning of the poem, which comprehends here something of the pathetic inadequacy of ordinary mortal thought and feeling to grasp the full nature of God's love, God's grace, God's kingdom.[14]

Cary Nelson comments, in *The Incarnate Word*, that as we enter the "space" of this poem, we enter into a circle that suggests "the boundless sphere of God's presence, the kingdom which the dreamer can glimpse but cannot yet enter."[15] And, insofar as the poem is an "emblem" for the pearl, which in turn suggests the kingdom (in the parable), this is true. Yet the poem, "figuring" the kingdom in its intricate circular form (like Suger's St. Denis), is equally about the danger in all such figuring. This is much of the point of the comic dreamer, who, moving always within this perfect form nonetheless only sees perfection "over there," across the river, in the figure of the Pearl Maiden, of the pearl she wears, or of the holy city itself. The figure makes the kingdom appear graspable, if only just out of reach—yet all the while we are unknowingly within it.

This divinity, the poet affirms, both surrounds and is within one always and yet is not something that can be grasped. Rather, it can only be metaphorically entered by experiencing it in the embodied, sacramental life. This kingdom is a lived truth that breaks through form, as in the moment that the disciples saw the resurrected Jesus in the broken bread at Emmaus.

Thus, *Pearl* is at least in part a poem about humility. Like

---

14. Muscatine, *Poetry and Crisis*, p. 55. See also Spearing, Davenport, and Nelson (especially on the 101 stanzas); compare Barbara Nolan, who recognizes a split between reader and narrator here but doesn't question the narrator's role and who sees, in the final stanza of the poem, the poet speaking "in propria persona" (p. 204), but does not adequately explain how this voice is so easily distinguished from our narrator's in the previous stanzas.

15. Nelson, *Incarnate Word*, p. 31.

Gawain struggling so desperately to be the perfect knight of the pentangle and inevitably failing, the poet here casts himself within his own emblem or jewel as a man who continually, and comically, fails to understand the emblematic nature of the world into which he is cast, and thus fails to grasp his "privy pearl" simply because he tries so very hard to do just that.[16]

The Dreamer, it appears to me, does learn something along these lines; the poem after all ends with the Eucharist and with his desire to be a "homely hyne": a servant and not a master, a possession, or part of the divine body and will, and not a possessor. But regardless of how the audience responds to the simple piety of the awakened dreamer,[17] it is clear that the poem as a whole struggles to reveal these truths to its audience. The 101 stanzas, one more than the perfect 100 we might expect, as well as the missing line (472), which Nelson (following Crawford) suggests is deliberate (the poet "may have avoided formal perfection for fear of excessive vanity offending God"),[18] both have a suggestion of signs about them, indications of small chinks in the surface of the jewel. More significantly, however, within this near-perfect form, in the poet's language itself, we find constant reminders that the kingdom is not something that can be "spotted": fixed in one place, given one simple meaning. The key words in the poem figuratively alter shape as the poem progresses, defying the dreamer's (and the reader's) attempts to define: to fix limits, impose boundaries, or possess.[19]

16. See Martin, *Art and the Religious Experience*, p. 43.
17. Part of the point of this conclusion might of course be that, when all is said and done, the Christian "truth" is a simple one. Paul Tillich, asked once to summarize his own systematic theology, simply broke into song: "Jesus loves me, this I know. . . ."
18. Nelson, *Incarnate Word*, p. 33; John R. Crawford, *The Pearl* (San Francisco: Grabhorn-Hayem, 1967), p. 113.
19. See A. C. Spearing, "Symbolic and Dramatic Development in *Pearl*," in *The Middle English Pearl: Critical Essays*, ed. John Conley (Notre Dame, Ind.: University of Notre Dame Press, 1970), p. 126. Nolan hints at this paradox of the *figura*, which succeeds only by being "shattered" or "crucified," but, following Dante, Bonaventura, Hugh and Richard of St. Victor, and Abbot Suger (among many others), her main focus is on figure as providing a way to the kingdom through its beauty and aesthetic "resemblance" to the divine. See *Gothic Visionary*, especially pp. 189, 202–4.

It is, of course, with boundaries and limits—legal, allegorical, etymological—that we often feel most comfortable, "knowing our place," as the saying accurately has it, or "knowing just where we stand." But the poem, despite its careful physical descriptions and despite its own clear, circular boundaries, rarely lets us feel satisfied as to where, exactly, we are, either physically or linguistically. Instead, we are invited to go "in Godez grace, / In auenture ther meruaylez meuen" [where marvels occur] (63–64). We journey with the dreamer, attempting to understand, to grasp what is beyond human definition, attempting too often, as Spearing says of the Dreamer, to impose our own preconceptions on the Pearl Maiden. We see our reality in a certain, simple way and are unwilling to have this altered. Davenport comments, concerning the dreamer:

> It is as if he is bound to cling to his earthly notions as a protection against the overpowering brilliance of the heavenly world; and his obstinate earthliness is felt often as a social deficiency, an inability to grasp the hierarchy and manners of the heavenly court, in which all are kings and queens.[20]

Critics have done an excellent job isolating the deficiencies of the Dreamer, charting the various wrong turns our guide makes. Yet, it is also true that the narrator at the beginning of the poem is the Dreamer who has already made the journey there and back, like Will in *Piers Plowman*, who as pilgrim is just setting out but as narrator has already arrived. But one of the points being made in these texts is, I think, that to have arrived means to begin: literally, to begin narrating, telling one's story (and for the reader, listening to it), but also figuratively, in that one is reborn, newly made at the end of the journey, signaling the beginning of a new journey in Christ, a journey that is utterly open-ended and dependent on the will of God. Thus *Piers* ends at Easter, as the liturgical calendar is used as a mirror for Will's story and awakening (all that lies after the story ends is what follows Easter, the Church Militant), and *Pearl* ends with the Eucharist and the nar-

20. Davenport, *Art of the Gawain-Poet*, p. 125.

rator's response to his own awakening, a response that, like the telling of the story itself, signals a beginning, a new life.

This is so primarily in its new recognition of the failure of all figures to reveal adequately the radical nature of the divine love. It is as if the journey itself can be related, but at the crucial moment only silence reigns. The narrator is broken, like the bread. All of his experience culminates here, and although life goes on (as the fact of the narrative implies), that life can no longer be adequately described. Something—Being—is realized, which shatters the journeyer's logic, and thus his ordinary discourse. Aquinas in a moment of mystical rapture sees all of his life's labor as straw for the fire; Dante at the moment of supreme vision is struck dumb and the reader is left with the silence of the revolving heavens.

The *Pearl* narrator, like Will, no longer sees what he had seen before—his pearl, himself, his world—in quite the same way. He is not the same man as the poem begins, and the beginning is, I think, intended to alert the reader to this, as it sets us down in a "spot" rather difficult to define or set limits to.[21] Is the narrator referring to a real pearl? A real "erbere"? Real "gresse," "grounde," a real "spot" from which he lost this "pryuy perle wythouten spot"?

Interpretations abound. Some critics are certain that the opening lines would undoubtedly have suggested to the medieval audience (however we choose to define that particular fiction) the well-known lapidaries, in which gems are emblems of spiritual qualities. Some would argue that there is no overt suggestion in the opening of the poem that the pearl is anything but a pearl, despite the marvelously sensual description ("so smal, so smothe her syde gaye") and the presence of "luf-daungere" (longing for a loved object); similarly, there are arguments about the "spot": a garden, graveyard, mound.[22]

21. Ibid., p. 34.
22. See especially P. M. Kean, *The Pearl: An Interpretation* (New York: Barnes and Noble, 1967); Edward Wilson, "Word Play and the Interpretation of *Pearl*," *Medium Ævum* 40 (1971), pp. 116–34; C. A. Luttrell, "*Pearl*: Symbolism in a

Interpretive Construction

The poem from its opening lines invites this confusion. If it is a real pearl, as it at first seems, then his sorrow seems excessive, as Wilson argues.[23] If he is referring to a small child, as most critics agree, then did he "really" lose her in "on erbere"? *This* garden, with all of its flowers? Luttrell has observed that the plants mentioned here are divorced from their proper season and geographical location.[24] Clearly, the "I" of the poem is in a location created—with some help, certainly, from earlier allegories, lapidaries, romances—by the poet himself. It is an imagined space, a spot existing only in the mind of the poet, and now the reader, from which spot an imagined journey begins.

All of this complexity and confusion create a certain distance between reader and narrator, as Nolan suggests: "From the narrator's point of view the garden seems to be real enough. But for the audience, its mystery assumes paramount interest."[25] Yet Nolan does not suggest that this separation we feel from the narrator leads us to clarify the further separation between this first-person speaker and the poet who has arranged this ambiguity. It is this deliberate ambiguity, I am suggesting, set against the apparently single level understanding of the narrator, that prepares the reader for the complexities that lie ahead. In a sense, with the beginning of the poem the reader has already entered the dream, where things are not quite as she expects them.

Yet, I say apparently single level because, as the reader knows on a second trip through the poem, the narrator is the awakened dreamer and so presumably recognizes that what he describes in this opening is less straightforward—less literal—than he makes it appear. It is then the narrator himself who is responsible for "setting us down" as the poem begins in the place of the dreamer, that is, in a spot that seems easily recognizable and defined but that on further inspection becomes increasingly unclear and mul-

---

Garden Setting," in Conley, *Middle English Pearl*, pp. 297–324, and Elizabeth Petroff, "Landscape in *Pearl*: The Transformation of Nature," *Chaucer Review* 16 (1981), pp. 181–93.
23. Wilson, "Word Play," p. 119.
24. Luttrell, "*Pearl*: Symbolism," p. 313.
25. Nolan, *Gothic Visionary*, p. 164.

tivalent. This apparently trivial clarification is important in that it reminds us that the changes undergone by this dreamer-turned-narrator inevitably surface in a text that defies the sort of single level interpretation that the original dreamer tries to impose. The text is, on one level at least, the narrator's *Pearl*: paradoxical and polyvalent. As such, it indicates the distance traveled from the time when the narrator was simply Dreamer.

Some of the tension concerning location inevitably revolves around the link words, which play so prominent a part in the process of the poem.[26] For example, any suggestion that a word can be limited to one meaning is immediately laid to rest by the first link word *spot*, if not by the referents of *pearl* itself. Throughout the first section (the first five stanzas), the poet carefully plays off two meanings of *spot*, setting up two themes or melodies that play off each other as if contrapuntally, while moving us through the poem. Each stanza travels toward its climax, that "pryuy perle withouten spot," and then circles back via the link word in the first line of the next stanza: "sythen in that spote hit fro me sprange. . . . To that spot that I in speche expoun. . . . Bifore that spot my honde I spennd" [clasped]. Yet, the circling is also a progression, a development through the narrative: we may seem to return to the same "spot," yet never do as our understanding of it alters with each new context. As with the poem as a whole, we seem with each stanza to return to our beginning "spot" but find it—or ourselves—altered by the journey.

Further, however, as I have suggested, each time we return to that link word, we recognize a distinctly different meaning: "without spot" suggests "without blemish, perfect"; "to that spot" suggests a strictly spatial reading; a spot of land, a specific locale. We find as we read that we weave our way back and forth between these two meanings, never able to rest in one, until we recognize that the meanings need not be kept so isolated from each other: the word is the same each time and simply has layers of meaning. Thus, the pearl "without spot" is perfect, unblem-

---

26. See O. D. Macrae-Gibson, "*Pearl*: The Link Words and the Thematic Structure," in Conley, *Middle English Pearl*, pp. 203–10.

ished, but also is without location, unfixed, and unfixable; this realization suddenly separates us from the dreamer, who is certain that his pearl is fixed, spotted right where he "wayted." This recognition brings a certain complex irony (and humor, I think) to the poem very early on: it is this dreamer who is "spotted" by us (and by the poet), that is, seen, understood, located in a fixed place, and also blemished because he is so firmly spotted, rooted to the earth and the perspective of the earth.

Yet I want to emphasize again that if we attempt to eliminate the physical perspective entirely, then we also eliminate the "spot" from which we inevitably begin. *We* must begin "spotted" because *we* are rooted to the earth. In this sense we are all of course "spotted": to be human means to be blemished, in part because we do take the "earth" or matter as our sole perspective. This, however, is not the real problem: the problem is the failure to recognize our own spottedness for what it is: we either deny that there is anything other than the earthly, material perspective and in that way, like the jeweler, become literalists and materialists, or we deny that the earthly has anything at all to offer us: we attempt to escape the earth and body and in that way fail to understand the sacramental nature of Christ's gift. We fail to understand earth's meaning. *Pearl* deals quite explicitly with the former problem but implicitly in its own "physical" (circular) structure and beauty acknowledges the truth of the latter as well. Paradoxically, the poem celebrates the material but only insofar as the material is seen from the point of view of the spiritual: from the Maiden's point of view. The physical beauty and splendor of the Maiden, of the setting, and ultimately of the New Jerusalem itself—descriptions of which constitute a large portion of the poem—all suggest the proper appreciation of the image.

This sudden shift in perspective that the reader potentially undergoes is, in miniature, the process and goal of the poem as a whole. Yet, we should recall that the reader may not go through this process, just as the dreamer may not. He or she may reduce the poem to its simplest terms or may simply reject the poem entirely, as a good number of Jesus' auditors did, wondering like

Nicodemus, "how can these things be," and deciding that they cannot. But in another sense, to say that the reader decides would be considered a misstatement by anyone who accepted the fact that true understanding and insight come only by grace—it happens to the reader as the reader "knocks"—that is, wrestles with the text.

Thus, it is also impossible to define when this happens to a reader, a problem that surfaces again in Blake. Just as the Pearl Maiden cannot force insight, cannot impose a breakthrough for the Dreamer, the poet cannot force a reader to leap: it comes or it does not, and it comes when it will. The text provides for it and in one sense demands a response, but it cannot force a "yes." As I suggest later, part of the point of the poem's humor, which arises from the failed narrator, is due to a certain skepticism of the poet's, skepticism not about the truth of the kingdom but about the possibility that the figure will lead to the kingdom.[27]

The clarity of the poem, then, lies far from the simple equivalence of pearl equals kingdom equals salvation, or whatever term we use to define the undefinable. There is clarity, but it is the clarity gained by the perspective of this kingdom itself, which is a vision that shows us that when we say *kingdom* we are inevitably missing the mark. It is instead an understanding that claims the whole man in its mystery.

As with so much of the language of Jesus, words are weighted with irony; there is a split between what the characters in the drama perceive and what we perceive. In the Gospels, this occurs with key words that become charged with new meaning through the acts and insight of Jesus: *bread, wine, vineyard; water, gates, ways, roads,* and *life* itself. Similarly here: when the narrator says, "To that spot that I in speche expoun / I entred in that erber grene," we might hear an ambiguity, a complexity that the narrator apparently misses.[28] Again, at the end of this first section

---

27. See Nolan, *Gothic Visionary*, pp. 40–42, 48–50. See also Ann Chalmers Watts, "*Pearl*, Inexpressibility, and Poems of Human Loss," *PMLA* 99 (1984), pp. 26–40.

28. The complexity lies in words like *erbere* and *spot* which already, by line

Interpretive Construction

as the dream proper begins: "I slode [slid] vpon a slepyng-slaghte [into a sudden sleep] / On that precios perle withouten spot" (59–60), we hear some rich humor in the simple preposition. The narrator seems to imply a literal reading here: He sleeps on, on top of, his pearl, which is buried beneath him. In retrospect, we might also hear him saying that he was "struck"—"slaughtered" as by a blow—into sleep "concerning" or "about" his precious pearl, also accurate. But, on further consideration, we might also appreciate the rather comic fact that he is sleeping "on" a pearl that is "withouten spot": that has no location at all. This sleep truly is a "death blow" to him but not at all in the way he has thought. Instead, it is a death he must face: the death not of his maiden, but of his own way of being in the world.

This question of location, of spot, remains a crucial one throughout the poem and will be a continual indicator of the dreamer's progress, or lack of progress, as he again and again believes that he has spotted his pearl, confusing the physicality of a dream—the trees, ground, river, and city—with the world to which he is accustomed. This material perspective is what the pearl maiden must defeat by inducing the dreamer to let go of his preconceived notions and viewpoint. He must be brought to a place where the ground under his feet is not so secure; where he is forced, finally, to acknowledge a mystery.

The beginning of the second section is in its own way a summary of this problem as we move from the waking state to the dream, from body to spirit, from "spot" to "adubbemente" (adornment):

> Fro spot my spyryt ther sprang in space;
> My body on balke ther bod. In sweuen
> My goste is gon in Godez grace,
> In auenture ther meruaylez meuen.
> I ne wyste in this worlde quere that hit wace,
> Bot I knew me keste ther klyfez cleuenz.

37, have become charged. See the preceding discussion on the narrator's role in this, however; it is a mistake, I think, to accuse him of a naivete that we associate with the dreamer.

> Toward a foreste I bere the face,
> Where rych rokkez wer to dyscreuen.
> The lyght of hem myght no mon leuen,
> The glemande glory that of hem glent,
> For wern neuer webbez that wyghez weuen
> Of half so dere adubbemente.
>
> [From that spot my spirit rose after a time;
> my body remained on the ground in sleep.
> My spirit through God's grace has gone
> on an adventure where marvels occur.
> I have no idea where in the world it was
> but I know I was conveyed to where cliffs rise sheer
> I looked towards a forest
> where I discerned beautiful rocks
> the light of them no one could believe
> the gleaming glory that shone from them,
> for there were never tapestries woven
> adorned half so dearly.]
>
> (61–72)

"Fro spot": again we hear more than the single literal meaning. From a particular location of course, but also from a "spotted," fixed, and blemished position. He begins to journey from a flawed perspective, suggested by his continual attempt even here to locate himself by the familiar. He may not know where in the world he is, but he certainly recognizes sheer cliffs, a forest, rocks. He knows that he is in a place of "marvels," where the rocks themselves glisten with a light that no man can believe (or understand: "leuen") and where the leaves unfold "as bornyst sylver" (77)—in short, what appears to be an earthly paradise—but the glorious and detailed physical descriptions themselves suggest what the key link words in this section and the one following make clear: his primary focus here is on "adornment" and wanting "more and more."

It is the sensual marvel of the dream locale that eases the dreamer's grief (ll. 85–86) and makes him hunger for more; similarly, it is this adornment which draws the reader in. The care-

Interpretive Construction 45

fully controlled alliteration working with the images creates in sound and sight a sense of the ease and glory of this spot:

> Dubbed wern alle tho downez sydez
> Wyth crystal klyffez so cler of kynde.
> Holtewodez bryght aboute hem bydez
> Of bollez as blwe as ble of Ynde;
> As bornyst syluer the lef on slydez,
> That thike con trylle on vch a tynde;
> Quen glem of glodez agaynz hem glydez,
> Wyth schymeryng schene ful schrylle thay schynde.
>
> [Adorned were all the hills' sides
> with crystal cliffs so clear in character.
> Woods lay shining about them
> with trunks as blue as the color of India (indigo).
> The leaves, which quivered densely on every branch,
> slid over each other like burnished silver.
> When the gleam from clear patches of sky glided over them,
> they shone most brightly with a lovely shimmer.]
>
> (73-80)

We, too, marvel and long for "more and more," long to enter more fully, to *be* there entirely, as if the language were itself a land where we might live. And this is precisely the tension the poem is trying to locate for us: to reveal to us the paradox of the figurative, spots that are without spot.

* * *

One appropriate, if early, climax to this word game occurs when the dreamer first addresses the Pearl Maiden, after watching her coming down the bank on the other side of the river. Again, as Gordon points out in his notes, the description of what the dreamer sees is both detailed and exquisite.[29] The link word now, rather than *adubbement* ("set" or "adorned") is *pyghte*, also suggesting set, fixed spatially; referring primarily to the "pearls" that adorn the woman but also to the Pearl Maiden herself, "set" on the other side of an apparently "real" or material river:

---

29. E. V. Gordon, ed., *Pearl* (Oxford: Clarendon Press, 1953), p. 56.

> That gracios gay withouten galle [flaw],
> So smothe, so smal, so seme slyght,
> Rysez up in hir araye ryalle,
> A precios pyece in perlez pyght.
>
> (189–92)

At the center of his vision is the Pearl Maiden herself, moving gracefully toward him, so beautiful—and apparently his *own*—that all else in that paradise is forgotten. Then at the center of the maiden herself (and at the conclusion of his description of her) lies the one pearl that is "more equal" than the others and that cannot, the narrator tells us, be described:

> Bot a wonder perle withouten wemme
> Inmyddez hyr breste watz sette so sure;
> A mannez dom moght dryghly demme
> Er mynde moght malte in hit mesure.
> I hope no tong moght endure
> No sauerly saghe say of that syght,
> So watz hit clene and cler and pure,
> That precios perle ther hit watz pyght.
>
> [A wondrous pearl without flaw was set
> so firmly upon her breast; a man's judgement
> might be utterly baffled before his mind
> could conceive its magnitude.
> I think no tongue could have power
> to describe that sight in adequate speech,
> so clean and clear and pure it was, where that
> precious pearl was set.]
>
> (221–28)

The vision is a stunning one, with its pearl upon pearl, figure upon figure, which matches the simultaneous layering of genres. All levels overlap in the land of figure; none is excluded. We can easily locate ourselves here within elegy, the courtly romance, the dream vision, the travelogue, the earthly paradise. We recognize a father discovering a lost daughter ("nerre then aunte or nece") and yet also, apparently a man—a lover—being ravished in a dream by the sight of a beautiful woman:

Interpretive Construction 47

> As schorne golde schyr her fax thenne schon,
> On schylderez that leghe vnlapped lyghte.
> Her depe colour yet wonted non
> Of precios perle in porfyl pyghte.
>
> [Her hair, that lay lightly on her shoulders, unbound,
> then shone like bright cut gold.
> The intense whiteness of her complexion was not inferior
> even to that precious set in an embroidered border.]
>
> (213–16)

However, at the center of this vision lies not the woman herself, as I have suggested, but the one flawless pearl with which the description closes. The pearl, as we later learn (if we do not already recognize this figure), is the emblem for the heavenly kingdom, set on the maiden's breast as a figure indicating her true location, where she is "set." As she tells the dreamer, she has become a pearl, that is, a member of the kingdom, and her wearing pearls is a sign of a condition that otherwise is inexplicable to us: like the flawless pearl itself, "So watz hit clene and cler and pure" (227).

It is at this point that the dreamer first addresses his maiden, and we see most clearly, even humorously, what happens when you pile layer on layer of meanings:

> "O perle," quoth I, "in perlez pyght,
> Art thou my perle that I haf playned [mourned],
> Regretted by myn one on nighte?"
>
> (241–43)

As the debate that now begins makes clear, the fact that he is (at least imaginatively) a jeweler and possessor of pearls is precisely his problem. His vision is fixed on the earth's gem; similarly fixed upon the "mote" in the maiden's argument, he is blind to the beam in his own eye. The dramatic reversal that now occurs in the poem is caused directly by this failure of his, a failure that we have been invited to share. In a sense, the poem sets us up once again. Although we find ourselves at moments separated from the dreamer (if we have been reading carefully), nonetheless we are invited to share his point of view, marveling with him over the exquisite landscape and sharing his astonishment and joy at locating this beautiful lost pearl. And despite our uncertainty about just what he has lost, whether it is pearl or child, there is little question that in these climactic lines we respond at least in part as a courtly audience would respond to a romance: whatever else the pearl was, she is now a ravishing woman, adorned in costly gems.[30]

Thus our expectations are great; we are aroused and eagerly await the union of these two, as does the benighted dreamer himself. But instead, we get a harsh reversal:

> That juel thenne in gemmez gente [noble]
> Vered vp her vyse with yghen graye [turned, face],
> Set on hyr coroun of perle orient,
> And soberly after thenne con ho say:
> "Sir, ye haf your tale mysetente. . . ." [spoken heedlessly]
>
> (253–57)

The disappointment here, shared by dreamer and reader, is a great part of the point in this poem. We are led by the sensual, the figure (the Pearl Maiden herself), to that which is ultimate (to Jerusalem, in fact) but only if we recognize the sensual as the embodied figure of a truth otherwise ungraspable.

This does not mean that the Pearl Maiden ceases to be a woman (or child); just as Beatrice remains Dante's Beatrice, she remains his Pearl, but her greater significance is her pointing the way to the holy city, the kingdom of God. Like Beatrice, and like all things of this "whole sensible world," as Bonaventura says, she is not intended to be a possession but a guide, a rung of a ladder by which "we shall mount up to God, that we may be true Hebrews crossing from Egypt to the land promised to our fathers."[31]

The *Pearl*-Poet, from all we can tell, is not one who frowns on

---

30. See Gordon's notes to lines 228 and 254, *Pearl*, pp. 56–57.
31. Bonaventura, *Mind's Road to God*, p. 11. For my qualifications to the use of Bonaventura, see note 19.

the flesh; the richness of the description here, and in *Gawain*, is, we sense, intended to be appreciated, walked in, we might say, like somebody's garden. The sensual is relished, but not, ultimately, for its own sake.³² As Auerbach comments, "the figural interpretation of reality, which . . . was the dominant view in the European Middle Ages,"

> was the idea that earthly life is thoroughly real, with the reality of the flesh into which the Logos entered, but that with all its reality it is only *umbra* and *figura* of the authentic, future, ultimate truth, the real reality that will unveil and preserve the *figura*. In this way the individual earthly event is not regarded as a definitive self-sufficient, reality . . . but viewed primarily in immediate vertical connection with a divine order which encompasses it, which on some future day will itself be concrete reality. . . .³³

It is figure we are witnessing in the Pearl Maiden. Similarly, the poem is figurative of the kingdom insofar as it is pearl—circular and "wemle"—but it is figure primarily by being also a shattering of the figure itself. The kingdom, it has been suggested in the Introduction, is found only in the rupturing of the form within which the kingdom is held and proclaimed. We again reach Emmaus: as long as reader and Dreamer see only pearl, they will fail to see (and grasp) kingdom. The kingdom must break through the form that contains it just as Jesus is revealed at the instant the bread breaks. Bread must be broken, the literal shattered, and yet without it no figure exists. The two live together in an inevitable and necessary tension. Out of that tension arises beauty: the pearl that is *Pearl*.³⁴

32. See Gatta, "Transformation Symbolism," p. 248, on the sacramental view of reality; see also Emert, "*Pearl* and the Incarnate Word," pp. 36, 49, 79, 129, and Petroff, pp. 181–83.
33. Erich Auerbach, "Figura," in *Scenes from the Drama of European Literature* (New York: Meridian Books, 1959), p. 72.
34. See Auerbach, "Figura," p. 72. Michael McCanles argues that "literal" and "metaphorical" are in fact inseparable. "Discourse of either sort becomes possible only when the literal and metaphorical meanings of words are allowed to be dialectical functions of each other while being sharply distinguished." He adds, "Literal meaning is itself a metaphor. . . ." See "The Literal and the Metaphorical: Dialectic or Interchange," *PMLA* 91 (1976), p. 285. (We approach Blake here, where such "opposition is true friendship.")

* * *

The debate between Dreamer and Maiden becomes rather like a game of tennis, with the Dreamer continually lobbing these unqualified and unclarified statements over the river to the Pearl Maiden, who returns them with spins and twists that transform his words so thoroughly that he can no longer see them in quite the same way. They remain his words, his concepts, but they come back multifaceted, polyvalent. A magician has transformed the round ball into a sparkling complex jewel in midair, yet, the dreamer keeps lobbing it back as if it were nothing more than a tennis ball.[35]

Yet at the same time, of course, this play is also a journey. We move through the dialogue, taking up themes or words that lead as if inevitably into other themes and words, with the linking words themselves functioning like a thread that guides us through the labyrinth. And again, the richness, the complexity of the strands as they interweave from stanza to stanza is such that it defies the reader to separate them. They cannot of course be separated, and this is precisely the poem's point. One figure points to another, *is* in a sense that other (metaphorically), until we realize that all figures, like all objects (and all words), are manifestations of the one word and figure that is who we ultimately are.

The Pearl Maiden, for example, at the beginning of their discussion, quickly suggests that his failure to understand the nature of perception is in some way also a failure of "cortayse" (courtesy), a theme that will dominate the discussion three sections later. Similarly, the failure to see correctly implies a failure of faith (as with the Disciples in Matthew 16), which in turn suggests pride, that deadliest of sins, as the Dreamer is unwilling to accept the truth of anything that he cannot understand through his reason:

"I halde that jueler lyttel to prayse
That leuez wel that he sez wyth yghe,

35. See Milroy, "*Pearl*: The Verbal Texture," p. 203, on languages "enshrining truth," and Hill, "Middle English Poets," p. 166.

And much to blame and vncortoyse
That leuez oure Lorde wolde make a lyghe,
That lelly hyghte your lyf to rayse,
Thagh Fortune dyd your flesch to dyghe.
Ye setten Hys wordez ful westernays
That leuez nothynk bot ye hit syghe;
And that is a poynt o sorquydryghe,
That vche god mon may euel byseme,
To leue no tale be true to tryghe
Bot that hys one skyl may dem."

[I praise that jeweler very little that believes only what he sees with his eyes, and very blameworthy and discourteous one who believes our Lord, who faithfully promised to raise your life though Fortune caused your flesh to die, would tell a lie. You who believe nothing unless you have seen it, set his words completely awry. And it is an instance of pride, which ill befits every good man, to believe no account to be true when put to the test except what his judgement alone can understand.]

(301–12)

Here, as so often in this debate, the Pearl Maiden is not interested in simply setting one point straight: she is trying to show how interconnected all strands of our lives are. And our words betray us: they show how, over and over again, we come to think that what we see before us is all there is and that it only has one meaning, exists on only one level, forgetting that the world's primary function is as figure "of the authentic . . . ultimate truth."[36] Because of his failure to understand the meaning of what he sees, and therefore of what he says (or vice versa), everything for the Dreamer is turned around or "westernays" in its importance. The mirror of the mind, as Bonaventura would say, is dulled, so that the physical alone is real.[37]

36. Auerbach, "Figura," p. 72.
37. See E. V. Gordon's footnote on "westernays," p. 57. See also Rudolf Otto, *The Idea of the Holy*, trans. John Harvey (1923; reprint, New York: Oxford University Press, 1958), p. 7 (on defining the "numinous"): "There is only one way to help another to an understanding of it. He must be guided and led on by consideration and discussion of the matter through the ways of his own mind,

* * *

As other critics have commented, the poem works as a poem in part because of our Dreamer's marvelous obtuseness: this functions as both entertainment and edification in the best Horatian manner.[38] The Dreamer longs to hear about the Maiden's life in the kingdom and so says, "I wolde bysech, wythouten debate, / ye wolde me say in sobre asente / What lyf ye lede erly and late" (390–92). Then, thirty lines later, he begins the debate himself by questioning the facts of her statements concerning her life as "Quen" in heaven. The Maiden then takes up his word ("Quen of cortaysye") and attempts to show him the limitations of his understanding: how the concept of "cortaysye" and "court" and "kyndom" (445–55) are analogies, *umbra* based on our knowledge of earthly life. We have little else to go on when talking about the divine.[39] Yet, the analogies inevitably break down. They cannot contain the truth of the divine realm and must be shown to collapse, lest we begin to worry about who shall sit next to Jesus in heaven. Thus the Pearl Maiden uses the analogies yet simultaneously transforms them so that a "quen" is not quite what we thought:

> "The court of the kyndom of God alyue
> Hatz a property in hytself beyng:
> Alle that may therinne aryue
> Of alle the reme is quen other kyng,
> And neuer other yet schal depryue,
> But vchon fayn of otherez hafyng,
> And wolde her corounez wern worthe tho fyue,
> If possyble were her mendyng."

[The court of the kingdom of the living God has an attribute in its own nature: all that may arrive there in that kingdom are either queen or king, and yet one shall never dispossess another, but each

---

until he reaches the point at which "the numinous" in him perforce begins to stir . . . our *X* cannot, strictly speaking, be taught, it can only be evoked, awakened in the mind; as everything that comes 'of the spirit' must be awakened."

38. See Davenport, *Art of the Gawain-Poet*, p. 21.
39. See Spearing, in Conley, *Middle English Pearl*, pp. 134–37. Of course the *fact* of the analogy suggests a certain faith in the reality and importance of the earthly life, a point that Auerbach stresses in his essay "Figura."

one (be) glad of the others' possession, and wish their crowns were
five times as precious, if any improvement of them were possible.]
(445–52)

As Gordon nicely comments, when the Maiden speaks of "cortesaye" and refers to Paul's analogy of the "Body of Christ" ("Of cortesaye, as saytz Saynt Poule, / Al arn we membrez of Jesu Kryst"), we recognize a significant stretching in the concept of courtesy, since Paul is speaking in 1 Corinthians of divine grace: spiritual gifts.[40] Again the Maiden (and poet) defies our attempt to split heaven and earth, reminding us instead that the mundane ("courtesaye" with its courtly and material associations) is always to be seen as embodying the spiritual. This in turn will connect with her later discussion of "less and more," until we see that "the grace of God is gret innoghe" (section XI). However, we journey there only because the Dreamer insists on seeing these key words in the context to which he is accustomed, forcing the Maiden continually to redefine by expansion, in order to undermine his definition. The world is a simple place to the Dreamer; things are what they are, and have set boundaries, clear meanings:

"That Cortayse is to fre of dede,
Yf hyt be soth that thou conez saye . . .
Of countes, damysel, par ma fay,
Wer fayr in heuen to halde asstate,
Other ellez a lady of lasse aray;
Bot a quene!—hit is to dere a date."[41]

[That Courteous One is too liberal in action, if what you say is true . . . by my faith, young lady, it would be fine to hold the rank of countess in heaven, or else a lady of less rank, but a queen! It is too exalted a rank.]
(481–92)

Here he complains that the "date" or limit set by the Maiden

---

40. Gordon, *Pearl*, p. 57.
41. See Gordon, *Pearl*, p. 63, on "date," and Davenport, *Art of the Gawain-Poet*, p. 44, on "defining." Note the continual doubt in the Dreamer's mind: if it's true what you say. . . . Compare l. 1185.

is "to dere": too exalted, too broad. Similarly, at the end of the Maiden's homily on the parable of the vineyard, wherein she attempts to break through his understanding of "less and more," his response is quick and to the point: "Then more I meled [spoke] and sayde apert: 'Me thynk thy tale unresounable'" (589–90)—as, of course, it is, that being much of the point of the parable. As Dodd summarizes, the parable is "a striking picture of the divine generosity which gives without regard to the measures of strict justice."[42] But our understanding of the response of the laborers, which the Dreamer so clearly echoes, can, I think, tell us more about the predicament of the Dreamer than Dodd's comment at first suggests.

The Dreamer insists that this parable makes no sense from any logical, rational, or businesslike point of view. Surely it is true that, as the Psalter says, "Thou quytes [requite] vchon as hys desserte":

> Now he that stod the long day stable,
> And thou to payment com hym byfore,
> Thenne the lasse in werke to take more able,
> And euer the lenger the lasse the more.
>   (595–600)

At the center of the poem, the Dreamer has reached an apparent dead end in the logical paradox of the parable. As Gordon interprets these final two lines, the Dreamer is saying something like "Then the less work done, the greater the capacity for earning, and so continually in a constant (inverse) ratio."[43] How can you possibly conduct any business with such a principle? But the parable claims, and the Pearl Maiden echoes, that this is how the Kingdom works: "'Of more and lasse in Godez ryche,' [kingdom] / That gentyl sayde, 'lys no joparde, / For ther is vch mon payed inlyche [alike]'" (601–3). "He lauez Hys gyftez as water

---

42. C. H. Dodd, *The Parables of the Kingdom*, rev. ed. (New York: Charles Scribner's Sons, 1961), pp. 94–95.

43. Gordon, *Pearl*, p. 66.

Interpretive Construction 55

of dyche" (607): that is, he pours out his gifts like water from a stream that never ceases to flow.[44]

But the Dreamer is like those in the parables who insist always on interpreting according to justice and the law, wherein, as Dan Via comments in his interpretation of this parable, "reward should be exactly proportionate to achievement." Such an interpretation of reality, however, implies "that they believed themselves capable of maintaining their position in the world, of deserving their reward." The parable breaks into this vision of the world and challenges the whole notion of winning the kingdom by one's efforts: reward comes not through one's achievements but instead simply through another's generosity, through "cortesaye," or "grace," from which the laborers are potentially excluded, Via concludes, "because of their impenetrable legalistic understanding of existence, grounded in the effort to effect their own security."[45]

This, of course, is precisely the danger that faces the benighted dreamer, a serious danger, in spite of the humor of his rather colloquial outbursts.[46] In his own comic way, he is a fourteenth-century equivalent of those laborers who cried for justice, of the hardworking elder son who is incensed at the treatment that the prodigal receives from his loving and merciful father. Robert Funk nicely clarifies the dilemma of such thinking:

> There is nothing wrong with such logic except that it fails to discern that it is man and not God who is on trial. It refuses to let God be God. The Pharisees are those who insist on interpreting the word of grace rather than letting themselves be interpreted by it.[47]

---

44. Compare the earlier use of this water-well image, in which the dreamer's sorrow ran like water from a well; note also the colloquial language of the Pearl Maiden. See Emert's discussion of the *sermo humilis*, "*Pearl* and the Incarnate Word," p. 145f., and Auerbach's essay on the topic in *Literary Language and Its Public*, Bollingen Series LXXIV (New York: Pantheon Books, 1965), pp. 25–67.
45. Dan Via, *The Parables* (Philadelphia: Fortress Press, 1967), pp. 153–54.
46. Compare the mingling of humor with a serious point in *Gawain*.
47. Robert Funk, *Language, Hermeneutic and the Word of God: The Problem of Language in the New Testament and Contemporary Theology* (New York: Harper & Row, 1966), p. 17. See also Davenport, *Art of the Gawain-Poet*, p. 125.

The issue may at first appear to be confused by the Pearl Maiden's sudden insistence, "The innocent is ay [always] saf by ryght" (section XII), but her references here to both Old and New Testament clarify the contexts within which she is speaking. The key question always is a simple one: "'Lorde, quo [who] schal klymbe thy hygh hylle, / Other rest wythinne thy holy place?' "[48] And the answer appears to be equally simple:

> "Hondelyngez harme that dyt not ille,
> That is of hert bothe clene and lyght,
> Ther schal hys step stable stylle":
> The innosent is ay saf by ryght.
>
> ["He who did no evil with his hands, who is pure
> and unsullied at heart, shall there set his foot at rest":
> the innocent is always safe by righteousness.]
>
> (681–84)

Yet as the Psalms also indicated, this saying is a hard one, for no grown individual can live in innocence:

> Anende ryghtwys men yet saytz a gome,
> Dauid in sauter, if euer ye segh hit:
> "Lorde, thy seruaunt dragh neuer to dome,
> For non lyuyande to the is justyfyet."
>
> [Also, concerning just men, a certain man, David,
> says in the Psalter, if you have ever seen it: "Lord,
> never bring Your servant to judgment, for no
> living man is justified before You."]
>
> (697–700)

The solution to this predicament is clear, if again paradoxical. The children are the innocent ones and thus are "saf by ryght": "To suche is neuer ryche arayed" (719). Therefore, you must become as a child, like the Pearl Maiden herself, in fact, in order to enter the kingdom:

> Ryght con calle to Hym Hys mylde,
> And sayde Hys ryche no wygh myght wynne

---

48. The reference here is to either Psalm 15 or Psalm 24.

Interpretive Construction 57

> Bot he com thyder ryght as a chylde,
> Other ellez neuermore com therinne.[49]

> [Justice summoned His gentle ones (the disciples)
> to Him, and said no one could win His kingdom
> unless he came to it absolutely like a child.]
> (721–24)

The climax of the debate itself is here, in this thirteenth section, where so many of the key images are gathered up and held, glistening in our minds like the many facets of a diamond. There is only one path back to innocence, the Maiden affirms, and that is the way of the cross. If you plead justice, "Alegge the ryght, thou may be innome," you may be refuted in your argument.[50]

> Bot He on rode that blody dyed,
> Delfully thurgh hondez thryght
> Gyue the to passe, when thou arte tryed,
> By innocens and not by ryghte.

> [But he that on the cross died bloodily,
> grievously pierced through the hands, grant you
> to go free, when you are tried by innocence
> and not by your own righteousness.]
> (705–8)

To travel by this path, through this gate, is to become like that earlier jeweler who sacrificed all, "solde alle hys goud, bothe wolen and lynne, To bye hym a perle watz mascellez" (731–32).

An attempt to sum up the various attributes of the kingdom is made here, through the central image of the pearl. The kingdom, the Maiden says, is something like this: imagine a perfect pearl, and you will at least have a figure for the life I now experience, across this river. Imagine its purity, clarity, perfection, and endless circularity; its grace, courtesy, and "commenness," as each alike shares in its bliss:

---

49. The break in link words here with the word *Jesus*, substituting for *Ryght*, is a way of indicating their unity.
50. See Andrew and Waldron, *Poems of the Pearl Manuscript*, p. 87.

> For hit is wemlez, clene, and clere [flawless],
> And endelez rounde, and blythe of mode,
> And commune to alle that ryghtwys were.
>
> (737–39)

This Pearl is given only by the Lamb, "that schede hys blode," as a gift of grace, showing each of us in this ultimate sacrifice how to "klymb thy hygh hylle."[51]

The pearl seen earlier on the Maiden's breast is also, of course, a sign or token of "pes," the image of where she dwells, the state she now calls home, the "reme of hevenesse clere" (735). It is, however, at this point that this significance becomes clear—clear, that is, if one can see through this complexity of figure within figure within figure. The Dreamer himself marvels over all these pearls:

> "O maskelez [spotless] perle in perlez pure,
> That berez," quoth I, "the perle of prys. . . ."
>
> (745–46)

As in earlier lines (241–43, for example), one finds here a man who has been seeking a single lost pearl and opens a door only to find not one pearl but a landscape full of them: 144,000 as it turns out, all dressed in pearls, set out in nothing but pearls, and all adorned with the pearl of great price. All are figures (as both pearls and brides of the Lamb) and are adorned with figures, standing within a larger figure, the holy city itself, all of which are varying attempts to get at the single truth and way.[52]

It is to his pearl that the Dreamer has been journeying all along, believing that he could reach her under his own volition: walking, swimming, perhaps buying his way in, as a literal reading of the parable of the pearl of great price might imply. The Maiden's point, on the other hand, is that the only bridge is one that we do not build. Rather, it is something that happens to us, breaks upon us by overturning all of our expectations as the Cross did for the Disciples, who did not get what they expected, and

---

51. See Nelson, *Incarnate Word*, p. 32, on the restoration of the "circle."
52. Ibid., pp. 39–40.

did not expect what they got. "He who seeks to find his life must lose it": a statement such as this can be understood literally ("thy corse in clot mot calder keve"), but a literal understanding alone will not suffice, will not put the pearl within reach. The Dreamer must see this, like everything else, figuratively: as a demand to give up his life in this world; cease to see himself as owner, as jeweler, becoming a "homely hyne" instead. These too, of course, are figures, ways of discovering the need for a radical change in perspective, which is the Maiden's goal, with language her tool. Discussions of "ryght," of "kynde," of "cortayse" and "quens"; definitions of "maskeles" and "grace" all lead to the same place. All are attempts at conversion, turning the Dreamer around in his sleep—which is to get him to Jerusalem, to his pearl, figures for a reality we cannot name yet always seek, which we find only by being found—through a letting go, a giving up, that is an acknowledgment that we cannot will our way home.

* * *

The Maiden says, we recall, that this kingdom is "endeles rounde," suggesting in that perfect circularity that you can begin at any point on its surface and find yourself connected to the center, simply by plunging in, figuratively speaking, head first: "I rede [advise] the forsake the worlde wode [madness] / And porchace thy perle maskelles" (743-44). However, one might also find that at any spot on the circumference of this divine circle, one is simultaneously at the very center: God, after all, is an infinite pearl, both center and circumference. And we discover this by entering into His world at any one of its infinite points.[53]

The poem, too, as pearl, is a world in which we can enter, as Blake would say centuries later, "upon the wings of thought," in order to find ourselves arriving at Jerusalem by way of any number of different yet connected threads; each word and image leads to this center (showing us this fact is part of its purpose).[54] Yet,

53. Ibid., p. 49.
54. Louis Blenkner has led the way for those who wish to see a mystical path being followed by the narrator; see especially his essay "The Theological Structure of *Pearl*," *Traditio* 24 (1968), pp. 43-75, in Conley, *Middle English Pearl*, pp. 220-71.

the key always remains a turning around of our perception of reality, the equivalent, in the terms of the poem, of moving from a "jueler" to a "homely hyne": a servant instead of a lord, and so possessed, rather than possessing. You thought you knew your "priuy perle"? Maiden says to Dreamer; you knew nothing at all, nothing but "mokke and mul."

The Dreamer, as we know, "has ears, but has failed to hear." Continually misinterpreting the figure right up to the very last, he plunges in not figuratively but literally, confusing a mirror for reality and thereby awakening himself rather rudely from his own dream. He is one of those who "insist on interpreting the word of grace rather than letting themselves be interpreted by it." Overcome by "delyt" at seeing his own pearl in the brides' procession, his mind "to maddyng malte."[55] A clearer and more concise explanation of his problem is more difficult to imagine than his own summation: "Quen I ses my frely [gracious one], I wolde be there. . . ."

However, in a final comic paradox in this most paradoxical of poems, it is this mad plunge into the symbolic landscape itself that awakens the Dreamer at last into both literal and figurative worlds. As Nelson nicely concludes,

> The dreamer confuses figure with fulfillment, but through God's grace (and the poet's), he is saved from the consequences of his reckless act. Instead of drowning in his delusions, he awakes uniquely aware of his figural mortality in the garden where his dream began.[56]

The awakening has led to a new understanding of his own place, even if at first rather grudging:

---

55. For an earlier, significant use of this term ("malte") see ll. 223–26, and the commentary by Hill, "Middle English Poets," p. 168.

56. Nelson, *Incarnate Word*, p. 46; compare Jonah in *Patience*. One reason for this "madnes" is the confusion he is experiencing between literal and figurative, reminding us of McCanles's argument (note 34) that literal and figurative are two linked aspects of one (metaphorical) whole. Thus the dreamer "literally" plunges into the river, but this literal is itself a figure in a dream, in which all acts are signs.

> I raxled, and fel in gret affray,
> And, sykyng, to myself I sayd:
> "Now al be to that Pryncez paye."
>
> [I stretched (myself), and fell in great dismay,
> and, sighing to myself I said, "Now all be
> to that Prince's pleasure."]
>
> (1174–76)

His own perception is reinforced by the return, in this final link word, to our opening line ("Perle, plesaunte to pryncez paye"), except with the meaning of "Prynce" shifted from the literal to the figurative, from this world to the next, a clear summation of the poem's path. This in turn leads, as it should, to action. At last, the Dreamer takes the plunge, sacrificing all he has, and is:

> Ouer this hyul this lote I laghte,
> For pyty of my perle enclyin,
> And sythen to God I hit bytaghte,
> In Krystez dere blessyng and myn,
> That in the forme of bred and wyn
> The preste vus shewez vch a daye.
> He gef vus to be His homly hyne
> Ande precious perlez vnto His pay.
>
> [On this hill I received this chance, lying prostrate
> for sorrow for my pearl, which I afterwards committed
> to God, with my own (blessing) and the precious blessing
> of Christ, whom the priest shows us every day in the form
> of bread and wine. He granted [or may He grant] us all to
> be humble servants and precious pearls to His pleasure.]
>
> (1205–12)

Recognizing that "this lote I laghte" can mean not only "this chance I received" but also "this *speech* or *word* I received" accurately sums up in verbal wordplay the message the Maiden has delivered to us as well, by way of the narrator-poet. Our chance, our grace too, comes by way of the word, which we must receive as we also subsequently receive the bread and wine. Receiving and truly accepting our word—our wound and fate—must lead to giving this over again to God, which is the act that transforms our words and wounds into sacraments: "I afterwards committed (it) to God." Our part is to give ourselves away in the combined, married blessing of Christ and self. In doing so what our own hands have labored over, the daily bread we bake, becomes Christ for us and for others. Our own labors return to us and transform us but only as we give them freely over, newly blessed and "raised" as though upon a cross.[57]

As Dodd summarizes the message of the parable of the pearl: "to know when to plunge makes the successful financier."[58] Or as Funk comments:

> He who hears the word of grace as a word addressed to him knows the meaning of the cross. For just as Jesus invests everything, including whatever title he had a right to claim, as well as his life, in the certainty of that word of grace, so he who hears the word will know what it requires of him. By hearing he has been claimed as a vessel of grace and plunged into the way of the cross.[59]

The passives in this final sentence suggest in their own way the paradox with which *Pearl* concludes: the Dreamer has at last "heard" (itself a mysteriously passive "activity") and in that hearing finds himself not claiming now but "claimed"—and he acts accordingly, committing his "perle" to God. He acts, but all his acts are gifts, a transformation made possible by this gift of "hearing" and "seeing" anew "vch a daye" in the Eucharist, itself a sign of the ultimate gift of God to man, the sacrifice of the cross.[60] As with those who journeyed to Emmaus with the hidden Lord, finding themselves blessed by His presence when He took the

---

57. On "lote" as speech, see Andrew and Waldron, *Poems of the Pearl Manuscript*, p. 110.
58. Dodd, *Parables of the Kingdom*, p. 86.
59. Funk, *Language, Hermeneutic*, p. 18.
60. See Augustine, *The City of God*, trans. Marcus Dods (New York: Modern Library, 1950), X, 20 (p. 325): "Thus He is both the Priest who offers and the Sacrifice offered. And he designed that there should be a daily sign of this in the sacrifice of the Church, which, being His body, learns to offer herself through Him." See also Joseph A. Jungmann, *The Mass of the Roman Rite* (New York: Benziger Brothers, 1951), pp. 188–95, and Joseph M. Powers, *Eucharistic Theology* (New York: Seabury Press, 1967), pp. 75, 88–90.

Interpretive Construction 63

bread and broke it, our awakened Dreamer too travels each day into the nave and sees himself blessed at the altar, his labor of bread and wine transformed like him by the simple act of sacrifice into the body and blood of Christ, that "gentle juel." "Mokke and mul" becomes pearl at last.[61]

* * *

The poem, as we might now recall, is both process and product, both a journey to a figurative place (which we have called Jerusalem) and, as pearl, that place or spot itself. As such, the reader, rather like the Dreamer himself, ends where he began, knowing "the place for the first time."[62] He sees in this spot (the garden, grave mound, or completed poem itself) the holy city, just as an individual journeys to the Mass and sees there his own labor elevated and transformed.

The Jeweler, of course, like us, becomes one of those laborers in the vineyard in the parable retold by the Pearl Maiden at the center of this poem, each of whom received a penny, regardless of the length of time he worked. Marie Borroff notes, "Since it is a daily wage, [the penny] was identified by the patristic writers with the 'daily bread' asked for in the Lord's Prayer. And this in turn was identified with the communion wafer, likewise round in shape, 'shown us every day' as the poet says (line 1210), by the priest at mass." As a sign of our common salvation in Christ, there is no first nor last: "[u]nlike the row of laborers, the 'lines' formed by those who move through the streets" in the vision of Jerusalem "have neither beginning nor end. Nor can anyone in them be thought of as first or last, since the entire group is constantly starting out, arriving, and moving at every intermediate point." Our normal categories, including those primary catego-

---

61. See also Nelson, *Incarnate Word*, pp. 47–48, Gatta, "Transformation Symbolism," pp. 241–42. On the importance of this eucharistic action in the conclusion of the poem see Rosalind Field's essay, "The Heavenly Jerusalem in *Pearl*," *Modern Language Review* 81 (1986), pp. 16–17. More generally, see also the stimulating essay by Carl Jung, "Transformation Symbolism in the Mass," *Collected Works*, vol. 11 (Princeton, N.J.: Princeton University Press, 1969), pp. 201–98, especially pp. 253–58.
62. T. S. Eliot, "Little Gidding," from *Four Quartets* (London: Faber and Faber, 1944), l. 242.

ries of space and time, collapse here. (Eternity, Borroff concludes, is not "perpetual duration but . . . release from linear time.") Only the Lamb stands out, leading the way, "since his voluntary self sacrifice . . . has made salvation possible and has established the Church through whose sacraments the individual soul attains it."[63]

Most important for this poem is what the figure points to: "the mystery of salvation" founded on the paradox of the cross, of sacrificing all. It is the labor, the poem reminds its readers, placed on everyone who would even witness the elevation. This is what the journey to the kingdom entails; this is the new perspective the poem demands.

Funk comments that the man who has correctly heard the word is "claimed as a vessel of grace," and this, we sense, is what has happened to our Dreamer-turned-narrator. As servant or "homly hyne," he is now in his master's pay, and all that he does will be done as a gift or offering to that Lord. As the narrator comments, on awakening he committed ("bytaghte") his pearl "to God . . . In Krystez dere blessyng and myn," receiving in turn "precious perles unto his pay."

We are reminded here, perhaps, of our struggles as the poem opened to define just what this pearl is. On one level, the narrator (recently dreamer) refers, we presume, to his daughter. On the simplest level, the poem has been about a man surrendering at last his hold on a dearly loved one, committing her to Christ's blessing. Yet, the narrator has said "Ouer this hyul this lote I laghte / For pyty of my perle enclyin, / And sythen to God I hit bytaghte. . . ." By way of the parable, it is easy enough to see that "this lote"—this fortune or lot—also refers to his pearl, but now not only the daughter, except insofar as the daughter represents the whole, the "pearl of great price" that itself in the

---

63. Marie Borroff, *"Pearl*'s 'Maynful Mone:' Crux, Simile and Structure." In *Acts of Interpretation: The Text in Its Contexts, 700–1600,* ed. Mary J. Carruthers and Elizabeth D. Kirk (Norman, Okla.: Pilgrim Books, 1982), pp. 165, 171. On the Eucharist, see again Jungmann, *Mass,* pp. 119–22, 129; Powers, *Eucharistic Theology,* p. 25–31, and Theodore Klauser, *A Short History of the Western Liturgy* (London: Oxford University Press, 1969), pp. 97–101.

parable stands for the "way to the kingdom," sacrificing all a man has and is.

Behind the narrator, of course, stands the poet himself, the "authority" of the poem, himself a "homly hyne" in his master's pay. He, too, as wordsmith has a "lote" to commit to God, a pearl to bestow and a pearl to receive "unto his pay." The pearl he bestows is the poem itself, which only becomes pearl as the process ends: that is, in the final line of the poem, which makes the structure whole, complete, and also circular. And, like the narrator's pearl (the daughter), the poem stands for all that a man has to sacrifice: it, too, is the way to the kingdom, the pearl of price, but only as it acknowledges the paradox of the cross: that the kingdom comes not just by seeing this elevation of the Host but by seeing in a way that means insight, that implicates the whole man, so that he faces the fact of sacrifice in his own life. As with Abraham, the poet reminds us that we must be willing to sacrifice our "only beloved son" (or daughter, or pearl, or poem) in order to become the "father of nations," the source of future blessing.

Thus, the poet has been laboring in the vineyard and must go with his offering to the table, where in turn it can be elevated and blessed, becoming in this sacrament a vessel of grace. It becomes, that is, a visible sign revealing that all of our acts, our constructions, are like the Eucharistic offerings given at Mass, offerings that are modeled on the sacrifice of Jesus at Golgotha. That is not to say that the poem itself is, strictly speaking, a sacrament. Rather, it is a figure of the Eucharist, suggesting in its own construction that all of our constructions are intended so to be seen.

The poet affirms that after his insight must come response, as for the Dreamer, who moves from the dream vision to his own sacrifice and finally to the Eucharist, which itself is the sign of sacrifice and sacrifice's meaning, both pointing to the cross and embodying it. Vision leads to act: the end of the journey marks the beginning of a new journey, witnessed in the giving up at poem's end and in the creation of the poem itself, which in its own paradoxical nature is a sign of the transformed narrator, who is now, metaphorically, pearl himself.

Yet the poem is a warning, finally, about taking sign and even sacrament as sufficient in itself for salvation. As suggested, in many ways by the fourteenth century the church found itself in much the same position as the Hebrews in the time of Jesus, with the cathedral, liturgy, and sacraments in the place of the temple, cult, and law. As the Protestant reformers were soon to declare, fulfilling the ritual is not enough. A transformation and a new way of life are required. The Word must break in; the old life must be shattered *continually*. As Hugh of St. Victor explains:

> The sacraments were instituted on account of instruction, that through that which is seen without in the sacrament in the visible species the human mind may be instructed to recognize the invisible virtue which consists within in the thing of the sacrament. For man who knew visible things and did not know the invisible could by no means have recognized divine things unless stimulated by the human.[64]

The "divine things" that man must recognize (and does recognize, it is claimed, in Jesus) are precisely the paradoxes and overturnings discussed in the Introduction and in this chapter. This invisible is, paradoxically, a way of seeing, a perspective on life that comes to us only by means of the visible. But this way of seeing reveals that the figure or sign must be seen through or shattered as we found in the parables, which begin "the kingdom of heaven is like" and then overturn our expectations. Winning this kingdom, the *Pearl* Dreamer discovers, is possible only through losing.

---

64. Hugh of St. Victor, *On the Sacraments of the Christian Faith (De Sacramentis)*, trans. Roy DeFerrari (Cambridge, Mass.: Medieval Academy of America, 1951), p. 157. Compare Athanasius' *De Incarnatione*, ed. and trans. Robert Thomson (Oxford: Clarendon Press, 1971), pp. 159–75, 181: "Since men had not recognized his providence in the universe . . . if they looked up on account of the works of the body, they might gain through him an idea of the knowledge of the Father, working to an understanding of his universal providence from its individual aspects." See also Jungmann, *Mass*, pp. 181, 188–95; Gatta, "Transformation Symbolism," p. 249; and Emert, "*Pearl* and the Incarnate Word," pp. 47, 49, 84–86, 129, 155–57, 204.

Interpretive Construction 67

Hugh suggests that God is the physician, man the sick person, the priest the minister or messenger, grace the antidote, and the sacrament the vessel or means of grace:

> For, since man by desiring visible things was corrupted, to be restored fittingly he had to receive an occasion of salvation in these same visible things, so that he might rise again through the same things through which he had fallen.

Like other vessels, words themselves are "outward sounds" given as "a sign of the word which shines within,"[65] by means of which we come to know the invisible. Similarly, the poem, while a process, a journey we enter upon, is also a single entity, an object with a form of its own, which we have entered like a temple or swallowed like the bread and wine, finding either way that as object it is itself a pearl, a figure of the kingdom, insofar as the visible is shattered, leading to insight and act. Thus, as figure, it is cast in the image of Jesus, the "gentle juel" or "parable of God." It is the way, or gate to the kingdom, insofar as it leads to the Eucharist and thus to the cross.

The poem, of course, is the manifestation of the poet's offering up all that he has to Christ. It is in this offering that his poem becomes a pearl, "wemles, clene and clere, / And endeles rounde, and blythe of mode."[66] Thus, the form of the poem is both the poet's acknowledgment of his gift as a figure or image of the kingdom (that is, as a pearl) and simultaneously the poet's means of inducing the reader to pass over imaginatively to the kingdom. As his offering, it is potentially a "vessel of grace," allowing the reader to move, like the Dreamer, from a literalistic and possessive viewpoint to a symbolic and sacramental one, in which everything seen is a figure of the unseen, including his own gift and life transformed by his act of giving, like the "bread and wine" that "the preste uus shows uch a daye."[67] This showing is

---

65. Hugh of St. Victor, *On the Sacraments*, pp. 160, 474; see also Augustine, *De Doctrina Christiana*, trans. D. W. Robertson (New York: Bobbs-Merrill, 1958), pp. 34–37.
66. See Nelson, *Incarnate Word*, p. 43.
67. See F. David Martin, *Art and the Religious Experience: The "Language" of the Sacred* (Lewisburg, Pa.: Bucknell University Press, 1972), pp. 66–67.

akin to the vision that the Dreamer (and reader) has of the city from across the river: it is intended not merely to be seen but to be seen through and then embodied. This poetic Jerusalem, borrowed so literally from John, must be seen as oneself.

Depending on his point of view, he will either see a barrier across which he must hurl himself or see himself there already, a part of the divine community even as he sits within the cathedral. We reach again, of course, the tension of the "realized eschatology," wherein a man believes that the kingdom has come upon him, yet also recognizes that it is still over there. He cannot cross the river since first "thy corse in clot mot colder keve" [your corpse must sink, colder, into the earth].

The reader, as I have suggested all along, is in a predicament not unlike that of the Dreamer. Is he going to try to swim to the new Jerusalem? Is he going to demand logic and law, arguing angrily, "Me thynk thy tale unresounable"? The poem tempts and entices us into its magical world, but we find that the deeper we enter, the more mysterious and paradoxical its beauty becomes, until finally, driven by "delyt . . . in yghe and ere," we might plunge madly into its surface, only to find ourselves unable to possess the vision of our dreams. It is there; we know it is there; we have spotted it, smelled it, and touched it, in the poet's words, but failed to grasp it. And perhaps at that point comes a dawning realization concerning the terrible and wonderful paradox of human existence: we possess what we love in the body—and yet we do not and cannot, except by giving it up. Here in the giving up of everything is the New Jerusalem John witnessed, the "new earth" where "the dwelling of God is with men" (Rev. 21:1–3). We, too, on such an awakening might respond like our Dreamer:

> I raxled, and fel in great affray,
> And, sykyng, to myself I sayd:
> "Now al be to that Pryncez paye."[68]
> (1174–76)

---

68. See Nelson, *Incarnate Word*, p. 46.

This frustrating moment—which is also, paradoxically, the moment of grace,[69] the moment we say "al be to that Pryncyes paye"—is rather like saying "I've got it!" only in that moment to awaken to the realization that you *haven't*, which in turn leads to an understanding of what having it really means: giving it up. At which point, of course, we find to our great joy and amusement that we do after all have it—or *are* it. He grants us to be "precious perles unto his paye." And, although nothing outwardly is changed—bread appears to be bread, wine remains in the form of wine—we find that we have been figuratively and truly remade in His image and in the image of His kingdom. We are made members of the divine body, of the spiritual temple, of which the earthly cathedral, like this circular poem, is similarly a figure. As Rudolf Schwarz has written, about the "sacred ring" in church architecture, "When the few gather in his name, a holy city is founded and the sacred universe is created anew. In these few the land and all space beneath the heavens becomes one single, sacred body. The earth is united with the Lord. She drinks his holy cup and eats him as bread."[70]

In the process of his education our Dreamer learns to distinguish literal from figurative, physical from spiritual, and as a result of this knowledge at last reaches the point where he can "let go," can, in the words of the parable, sell all he has in order to purchase the one pearl, the "kingdom." Yet he also learns that although the body might be "mukke and mul" and must at last die, all that we are and do as humans remains embodied. The "figurative" act of "selling all one has" must be an act that exists in the human world; otherwise it is no "act" at all.

It is at this point that the poem's political dimension exists, a point of clear importance to the poet, who dwells often (as he does similarly in *Sir Gawain*) on questions of class and labor, and in particular on the duties and responsibilities of the nobility: what it really means to be a countess or queen. It is after all no

---

69. See Gatta, "Transformation Symbolism," p. 256.
70. Rudolph Schwartz, *The Church Incarnate: The Sacred Function of Christian Architecture* (Chicago: Regnery Co., 1958), pp. 56–57.

coincidence that at the center of this circular poem stands the Pearl Maiden's discussion of the parable of the laborers in the vineyard, a narrative that subverts all of our common sense notions of justice and proper rewards. "The first shall be last," the Maiden reminds the jeweler:

> Thus pore men her part ay pykez,
> Thus thay com late and lyttel wore,
> And thagh her sweng wyth lyteel atslykez,
> The merci of God is much the more.
>
> [Thus poor men always gather their share,
> though they come late and were insignificant (on earth),
> and though their labor is soon (*or* with small result) spent,
> the mercy of God is that much the greater.]
>
> (573–76)

All of this follows the jeweler's repeated attempts to cling to his own precious pearl, which truly amounts to clinging to himself, a desire that leads him ultimately to leap into the river as if he has the power to reach this New Jerusalem simply through his own physical labor, an act that is the equivalent of building Babel. Only the failure of this egotistical attempt awakens him to his own complete isolation.

From another perspective, the poet's, all of this labor stands in marked contrast to the jeweler's labor, so that one point of the poem is to demonstrate the "types" of building, which we can call (in a variation on Blake) building Babel and building Jerusalem. The latter remains labor—a poem is "built" line by line, stanza by stanza, and then exists before us as a product—and yet it is labor that transforms both the laborer and the one who chooses to enter into the finished product. The jeweler attempts to cling to what he views as his product, his creation—the pearl-daughter—finding his own value locked up in what he has physically produced (forgetting of course that the pearl, whether daughter or gem, is not in fact his "production" at all). The narrator-poet in contrast offers up his labor, recognizing that his pearl—including the poem itself, and all it stands for—is not truly "his." Thus the jeweler creates pearls that he wants to possess and own and unite with as a way of losing his terrible isolation on that "erber grene," believing that his physical labor can in itself bring him to the New Jerusalem and thus end his solitude. In contrast, in this offering up of his labor, the narrator-poet discovers that he himself becomes what he has made: in the true self-sacrificing labor he too becomes pearl and in that way gains all that he had thought he had lost. And this circular poem subsequently stands as a sign of precisely this act—as a sign of the man himself, of the jeweler-dreamer turned narrator-poet—just as the circular wafer of the Eucharist stands daily as an embodiment of the sacrificial labor of Jesus. What was broken is made whole.

What then is this "body of Christ" that the poem suggests we become? It is the labor of sacrifice that we call love, the true labor on which all other labor is modeled and figured on. It is the daily work we do with our hands and spirits and minds whose motivation is not the building up of our own separate selves but is instead the breaking down of that limited self through an imaginative plunge outward into the world. Only then do we discover that this apparent death and destruction are simultaneously the birth and building of a unified human world.

* * *

The architecture of this poem is the figure of this divine, sacred body.[71] Yet as figure, the poem is also the way, which at some point will burst its own form, opening like a gate to the New Jerusalem with its golden, translucent walls. And so for this poet Jerusalem is with us, *is* us, and is yet ahead:

> Through his simple stance this one man expresses what all dimly sense. Each feels the pull of the earth and the overpowering ascent of life, each senses that he has been sent on a journey and also that another pair of eyes would meet his own, were he to lift them from

71. Nelson, *Incarnate Word*, p. 49, quotes Jerome ("Through a circular room and by a circular staircase we ascend to the upper chamber of the Temple") and then adds, "Like the temple, *Pearl* is round in three dimensions—a microcosmic model of the spherical cosmos."

the center. All this will one day come to pass but the time is not yet ripe for it. . . .

Everything is still asleep in the germ and the things are still lying close together, illumined by an inward light. Nothing has as yet cut through this first plan to disturb it but already there are contained in it the powers which will one day rend it asunder—the commandment to grow and burst the dome. The time of bliss is short and when it is over man stands again in the sun, amidst the things, conscious of his body and of its meaning. He realizes that he is alone and that he has been sent on a far journey.[72]

72. Rudolph Schwartz, *The Church Incarnate: The Sacred Function of Christian Architecture* (Chicago: Regnery Co., 1958), p. 66.

3
"Delight into Sacrifice"
Resting in George Herbert's *Temple*

As many as I love, I rebuke and chasten: be zealous therefore, and repent. Behold, I stand at the door, and knock: if any man hear my voice, and open the door, I will come in to him, and will sup with him, and he with me. Rev. 3:19–20

> *Yet take thy way; for sure thy way is best:*
> *Stretch or contract me, thy poore debtor:*
> *This is but tuning of my breast,*
> *To make the musick better.*
>
> *Whether I flie with angels, fall with dust,*
> *Thy hands made both, and I am there:*
> *Thy power and love, my love and trust*
> *Make one place ev'ry where.*
> "The Temper [I]"

The *Pearl* as poem, we find, is a visible sign of the man remade. From "muck and mul" the dreamer too becomes pearl in a radical transformation of how he sees the literal truth. He also thereby becomes the narrator, as the transformation is that which makes the poem possible, makes possible a product that is a sign of this same transformation.

In Herbert, too, the poem-as-sign (as *Temple*) reveals this sacrificial way. As a sign the poem's message (as in *Pearl*) is the message of the Last Supper and of Golgotha: there is no way out of journeying if one wishes to find rest; no way out of being broken if one seeks wholeness. There is also, these poems suggest, no way out of speech if one seeks for "silence of God"[1]—understanding speech here to stand broadly not only for visible language but also for vocation. For Herbert, the poem is a sign of that calling. Only through the visible, the uttered, can we find the invisible and silent, as Augustine and Hugh of St. Victor suggest; the embodied beauty must, like Jesus, offer itself up. And it does this through the metaphor, whereby the image is revealed as that which shatters our logic, our expectations, our self-constructions. Metaphor undermines our attempts to establish permanent residency in the physical alone, or what we like to call the real. *The Temple*, then, is a metaphorical building that exists to be seen through. "The metaphorical interpretation presupposes a literal interpretation which self-destructs in a significant contradiction."[2]

If the journey in *Pearl* is initiated by the father's loss of a daughter, it is equally true that in many ways the journey that builds *The Temple* is begun with the son's loss of the father (when Herbert was three), an absence that can never be made fully whole again. And it is perhaps not too much to claim that this sense of absence and loss was reinforced by the death of Herbert's mother later in his life and by the increasingly uncertain world that was England in the 1620s and 1630s.[3]

"Beyond communication lies communion," William Kerrigan writes of Herbert. Language in *The Temple*, the language too of sermons, and even of the Gospels, is the attempt to overcome or transform mourning or absence: to find and claim the risen body. The language of metaphor in particular is the language of a rediscovered relatedness. And yet, although Herbert may write

---

1. On this phrase, see Joseph Anthony Mazzeo, "St. Augustine's Rhetoric of Silence," in his *Renaissance and Seventeenth Century Studies* (New York: Columbia University Press, 1964), pp. 1–28.
2. Paul Ricoeur, *Interpretation Theory: Discourse and Surplus of Meaning* (Fort Worth: Texas Christian University Press, 1964), p. 50.
3. See Christopher Hill, *The Century of Revolution: 1603–1714* (Edinburgh: Thomas Nelson, 1961), p. 27; William Kerrigan, "Ritual Man: On the Outside of Herbert's Poetry," *Psychiatry* 48 (1985), pp. 71–77; and Amy Charles, *A Life of George Herbert* (Ithaca, N.Y.: Cornell University Press, 1977), pp. 28–29, 132–34.

that verse is "when I am most with thee" ("The Quidditie"), verse also invariably acknowledges this absence. Always there is, it seems, an other, a "thee," to whom we must address ourselves. Seeking peace or union with the father and mother remains an unfinished business.[4]

The word *sermon*, as Pastor Herbert would have known, means a speech, or discourse, and in its metaphorical roots suggests an attaching or joining, especially in speech.[5] As the pastor would also know, it is word that ritually leads to sacrament: the Old and New Testament lessons, then the sermon itself, which prepares the members for the celebration of Christ's sacrifice. Sacred poetry, like the sermon, like all of the stories and conversations that fill Biblical and theological narratives, leads finally to this union at the table, the silence of communion. And then, of course, out into the world again, where language, Herbert says, has been "chaos since the time of Babel."[6] "The Church Militant," we recall, follows "Love III" in Herbert's poetry.

Of course what the central sacrament of Christian worship suggests is that union is finally made possible only through sacrifice. Here is the ultimate sign of God's love: He gave his only Son. Christ's own sense of abandonment by the Father is the necessary prelude to the resurrection and reunion. And it is clear that Herbert believes we must join him there, like the mournful thief who seeks comfort as he hangs beside Jesus and is then rewarded: "Today thou shalt be with me in paradise" (Luke 23:43). We too are that thief. Our delight in and longing to steal all the world's pleasure must be turned to spiritual profit as we acknowledge our own brokenness.

In his introduction to *The Temple*, Herbert will call this process

---

4. Kerrigan, "Ritual Man," p. 72.
5. William Morris, ed., *The American Heritage Dictionary of the English Language* (Boston: Houghton Mifflin, 1973), p. 1538.
6. See William H. Pahlka's *Saint Augustine's Meter and George Herbert's Will* (Kent, Ohio: Kent State University Press, 1987), p. 141. The Herbert quotation is from one of his memorial poems to his mother; see Mark McCloskey and Paul R. Murphy, trans. and eds., *The Latin Poetry of George Herbert: A Bilingual Edition* (Athens: Ohio University Press, 1965), p. 125.

one of turning "delight into sacrifice."⁷ The architect Rudolf Schwartz, in *The Church Incarnate*, has similarly described such buildings in his "Fourth Plan." "Their space," he says, is consumed in representing the way.

> They have no home. The form makes them fugitives on the earth, it consumes them in representing an endless process of consummation. The earth is but the material which bears their train, it is not a staked claim. . . . The things which other people take so for granted—that man, sheltered in God, also has a home in the world, that wherever there is sacred form, a reverent delimitation occurs, and that the building of a church means primarily the enclosing of a piece of the world which has now become as God originally intended it to be—all these ideas are foreign to this people. The goal is eternal and sacred, the form reaches out to it as the form of the sacred means to the sacred end. But even simply regarding it as "form" (which indeed it is, in a preeminent sense) would be a defection, this would divert the eye away from the goal and the form would instantly disintegrate. . . . This form does not suffice in itself. It is bearable only as an exalted chainwork in the light, risked toward the eternal goal.⁸

So too in Herbert does "form not suffice in itself." We recall Augustine's warnings (in *On Christian Doctrine*) about using, not enjoying, the vessels that carry us home.⁹ Or, modifying this

---

7. *The Works of George Herbert*, ed. F. E. Hutchinson (Oxford: Clarendon Press, 1941), p. 6. All quotations from Herbert (unless otherwise indicated) refer to this edition.
8. Rudolph Schwartz, *The Church Incarnate: The Sacred Function of Christian Architecture* (Chicago: Henry Regnery Co., 1958), pp. 126–27.
9. St. Augustine, *On Christian Doctrine*, trans. D. W. Robertson, Jr. (New York: Bobbs-Merrill, 1958), pp. 9–10. For another example of Herbert's use of Augustine, see Richard Todd's *The Opacity of Signs: Acts of Interpretation in George Herbert's The Temple* (Columbia: University of Missouri Press, 1986). See too John E. Skillen's review of Todd's book in *Christian Scholar's Review* 18 (1988), pp. 81–84. Skillen writes (in part as a corrective to Todd): "For created things successfully to serve as signs of the *invisibilia Dei*, to serve as vessels to assist us on our journey to the heavenly Jerusalem, they must be rendered provisional, recognized in their insufficiency, used and not enjoyed for their own sakes" (p. 83). For an extensive treatment of the relationship between Herbert and Augustinian aesthetics see Pahlka, *Saint Augustine's Meter*, esp. pp. 141–43, and 163–69.

Augustinian definition of language-as-sign, we might call the poems of *The Temple* a "waking dream," borrowing from Murray Krieger's borrowing from Keats, understanding that as temple the work is complete, a finished structure, and in that sense is embodied; and yet as sign it is awake to its failure to be home and instead speaks only of preparation and expectation, finding home and kingdom to be something unfixed, undefinable, like the kingdom of the New Testament parables.[10] There is no rest here; instead its sweetness must become sacrifice for the reader as for the narrator. This temple sets the reader down on the road.

* * *

St. Paul quickly recognized a problem that was developing in the young churches to which he ministered. "Is Christ divided? Was Paul crucified for you? Or were ye baptized in the name of Paul?" (1 Cor. 1:13). Do not mistake me for the final truth, "For we preach not ourselves, but Christ Jesus the Lord" (2 Cor. 4:5). My word is only a light reflected from the divine Light:

> For God, who commanded the light to shine out of darkness, hath shined in our hearts, to give the light of the knowledge of the glory of God in the face of Jesus Christ. But we have this treasure in earthen vessels, that the excellency of the power may be of God, and not of us. (2 Cor. 4:6–7)

George Herbert too was a minister of the Word, a "Deputy of Christ";[11] he recognized with Paul that his life was intended to be a broken vessel for this truth, through which Christ could enter His church. There can be no separation between the man and his vocation, Herbert affirmed early in *The Priest to the Temple*: "After a man is once Minister, he cannot agree to come into any house, where he shall not exercise what he is, unlesse he forsake his plough, and look back" (226). There can be no separation here, for the man has become wholly Christ's. The heart has been remade; he has sacrificed all, has emptied himself only

---

10. Murray Krieger, "A Waking Dream," in Morton Bloomfield, ed., *Allegory, Myth and Symbol* (Cambridge, Mass.: Harvard University Press, 1982), pp. 1–22.
11. "A Priest to the Temple," chap. 1. Hutchinson, *Works of George Herbert*, p. 225.

to be filled with Christ, becoming his temple. "And therefore," Herbert writes, "St. Paul . . . in the first of the Colossians plainly avoucheth, that he fils up that which is behinde of the afflictions of Christ in his flesh, for his bodie's sake, which is the Church" (225).

All of the poems in *The Temple* in one form or another point to this rebuilding,[12] and many suggest specifically the role of "the afflictions of Christ" in the remaking of the man. The poet-priest, it might be said, combines Moses and Jacob: his raising of the altar in the form of the poem is the sign of his having "passed over the Jordan" and then, after a wandering, returned, but only after wrestling with the angel. The building of the poem becomes a metaphor for this wrestling, so that it is in (or through) the poem that he is renamed. No longer is he simply George Herbert, parson of Bemerton; he now becomes the "George Herbert" of the poems, the persona who exists only in the poems and who continues to exist as a figure. Like Jacob, who was newly named, he becomes a sign of the sacrificial way.

The poet-priest raises a temple, builds an altar upon which to sacrifice, and yet must make clear that "it is not ourselves we proclaim. . . ." Like the body, the building is a finished product that embodies a process that is to be repeated within every individual. Yet as product it denies its own completed state. Thus, as Harold Tolliver notes, although Herbert "thinks in terms of interpenetrating, filled places, and mutual habitations of body and spirit," and although "[t]he temple is the chief place of pres-

---

12. I am indebted, of course, to Stanley Fish, whose work on Herbert, although controversial, has been both influential and stimulating. See both *Self-Consuming Artifacts: The Experience of Seventeenth Century Literature* (Berkeley and Los Angeles: University of California Press, 1972), pp. 153–223, and *The Living Temple: George Herbert and Catechizing* (Berkeley and Los Angeles: University of California Press, 1978). Equally significant, if less directly relevant to my work, are Helen Vendler's careful readings in *The Poetry of George Herbert* (Cambridge, Mass.: Harvard University Press, 1975), and Arnold Stein's *George Herbert's Lyrics* (Baltimore: Johns Hopkins University Press, 1968). For further refinements and developments of Fish's positions, as well as an excellent critique of Fish and Vendler (among others), see Barbara Leah Harman, *Costly Monuments: Representations of the Self in George Herbert's Poetry* (Cambridge, Mass: Harvard University Press, 1982), pp. 1–38. On Fish, see esp. pp. 19–20, 33.

ence . . . all means of bringing God into localities are imperfect, and for the poet no placement less than paradise can be fully satisfactory."[13]

Building is like the act of reading, in which one begins, moves through both time and space (across, down the page), knowing that at some point—some appropriate point, ideally—one will finish: the experience will be finished, the temple erected, the poem known as a whole. It is potentially, like the temple raised at Jerusalem, a structure worthy of Yahweh. As structure, as form, it pleases and gives satisfaction by seeming whole, complete, and symmetrical. And yet, as Schwartz says, "The form makes them fugitives on the earth." For as sign the form's message is that of the New Testament parables, which in turn are contained in the signs of the Last Supper and the Cross. In this understanding of kingdom, "the fiction of safe territory" must be relinquished, as Barbara Harman nicely comments (on "The Collar"). "To return is to establish a relationship with God, not in a world where order is necessary, but in a vulnerable present where images cannot be secured."[14]

In Herbert, we might then say, Augustine's theory of language links with Ricoeur's theory of the parables as paradoxical, polyvalent metaphors of kingdom. In Herbert, that is, it is metaphor that teaches that our own buildings do not suffice. Yet it is also true, as Ricoeur comments, that we must build in order to learn just this lesson. In a reference to Hegel, Ricoeur notes, "The world of religion is the everlasting process of giving forms and abolishing forms. . . . Religion is the place where the manifestation of the Spirit and the death of its representation may be seen."[15]

13. Harold Tolliver, "Herbert's Interim and Final Places," *Studies in English Literature* 24 (1984), p. 106.
14. Harman, *Costly Monuments*, p. 88.
15. Paul Ricoeur, "The Specificity of Language," *Semeia* 4 (1975), pp. 140–41. I am not suggesting that Herbert is a pre-Hegel Hegelian. Yet as Fish has already demonstrated, the dialectic or tension between form and spirit is clearly evident in such works as Herbert's *Temple*. The goal of this dialectic, of course, differs from Hegel's.

Only through building comes the shattering that is the insight itself—is kingdom. Only from building comes the disruption of building or the knowledge that building does not suffice; yet this insight is itself the logic of the kingdom, as Ricoeur also notes.[16] And in the insight comes temporary rest, or the momentary completion of the building (specifically, here, the poem). The form is finished, the poem made whole, but (to circle back) it is only made whole in the knowledge that there *is* no rest, no completion; that the "hill lies further on," as Herbert declares in "The Pilgrimage." Kingdom is located in the sudden awareness that kingdom by definition cannot be located. Harman again nicely comments, "If it is man's inclination to fix, and make peace with, experience, it is God's inclination that he shall not."[17]

Herbert's task, then, is to build the earthly tabernacle (*The Temple*), yet to foil any attempt to rest within it. "Delight" must become "sacrifice," in ways I shall explore throughout this chapter. The reader, like God's own men, shall be "rich and wearie" ("The Pulley"), not allowed to adore God's gifts instead of God himself.

Building, therefore, never truly ends: the journey, like Herbert's "Pilgrimage," concludes only in death, whether literal or metaphorical: that is, whether the death of the physical body or that of the limited self or ego, which foreshadows the consummation that still lies before us.[18] Until then, no rest is final, as poem succeeds poem in a building that is really an unbuilding, a continual self-sacrifice in which the poem, like the poet-priest himself, is intended only to be used, not enjoyed. The form must

16. Paul Ricoeur, "The Logic of Jesus, the Logic of God," *Anglican Theological Review* 62 (1979), pp. 37–41.
17. Harman, *Costly Monuments*, p. 95.
18. See 2 Cor. 5:1: "For we know that if our earthly house of this tabernacle were dissolved, we have a building of God, an house not made with hands, eternal in the heavens. For in this we groan, earnestly desiring to be clothed upon with our house which is from heaven. . . ." On Herbert's "Pilgrimage," see Harman's fine analysis, *Costly Monuments*, pp. 138–51. Of the poems "Artillerie" and "The Temper," she comments, "the speakers of these poems are not mansion builders; they are pilgrims . . . the openness to self-correction is a prerequisite to journeying, but is also what journeying *means*" (p. 161). For my qualifying of Harman's argument, see the discussion of "Affliction (I)" and "The Collar."

George Herbert's *Temple*   81

deny its own apparent finality, must itself be sacrificed[19] like the body of Christ, whose own incarnation into our form and subsequent death was God's ultimate sign of who He is, of what it means to love, to be Love. Here is true journey's end for Herbert, as the procession of poems in *The Temple* toward "Love (III)" makes clear.[20]

* * *

As in *Pearl*, the complexity of this paradoxical truth of love is suggested in the way words, images, and themes are interwoven throughout the work as a whole. Nothing stands isolated, finally; all the threads lead to the same place, and so although we can isolate particulars (the concern with language; with sacrament; with the journey/pilgrimage; with love, sacrifice, will, and grace; with the heart, building) we find that if we follow any one thread long enough it will lead us to all the others. All are contained in the temple (itself a metaphor contained by the Body of Christ), just as in *Pearl*, where everything is contained within *that* particular sign.

But it is even better, perhaps, to remember that all the parts are contained within each part (a truth made known by the reader's containing *The Temple* as a whole). In this light "The Altar" is seen as the beginning of a journey (through *The Temple* and toward "Love"), and thus as way, and yet also as goal: both means and end. "Altar" is contained by *Temple*, yet it also contains temple, *is* the temple of the heart remade. This is the journey's end at journey's beginning, a truth recognized in the Christian

---

19. See Heather A. R. Asals, *Equivocal Predications: George Herbert's Way to God* (Toronto: University of Toronto Press, 1981), p. 11. Asals here focuses on language itself as the sacrifice in *The Temple*: Herbert as poet-priest "breaks the host of language of itself; he breaks the Word itself"—this being, typologically, the equivalent of the release from Egypt and the ascent to "celestial Canaan."
20. Even with the inclusion of "The Church Militant," it is clear that the main body of *The Temple* culminates in "Love (III)." "Church Militant" simply reinforces the sense of pilgrimage that runs throughout *The Temple* as a whole: we think we have arrived, found rest (and silence) as we reach the final lyric, only to discover that we were wrong (again). "Love (III)" depicts a future, eschatological moment; for now, however, we are left with the Church not Triumphant but Militant. For the link with the catechism, see Fish, *Living Temple*, pp. 137–54.

calendar, wherein Christ is made available every day, intersecting time with the timeless at every possible point. As Heather Asals comments, "Herbert's language is *both* of Egypt and Canaan," as journey and end coincide in Christ, who alone gives rest.[21]

We shall see how some of these threads weave themselves towards their goal, itself variously defined as Love, as Rest, as Paradise, as Christ. For example, in "The Altar," which is poem and heart as well as altar (as the shape forces the reader to see), each of these forms is simultaneously the sacrifice for the poet (his gift) and the place of sacrifice for the reader: the spot where delight is remade (by grace), through the poem as vessel:

> A broken ALTAR, Lord, thy servant reares,
> Made of a heart, and cemented with teares:
>   Whose parts are as thy hand did frame;
>   No workmans tool hath touch'd the same.
>   A HEART alone
>   Is such a stone,
>   As nothing but
>   Thy pow'r doth cut.
>   Wherefore each part
>   Of my hard heart
>   Meets in this frame,
>   To praise thy Name:
>   That if I chance to hold my peace,
>   These stones to praise thee may not cease.
> O let thy blessed SACRIFICE be mine,
> And sanctifie this ALTAR to be thine.
>
> (p. 26)

From the beginning, the poet does not allow the reader to escape from paradox. While we see the altar being reared on the page as we read, we must recognize that what is happening on the page merely points to the true subject of the poem, as letters and words are signs for "heart" and "tears." They are metaphors, just as "tools" and "stones" are metaphors in the new vision of Jesus and Paul. Thus the form of this altar, as many critics have

---

21. Asals, *Equivocal Predications*, p. 7.

pointed out,[22] is distinctly Old Testament (or classical) in style, not, as one might expect, at all resembling the table of the Reformation. The form, made up of letters and words, is simply the image of the physical object, like the "real" altar, which is intended only as a sign to the true sacrifice taking place through the individual, even as the Old Testament itself is read typologically as a sign. The altar, then, is broken as metaphor, spiritually, in affliction. Only thus can it be remade, and finally raised, like Christ, as a whole—as we see it, figuratively, on the page before us.

Similarly, the nature of the builder is called into question, as throughout the poem the nature of the nominative changes. "Thy servant reares" the altar, yet the parts "are as thy hand did frame"; and the parts, it turns out, are the heart that "thy pow'r did cut." As in "Love Unknown," it is necessary for the poet to have his own heart placed on the altar to be broken like the body of Christ, for the heart has "turned to stone" and become "hardened." Paradoxically, it is when the heart is most like a building—made of stone, that is—that it is least like a temple. To become temple, it must cease to be fixed, solid, certain, and self-contained.[23] The poem itself is this breaking process for the poet and in the process becomes altar, as the shattered heart, broken now in this journey, "meets in this frame" of the poem "To praise thy name."

The shifting of subject and predicate in the final two lines, and the rhyme-emphasized pronouns, together sum up this complex process: "O let thy blessed SACRIFICE be mine / And sanctifie this ALTAR to be thine." Thine and mine meet; rest is found in this connection of oneself with Christ, which happens only through the sacrificial act (itself a gift of God), as in both lines

---

22. See, for example, the analysis by Joseph Summers in *George Herbert: His Religion and Art* (Cambridge, Mass: Harvard University Press, 1954), pp. 141–42, where he reveals Herbert's sources in Old Testament passages. See also Rosemund Tuve, *A Reading of George Herbert* (London: Faber and Faber, 1952), p. 69, and Fish, *Self-Consuming Artifacts*, pp. 207–15.

23. See Harman, *Costly Monuments*, pp. 187–90.

he alone acts and causes alteration.[24] As in *Pearl*, as completed action the poem becomes object, but object whose task is to function as vessel for the reader, a way to the kingdom. As Schwartz comments, "This form does not suffice in itself." Like the volume as a whole, then, the poem is building in two senses, as verbal and as noun, as process and as product.[25] As product, its object is to deny its own space: altar, like temple, exists most truly as process and not as place.

Sacrifice as event culminates in sacrifice as object: the Host broken at the altar is the offering of the church ("let thy blessed Sacrifice be mine") sanctified by God's grace and then received back. This objectified accounting or series of actions is what Herbert continually suggests takes place through the heart and act of the believer, or of the reader, for that matter. As we read we are both within the church (as a body of poems) and yet moving toward it (as a completed object, as an eschatological truth): when built, it exists in our hands as object, but more truly we should exist within it—or as it. We are the temple that has been built as we journeyed, as delight is alchemized to sacrifice.

Such is the goal throughout: an internal journey and transformation that is simultaneously outward, propelled by the labors of the priest and poet. Inner and outer are one inseparable process. The vessel, the physical object or poem, like the church's vessels themselves (and like the pastor, and finally like Jesus), becomes the way to this truth. Light breaks within us; insight comes as bread is broken before us. Here in sacramental labor the new earth is daily made visible, so that "[w]hether I flie with angels, fall with dust . . . Thy power and love, my love and trust / Make one place ev'rywhere." Here is the union of Thy and my, coupled in the repetition of *love*. Delight in form becomes sacrifice in the heart as reader, like narrator, is remade by

24. Sacrifice (of the heart) was thought to be (like all else) a gift of God's grace. See Norman Pettit, *The Heart Prepared: Grace and Conversion in Puritan Spiritual Life* (New Haven: Yale University Press, 1966), pp. 23, 57–58, 62. See also William Halewood, *The Poetry of Grace: Reformation Themes and Structures in English Seventeenth Century Poetry* (New Haven: Yale University Press, 1970), p. 63.
25. See Fish, *Living Temple*, pp. 58–68.

the poem's paradox, itself a reflection of the kingdom's paradox, whereby a man must "lose his life to gain it."

* * *

William Halewood equates Herbert's mode with "the Reformation reading of life," which, he argues, "concentrates heavily on shock and surprise":

> It sees the human situation as paradoxical and improbable in every significant circumstance—that is, in every circumstance relating to salvation—and the ways of God amazing in their contradiction of reasonable expectations. It is devoted, in fact, to exposing the unreasonableness of expectations that man accepts as reasonable and to declaring the exclusive rightness of a version of reality that reason wants to reject.[26]

As with *Pearl*, Herbert affirms that although "the goods of heaven are all that matter," these "are not to be achieved by human effort or human merit, which can never suffice to make man worthy of heaven's rewards. Man," Halewood concludes, using a common metaphor in both Herbert and *Pearl*, "cannot sell himself or his goods to God. . . ."[27]

The desire of the Psalmist remains strong in Herbert: "One thing I have asked of Yahweh, / That will I seek after; / That I may dwell in the house of Yahweh / All the Days of my life" (Ps. 27:4). Yet equally clear to Herbert is the paradoxical fact that "unless the Lord builds the house, / Those who build it labor in vain" (Ps. 127:1). And like the parables, and like the *sermo humilis* defined by Auerbach in his reading of Augustine (and used in *Pearl*),[28] Herbert too uses the most common and simple images and syntax not only to create the persona of the "humble

---

26. See Halewood, *Poetry of Grace*, pp. 96–98. Recall too that the poem-as-act is dependent on the sacrament, and ultimately on Christ, in order to be "way." Without the body as "visible language," that is, without the Incarnation and Crucifixion (and Resurrection), the temple does not exist. See my later comments on Herbert's lyric "The Pearl."
27. Ibid., pp. 96–97.
28. Erich Auerbach, *Literary Language and Its Public in Late Latin Antiquity and in the Middle Ages*, Bollingen Series LXXIV (New York: Pantheon Books, 1965), pp. 40, 45, 50–66.

parson" so greatly loved by centuries of Anglicans, but also, as Funk claims for the parable, to evoke "a radically new relation to reality in its everydayness":

> The parable does not turn the auditor away from the mundane, but towards it. He discovers that his destiny is at stake precisely in his ordinary creaturely existence. By means of metaphor, the parable "cracks" the shroud of everydayness lying over mundane reality in order to grant a radically new vision of mundane reality.[29]

Over and over in the midst of a journey, Herbert says, God will "cross-bias" him. In "Love Unknown" the remaking of the heart takes place as a series of afflictions that the narrator fails to fully understand until it is explained by a "Friend." "Deare," he says, "could my heart not break, / When with my pleasures ev'n my rest was gone?" (p. 130). Two poems before this, in "Giddinesse," the poet prays for just this denial of rest, this need for continual rebuilding:

>   Lord, mend or rather make us: one creation
>   Will not suffice our turn:
>   Except thou make us dayly, we shall spurn
>   Our own salvation.
>
>   (p. 127)

If salvation is figured in much of Herbert as a building operation, here he recognizes the tragic paradox that, without continually "making" us by denying us our own efforts at building, we shall in that very building "spurn" God's building going on within us. Building, by necessity, Herbert claims at his most radical, must in fact be an "unbuilding" operation by God; otherwise building is simply Babel.

Thus two distinct and intersecting activities make up the building that is the individual poem and *The Temple* as a whole: the poet builds, adding line on line, poem on poem, while within that building (which itself is a metaphor for an internal process)

---

29. Robert Funk, *Language, Hermeneutic, and the Word of God: The Problem of Language in the New Testament and Contemporary Theology* (New York: Harper & Row, 1966), pp. 194–95.

God is subverting, undermining, exploding every attempt at self-affirmation, certainty, fixity: every attempt to find rest in one's own creation or form. Only with a final movement by the poet toward submission (made possible, he affirms, by God's grace), abandoning all attempts to establish an autonomous self, only then does the building become complete, and the poem find culmination as the poet finds a temporary rest. As Anthony Burgesse warned, in his *Scripture Dictionary* (1659), "whosoever builds his salvation upon his parts, his duties . . . this mans foundation is self." Instead it must be God "who makes . . . this glorious building," for men by their own power "could never become a fit habitation for the Lord to rest in. We are not born but made the house and building of God."[30]

Of course the action of God in the poem is itself, in one sense, metaphorical, since it is the poet who causes God to subvert the building process in the poem or to complete the process, as in "The Collar" or "Deniall." Nowhere is the poet's paradox clearer, as A. D. Nuttall has suggested.[31] The poem is a willed object in Herbert, existing solely as a sign for sacrifice, for the need to submit one's will to the will of God. If lines do not rhyme in "Deniall" that is the poet's choice, as it is the poet's choice to conclude the poem with "rhyme."

30. Robert Burgesse, *The Scripture Dictionary*, STC 5656. Quoted in Fish, *The Living Temple*, p. 164. See also Barbara Kiefer Lewalski, *Protestant Poetics and the Seventeenth Century Religious Lyric* (Princeton, N.J.: Princeton University Press, 1979), pp. 100–3; Daniel Rubey, "The Poet and the Christian Community: Herbert's Affliction Poems and the Structure of *The Temple*," *Studies in English Literature* 20 (1980), p. 115; and Annabel M. Endicott, "The Structure of George Herbert's *Temple*: A Reconsideration," *University of Toronto Quarterly* 34 (1965), p. 229. Endicott quotes a sermon of Lancelot Andrewes: "The nailing of Christ's body paradoxically constituted his *un*building" (London: *XCVI Sermons*, 1629), p. 484.

31. A. D. Nuttall, *Overheard by God: Fiction and Prayer in Herbert, Milton, Dante and St. John* (London: Methuen, 1980), pp. 60–61. "Herbert," Nuttall summarizes, "has striven to eliminate himself; it is a given, and yet what is given is already God's—so not given . . . Herbert's theology implies that ordinary language is unusable. Yet he has succeeded by words also in telling us just that." William Pahlka's study constitutes a lengthy response to precisely this paradox. *Saint Augustine's Meter and George Herbert's Will* (Kent, Ohio: Kent State University Press, 1987).

Yet without the sign that the poem is, both in its form and in its content, we have no way of knowing the truth; this is the primary significance of the Incarnation, upon which model the poems are based. Jesus acts, but his acts are perceived to be done not by "his will" but according to the will of God. In Christ these are one and the same. In this way all of his acts are read as signs of the kingdom, the "new earth" promised in John, where "God's dwelling is with men." Like the Apostles after Pentecost, the poet, Herbert suggests, works miracles "in the name of Jesus Christ of Nazareth" (Acts 6), only because Jesus came first and became the way, by sacrificing himself as a "sign for the whole world." Every sign then, although made by the Apostle (priest or poet), is made possible only by the will of God working through the human vessel.

The completed poem is made whole only by grace, and its crippled wholeness is itself a sign of that grace. The poem's identity, like the poet's, incorporates its own metrical, syntactic, or rhymed woundedness: this flaw that is the outer sign of the wrestling our wills do with God's angel, who often appears to us more as a demon, an affliction (to use one of Herbert's favorite words). The poem, like all of our labor, and like all of us, is akin to the calling of Jacob, whose own wrestling is a sign of his struggle to give himself over to his true identity at the crucial moment of his life. The "man" he wrestles with in the night is his brother, his God, himself. He wrestles and "wins," and yet in so doing he must die as Jacob, walking forth in the morning light as the crippled Israel, a name that means both "God rules" and "he who strives with God" (Gen. 32:24–31).[32]

In other words, you do not, Herbert would claim, simply will a great poem. Like the presence of Christ in the sacrament, it

32. See *The New Oxford Annotated Bible* (RSV) (New York: Oxford University Press, 1973), p. 41. Pahlka's study of Herbert's metrics reinforces this idea of the poem itself as a sign of the ambiguity embedded in the name: to strive with God, as Jacob does, is to embody simultaneously the truth that God rules. Jacob ultimately becomes this knowledge through his own strife. See *Saint Augustine's Meter*, esp. p. 167 ("Herbert's poetics is based on a union of sin and love") and pp. 207–8.

comes as a blessing, but one that follows—and can only follow—our own struggles. In "The Banquet" Herbert concludes of his own verse making:

> Let the wonder of his pitie
>   Be my dittie,
> And take up my lines and life:
> Hearken under pain of death,
>   Hands and breath;
> Strive in this, and love the strife.
>
> (p. 182)

Yet, suggests Herbert, the real paradox of human life is that much of this labor and strife arises from our inability to acknowledge and receive simply what God offers to us. We are, as Paul said, flawed vessels. We are welcomed to the banquet; it is our failure to accept this gift that makes us the ambiguous creatures that we are, mostly dull and opaque yet with the occasional brilliant transparency of Christ. And this too we must offer up: our own ambiguity, our attempt to labor for our own ends and not for the divine.

The struggle to get the poem built becomes the subject of the poem itself, as the poet, like the narrator, must not build willfully but instead must allow the miracle to happen somehow through his hands. The humor that surfaces in Herbert is present because the poet is conscious of this paradox whereas the persona often is not, as in *Pearl*.[33]

The striving to build, then, is simultaneously the striving to give up, or let go, in Fish's sense.[34] It is the sacrifice made by the *Pearl* Dreamer in order to *be* a pearl to his "princes paye," a sacrifice that alone makes possible the miracle that is the poem, that turns dreamer into narrator. And the act of building is simultaneously journey or pilgrimage, culminating in this sacrifice

---

33. See Harman, *Costly Monuments*, pp. 65–88, on "The Collar," and other poems in which the poet as he writes is not in the same "place" as his narrator.
34. See *Self-Consuming Artifacts*, esp. pp. 216–23.

(of the "old man" or "Jacob"), which is the metaphorical equivalent of the equally metaphorical temple building: the terms are interchangeable, and move, like the heart, toward Love.[35]

The sense of movement in so many of the poems, of give and take between the narrator and an outside, divine force, is perhaps clearest in a poem like "Affliction I," which is cast as a narrative journey ("when first thou did entice me . . .") that is subverted not just once, but continually, "daily," as Herbert suggested in "Giddinesse." This undercutting of expectation is evident not only in the simple narrative itself ("When I got health, thou took'st away my life"), which is paradoxical enough, but in the constant turning of the narrator back upon himself as he searches to find some steady foundation on which to stand. Three of the final four stanzas begin with *Yet*: it is not enough to reverse once; it must be done repeatedly. Thus, when the poem enters the present, when the narrative catches up with itself, it is only to place the narrator in a position of utter abandonment, uncertitude:

> Now I am here, what thou wilt do with me
>   None of my books will show.
>   (p. 48)

And even this does not bring him to rest. There is a final apparent submission that is clearly imposed by the will of the narrator, followed by a last-ditch, half-hearted effort to throw over the entire game (a small version of "The Collar"), and then at last the collapse into paradox:

> Yet, though thou troublest me, I must be meek;
>   In weaknesse must be stout.
> Well, I will change the service, and go seek
>   Some other master out.
> Ah, my deare God! Though I am clean forgot,
> Let me not love thee, if I love thee not.
>   (p. 48)

---

35. On the heart as a temple, see Lewalski, *Protestant Poetics*, pp. 100–3.

In a sense, all the poems are a simple repetition of *this* repetition, this prayer. If I *do not* love you, then my punishment is contained in that same negation. Damnation, as Milton's Satan knew so well, is simply the absence of God, caused by an arrant willfulness that will not submit to this conditional.

The poem is able to come to rest in this terrifying paradox in part because the same stanza has established so clearly the warmth and almost filial attachment that exists between narrator and "master." The simple interjections here—"Well," "Ah"—are much of the point of the poem, as we are forcibly reminded of the speaker's presence and of his interruption in the middle of God's game. As with *Pearl*, much of the delight lies just in such interjections, as the narrator plays an everyman role which a reader can both identify with and find amusing: the voice remains personal, touching, affecting. But it is finally important because the very interruption reminds us that this is, finally, God's game: the narrator is servant, not master; as in "The Collar," it is his to obey. Many of the poems exist because the narrator cannot help but get his fingers in the works: he wants to do the building, the planning, because simply to let go is, apparently, to exist with no foundation at all. It is to live in midair. Barbara Harman similarly summarizes the action in this poem:

> If God is he who cross-biases the self, it is not because he has specific plans which counter the plans one has for oneself. Rather, God cross-biases by countering every attempt by the self to have plans, to determine who he is, to define the terms of existence. If it is man's inclination to fix, and make peace with, experience, it is God's inclination that he shall not.[36]

Of course, if the existence of the poem depends on such interjections by the narrator, as he attempts to affirm his own life, it is also true that the existence of the poem is a sign that this final submission is not unrewarded. As in *Pearl*, the poem is a sign of the gift that comes from affliction; it is a tangible repre-

---

36. See Harman, "George Herbert's 'Affliction (I):' The Limits of Representation," *ELH* 44 (1977), p. 273.

sentation of that which is won by losing all. Harman, closely echoing recent commentaries on the parables, claims that in "The Collar,"

> The idea that it is possible to represent the self in ways either coherent or safe is reduced to the status of a cherished fiction, and is, at last, relinquished.... What replaces it is a view of the world almost violently open, made vulnerable by interpretation, sensitive to the free play of meaning, unbounded, unsafe, and, I would add, inhospitable to the representation of the self.[37]

Yet, although this is, I think, profoundly accurate, it is also true that with that final relinquishment comes the satisfying completion of the poem itself, a satisfaction that is both aesthetically grounded and, Herbert would say, theologically, or even ontologically, grounded, with the beautiful itself being a sign for this truth. If God ultimately rules, it is because this God, this beauty, is who we most truly are.

In this renunciation, then, in this sudden whirling reversal and denial of the limited self, the kingdom breaks in in the form of beauty and we are home free. This, after all, is why the renunciation is made: one gives up everything and finds that the promise has been kept. A rhyme is found and a poem completed. A door is opened, and Love takes you by the hand. And this final satisfying *rest* (recalling the word's musical referent) is found only through the renunciation. Renunciation makes possible both the recognition of beauty and at the same time the completion of form wherein beauty is located: the rest or silence toward which all things move (Mazzeo comments that for Augustine, "All dialectic, true rhetoric, and thought itself were but attempts to reascend to that silence from which the world fell into the perpetual clamour of life as fallen men know it").[38]

What finally is so profoundly satisfying about Herbert is not that he can tell or even show this fundamental Christian paradox

---

37. Harman, "The Fiction of Coherence: George Herbert's 'The Collar'," *PMLA* 93 (1978), p. 875.
38. Mazzeo, "St. Augustine's Rhetoric," p. 23.

George Herbert's *Temple* 93

(to give all is to receive all) but that he makes this happen again for the reader: he "simultaneously enlightens and gladdens," as Augustine said. The reader experiences "truth and goodness" as beauty in the successful and satisfying completion of the poem. Delight, then, is not just "turned into sacrifice"; delight is sacrifice and sacrifice is delight when it is correctly perceived through its source, that being the divine love. "The world is God's poem," Augustine claimed, and all beautiful objects, including those of the artist, who continues God's work, are but means of ascent to "self-subsistent beauty,"[39] that being the silence of God himself. Beauty is only beauty when it shows forth the source of beauty, as did the Incarnation, the life and death of Christ, in its perfect "illumination of goodness and truth." Aesthetics, like all else, must be both incarnational and sacrificial. Here alone is located true delight.

Thus it is fitting that in the very moment of renunciation comes the gift; at the moment that the journey is abandoned, one has arrived home and the poem is completed. This happens over and over at the end of Herbert's poems. A building is made complete, sound, but only because its builder has given up his initial attempt to make himself at home in his images. He has successfully labored through the night in dialogue with the divine, only to find at last that all his work has revealed to him a simple truth: God rules.

* * *

While the progress of the poem reveals the remaking of the narrator's heart into a temple, it is simultaneously working upon

---

39. Ibid., p. 25; *Civitas Dei* XI, chap. 18; *De Vera Religionis* XXIV, 45. As a corrective to Ricoeur's sense of metaphor, in which the "is not" implies a constantly deferred reality, Stephen Happel suggests that this "fails to take account of the way that art can 'trick us' into sharing its vision for the world. This 'shared vision' is true both of the subject who is experiencing the art and of the artwork itself. Sometimes seduced by the pleasure of an artful sound, movement or sight, we become part of the world we have temporarily entered." This notion of artistic seduction is, of course, very close to Herbert's understanding of turning "delight into sacrifice," which is the central function of the poem. Thus reality is not deferred so much as it is recognized as being inherently sacrificial. See "Worship as a Grammar of Social Transformation," in George Kilcourse, ed., *Proceedings* (Philadelphia: Catholic Theological Society of America, 1987), vol. 42, p. 82.

the reader. Here is where poet and priest combine, as is suggested in one of Daniel Featley's sermons quoted by Barbara Lewalski. This "spiritual and inward temple," Featley claims,

> Needeth continually to be built, repaired, enlarged, and adorned: for to *build* it in the ignorant, to *repaire* it in the relapsed, to *enlarge* it in the proficient, and *beautifie* and adorne it in those that are perfect, is the . . . whole duty of the *man of God*.[40]

Radical examples like those chosen by Harman ("Affliction (I)" and "The Collar") perhaps present the clearest case for this process, yet others follow a similar pattern; in fact, it is in poems like "The Pearl, Matt. 13:45," that one most easily sees a narrator who begins from a newly won submission to retell the story of the journey, at least in part for the sake of the listener.

"The Pearl" is told in the voice of a man who has made a decision. Statements are direct and clear, and the poem builds along easily discernible lines: "I know the ways of Learning . . . I know the ways of Honour . . . I know the wayes of pleasure . . . I know all these. . . ." Yet by the poem's end one senses that Herbert has successfully remade the parable on which the poem is based, and in doing so, has momentarily remade himself (and potentially the reader as well). The merchant here, like the Jeweler in *Pearl*, "sells all he has" for the sake of the kingdom, knowing full well "Both the main sale, and the commodities; / And at what rate and price I have thy love." The price, here, the "all," is the ways of the world: learning, honor, pleasure, listed in great detail in separate stanzas in order to make the cost felt. Nine pentameter lines, one lengthy syntactic period culminate in one short, monosyllabic dimeter reversal that sells all the richness of the poetic world and its visible language:

> I know the wayes of Pleasure, the sweet strains,
> The lullings and the relishes of it;
> The propositions of hot bloud and brains;
> What mirth and musick mean: what love and wit
> Have done these twentie hundred yeares, and more:

---

40. Lewalski, *Protestant Poetics*, p. 101.

> I know the projects of unbridled store:
> My stuff is flesh, not brasse; my senses live,
> And grumble oft, that they have more in me
> Then he that curbs them, being but one to five:
>   Yet I love thee.
>
>   (p. 89)

There is a world in these nine lines; the poem only succeeds, finally, because Herbert successfully convinces us (especially in this stanza) that he knows precisely what he is giving up. Alliteration, metrical variations, and parallelisms all work toward one end here: that we might feel the "sweet strains," "what mirth and musicke mean." The lines themselves stretch out, as if reveling once more in this sweet temptation of "twentie hundred yeares, and more." That it is impossible to get enough is precisely the point: "Pleasure" (including aesthetic) is never satisfied; it has no ending, no true rest. The only possible rest comes in the reversal, the short yet satisfying rejection, which concludes the sentence, the rhyme, the temptation: "Yet I love thee."

However, as in "Affliction (I)," this trio of reversals (each again signalled by "yet") still is not enough, because throughout the implication is that the speaker himself makes all the decisions, does all the acting, while God passively awaits his love. Until the final stanza, the speaker is always subject and God the object, yet this, too, is inverted by the poem's end in one final "twist," which is the syntactic equivalent of the "silk twist let down from heaven":

> I know all these, and have them in my hand:
> Therefore not sealed, but with open eyes
> I flie to thee, and fully understand
> Both the main sale, and the commodities;
> And at what rate and price I have thy love;
> With all the circumstances that may move:
> Yet through these labyrinths, not my grovelling wit,
> But thy silk twist let down from heav'n to me,
> Did both conduct and teach me, how by it
>   To climbe to thee.
>
>   (p. 89)

The "silk twist," as commentators have recognized, is both Ariadne's thread that guided Theseus through the labyrinth and the Incarnation: "The Cross of Christ is the Jacob's ladder by which we Ascend into the Highest Heavens," according to Traherne.[41] Yet it is also the "twisting" itself, this turning about or conversion, that comes syntactically with the "yet," which signals a shift in the stanza's direction, as it does simultaneously within the speaker. It was only through this intermediary (silk twist = cross) that the narrator gains the insight necessary to ascend, and that insight is an acknowledgment of sacrifice: he must take up his own cross and "climb . . . by it." The cross is both a sign that teaches and a demand for action ("conduct": "sell all you have and follow me"). Without this sign, this "twist" in our normal logic that tells us that we are made "men" by striving, accumulating, possessing, there is no way home, only "repining restlessnesse" (p. 160). In this poem, without this sign of God's ultimate love, the sentences (and thus the poem) have no end; there would be no way for the speaker to say, "Yet I love thee"—to make his reversal, his sacrifice—without the gift of the sign of the cross. Instead, there would be ceaseless and meaningless motion: history without the Incarnation.

Thus, the poem most properly ends with the burden put on God's grace (not "my grovelling wit," which we have seen in action for three stanzas), even while recognizing the need for appropriate response ("conduct") from the individual, who still must "climb." Syntax says it all here:

> *thy silk twist* let down *to me*
> Did both conduct and teach *me*, how *by it*
> To climb *to thee*.

God becomes both agent and recipient of action in this intricate sentence, which mirrors precisely the importance to Herbert of the Incarnation. If we take the *thee* addressed as Christ, then nominative, dative, and ablative all coincide with agent: the

---

41. *The English Poems of George Herbert*, ed. C. A. Patrides (London: J. M. Dent, 1974), p. 104.

means and goal are equivalent. Thus, even while the narrator ends in action ("climbing"), the action is set in a timeless infinitive phrase, syntactically dependent on all that comes before. The emphasis is placed not on the actor (the speaker climbing) but on the instrument (the twist), the action itself, and the direction of that action (to thee): the "I" is effaced.

As in the final complex stanza of *Pearl*, where action by the speaker is intentionally a giving up of action, here, too, we have a syntactic representation of the poem's point, based, like the medieval poem, on the underlying truth of the parable. On the surface it might suggest the possibility of a man's simply buying his way into the kingdom; instead the parable attempts to figure the truth of the cross. You want love: real love, ultimate love? Sell all you have and follow me.[42]

Many of Herbert's poems seem, like "Affliction (I)," to wander only until grace comes, bringing completion and rest. "Deniall" is one of the clearest examples. Here we find a narrative set in the past ("When my devotions could not pierce / Thy silent eares") with a continual emphasis on the "I," who stands through much of the poem in the nominative case, attempting continually to storm heaven's walls, an attempt that leads him only to "disorder." A reflection in the present ("O that thou shouldst give dust a tongue / To crie to thee, / And then not heare it crying!") shifts to a result in the past: "Therefore my soul lay out of sight, / Untun'd, unstrung" and finally to prayer, at which point the narrator's past and present converge, as he still laments the disorder in his heart:

> O cheer and tune my heartlesse breast,
>   Deferre no time;
> That so thy favours granting my request,
>   They and my mind may chime,
>   And mend my ryme.
>   (p. 80)

---

42. These phrases too, of course, are metaphorical. The "sell" and "follow" are equivalent: they amount to the same thing, which is conversion, or a radical turning around of what is the basis of one's life.

Here in the asking the future becomes present: "may" drops out in the final line and becomes fact as the "ryme" is indeed mended even as he asks.

In this final stanza the narrator reverses the subject-object order, as "*thy* favours grant *my* request," which leads to a proper joint operation, as we saw worked out in the final stanza of Herbert's "Pearl." "They and my mind may chime" together, and in that harmony comes, at last, "ryme." The poem comes home to rest, as God works through the human vessel.[43] Yet we note that the disorder, the rhymelessness remains as part of the poem: the whole that we are inevitably includes the crippled self we once were and we in some way continue to be. Like Christ's, our wounds are ours forever.

"Employment" and labor, it is clear, depend not on one's own will but on one's will converging with the will of God until inner and outer disappear. The poem cannot be completed, ordered, until grace, which alone allows for this convergence, comes. But the problem is a real one. Grace does come but apparently unpredictably. Did the initial devotions (the first stanza) fail because (as the syntax implies) they were too willful? Crying to God is not, apparently, enough: a turning of the heart is needed, the sort of turning witnessed in the final stanza, where a proper relationship between poet and master is reestablished. Yet this turning itself must be seen as a gift, coming only when the man's spirit is thoroughly beaten down ("My feeble spirit, unable to look right . . .").

It is worth stressing here that the poem as written exists as a visible sign of this relationship between God and man: the syntactic reordering that has taken place within the heart, by grace, Herbert would argue, and not by his own will. This is why the poem is so often (or becomes so often) a prayer in Herbert. The prayer is an acknowledgment of need, of outside aid.

We are reminded, perhaps, of Herbert's "Pilgrimage," in which again a man journeys hopefully toward God only to be

---

43. See Mark Taylor, *The Soul in Paraphrase: George Herbert's Poetics* (The Hague: Mouton, 1974), pp. 79–82.

broken down again and again, defeating the very notion that one can make progress on one's own.⁴⁴ So too, in "Deniall," the progress of the poem becomes a metaphor for the life of an individual, particularly in regard to a calling or employment (the poem follows immediately after "Employment II" in the first edition), as the correct "tuning" of the breast stands for both a right relationship to God through grace and, simultaneously, the fulfillment of one's vocation (here, as both poet, who without rhyme ceases to *be* poet, and as priest, who has the task of showing the way to truth, to build in others' breasts).

Perhaps the most radical expression of this movement toward silence (a silence that is both submission and yet completion at the same time) comes in "The Holdfast," which again is a journey, with each stanza showing a new loosening of one's foothold on the side of a mountain. Each new response, the poet implies, although it seems to be submission, is in fact a self-willing (as the opening word *threatened* suggests), which amounts to a foundation built by ourselves, and not one given to us through radical surrender. Thus each attempt at building by the narrator is immediately undercut by this "friend" (who in Herbert always turns out to be Christ):

> I threatned to observe the strict decree
>   Of my deare God with all my power & might.
>   But I was told by one, it could not be;
> Yet I might trust in God to be my light.
> Then will I trust, said I, in him alone.
>   Nay, ev'n to trust in him, was also his:
>   We must confesse that nothing is our own.
> Then I confesse that he my succour is:
> But to have nought is ours, not to confesse
>   That we have nought. I stood amazed at this,
>   Much troubled, till I heard a friend expresse,

---

44. "The final lines of 'The Pilgrimage,'" Barbara Harman comments, "suggest that meaning, closure, and psychic coherence are unavailable in this life." See *Costly Monuments*, p. 145. Closure does in fact come with the poem's end and the rhyme's completion, but, as this poem demonstrates, that closure is itself a sign that such rest is temporary at best.

> That all things were more ours by being his.
> What Adam had, and forfeited for all,
> Christ keepeth now, who cannot fail or fall.
> (p. 143)

The key line here is "I stood amazed at this," as it brings the narrative—and narrator and thus the poem—to an abrupt halt. Proceeding along smoothly enough, improvising through each stanza in his attempt to fine-tune his will to God's, the narrator is at last confronted with a paradox he cannot circumvent. Yet as the poem appears to end in a breakdown of the will (how can I act or move?) it supplies, out of this death, yet another realization, and one that, by another paradox, renews hope. Letting go is gaining all, but there can be no halfway measures. An utter denial is demanded, not just "confesse that he my succour is."

Like the labor of building an altar with uncut stones, even language must at last be emptied of human will, even as we know that language is our tool for recovering what was lost, for covering absence with metaphorical, imaginative connection. On our own we build Babel. The paradox remains: strive in this, and love the strife.[45]

We cannot will grace; we cannot even will not to will.[46] We cannot, in other words, complete any action ourselves, including, for Herbert, the poem itself, without grace's descending. Yet grace does come, not because the poet cries out for it or labors (as in "Deniall," the cry does not cause salvation), yet nonetheless in response to such labor.[47] The journey, we might say, that each poem is, does not cause the satisfactory (if temporary) end, yet setting out remains necessary to reaching the end. Without the

---

45. See A. D. Nuttall, *Overheard by God: Fiction and Prayer in Herbert, Milton, Dante and St. John* (London: Methuen, 1980), for a radical treatment of this issue in Herbert. See also Harman, *Costly Monuments*, pp. 53–55.

46. For comments concerning the influence of Calvinism on Herbert, see, for example, Nuttall, *Overheard by God* (esp. pp. 42–45, 53–54); Halewood, *Poetry of Grace* (esp. pp. 106, 110); Taylor, *Soul in Paraphrase*, pp. 92–95; and Louis Martz, *The Poetry of Meditation: A Study in English Religious Literature of the Seventeenth Century* (New Haven: Yale University Press, 1954, 1962), pp. 249–320.

47. Mark Taylor makes a similar point; the finished poem exists as a sign of grace. See *Soul in Paraphrase*, p. 10.

setting out no conclusion is possible; no poem would exist.[48] Again, the worldly, incarnate labor is necessary for the transformation of that same bodily existence. We must wrestle with our demons and angels in our daily labor, knowing that this wrestling is itself much of what vocation *is*. This figurative strife is the kneading that is necessary for bread to be bread.

As in *Pearl*, so many of Herbert's poems are first-person narratives of a past event in which this process of remaking went on and was successfully concluded. The present event (the poem itself) exists as a sign of that successful rest, even if that rest is simply the clear revelation that fixity and definition do not exist, except as eschatological goals. "Jordan II," for example, becomes a dialogue between a poet and his "friend," with the poem itself witnessing to whether or not he has heard correctly the advice given by the friend (Christ) at the poem's end. The issue here, although specifically related to the work of the poet, is no different from the other poems we have looked at. Once again submission, selflessness, is the turning required by the friend:

> As flames do worke and winde, when they ascend,
> So did I weave my self into the sense.
> But while I bustled, I might heare a friend
> Whisper, *How wide is all this long pretence!*
> *There is in love a sweetnesse readie penn'd:*
> *Copie out onely that, and save expense.*
>
> (p. 103)

The *Whisper* here reminds us of "The Collar," and in fact the situations are similar: there too the narrator had "woven himself" into the sense and was rescued from spinning his wheels endlessly only by this quiet voice that brings everything to a halt, because in the voice is found the goal: "a sweetnesse readie penn'd."

The dilemma for the religious poet is a serious enough one (and the poet merely stands in for all men confronted by the

---

48. There is also a sense in which no conclusion *is* possible, as Harman stresses in *Costly Monuments* in her analysis of "Pilgrimage," in which the end of the poem (satisfying as it is) tells us that rest comes only through death; the appearance of pilgrimage's end is an illusion.

demands of Christ): one must work, or journey, in order to reach salvation, yet one is not saved by works (the "long pretence" of the poems). Yet again, works are an indication of grace bestowed: from a remade heart will flow blessings, good works, love. This is what it means to "copie out" the "sweetnesse" in love. It is to become a vessel of grace oneself. And only in this way do one's works become a temple, finding in the temple, that is, what the narrator himself discovered: that there is no rest here, only a road that leads to a cross.

Or, rather: that rest *is* the cross's road. The cross is an act of fulfillment and completion ("it is finished") that, although in one sense finished, in another sense is always continuing, insofar as this sacrificial love is the central and eternal process of the universe. The *lack* of rest that the poem reaches in its own completion is itself a sign of this paradoxical knowledge, as poems like "Pilgrimage" and "The Pulley" most clearly attest.

Often the poems reflect journeys to that recognition of utter dependence: only at the end do we see that this metaphorical home had been found already and that the poem is a re-creation (by the narrator, already remade) of exactly this process, this stripping of the self's own constructions by means of paradox. The remaking of the man is evidenced in the poem, which then functions as an emblem for the reader to see and experience what the narrator has seen and been. The poem becomes the reader's journey, which is a building line by line that culminates in a turning around. As in *Pearl*, a point of view is altered by one's entry into the process. And again, as in *Pearl*, what the reader or narrator grasps is not the abandonment of the physical (aesthetic or otherwise); after all, it is precisely in the pleasure of the poem itself that this insight comes and that "delight" is made into "sacrifice." It is, then, our own labor as writers and readers that helps bring about the transformation. And what is transformed or "destroyed" is not the physical but the terrible compulsion we feel toward the physical, our desire to fill our loneliness and hunger with it. Our addictions are crucified.

Thus Herbert's rest, like the promised new earth, is not in a distant location but is instead right here in a state of continual vulnerability, like that Christ displays on the cross. Jesus denies nothing that was said of him, and accuses no one, because He is all of us. He knows all of these sins and acts on none. Instead, the desire to cling, to lose this terrible absence of God through power and wealth, flows beneath Him like water or blood. His real humanity is the wound He carries into eternity, as he shows to Thomas, and that we are likewise invited to carry. In fact, those wounds are the source of our salvation. We too are stripped by our callings, and we too must learn that the sufferings inflicted on us as we strive are not simply the acts of a misguided world or of faulty or missing parents. We cannot blame the other. That world is us and is also the body of Christ. However absent He might seem, when we wrestle with what is deepest in us we wrestle always with the divine in us.

The "emblem" poems are perhaps the clearest sign of the way I suggest many of the Temple poems work on us. "Paradise," for example:

>   I blesse thee, Lord, because I GROW
>   Among thy trees, which in a ROW
>   To thee both fruit and order OW.
>
>   What open force, or hidden CHARM
>   Can blast my fruit, or bring me HARM,
>   While the inclosure is thine ARM?
>
>   Inclose me still for fear I START.
>   Be to me rather sharp and TART,
>   Then let me want thy hand & ART.
>
>   When thou dost greater judgments SPARE,
>   And with thy knife but prune and PARE,
>   Ev'n fruitfull trees more fruitfull ARE.
>
>   Such sharpnes shows the sweetest FREND:
>   Such cuttings rather heal than REND:
>   And such beginnings touch their END.
>   (pp. 132–33)

The narrator is (figuratively) in God's garden, which is also Gethsemane. The poem too, like the man and like Jesus, shows the effects of pruning. The poem then echoes the narrator's reliance on God to work as a gardener—as an artist, in fact—in order to bring the speaker to his proper "end." Without this stripping away, the poem does not exist, and the poet, by implication, likewise fails in his calling: fails, that is, to submit, to give himself over to God. Without the "affliction" sent by God, the poet builds and builds but only in repeated circles: "Frend" never becomes "end," and so "Paradise" (figured in the completed poem) is never reached.

The notion that the physical movement through a poem on a page (or the mental movement, the act of reading) can be taken as a metaphor for a spiritual or psychological process is of course not new with Herbert, nor does it die out with Herbert (Yeats may be the most conscious, and greatest, practitioner of such emblem art since Herbert).[49] Yet it is clear that for Herbert such literal "cuttings" as we find in "Paradise," in "Deniall," and in "Grief" have a much more profound significance than in his apparent sources, where the correspondence between the image on the page and the truth is often suggested quite simply.[50]

In "Easter Wings," for example, simplicity of diction and syntax and an apparently guileless physical representation of the "wings" of the poem's title should not obscure the more profound underpinnings. Here if anywhere the reader, simply by entering into the poem, inevitably moves with the poem through its "affliction," its "fall" and "thinning," only in order to find herself "turned around," as in one of Yeats's gyres, where the poem empties out through its center into God.

The "visible language" in a poem such as this is first recognized by a reader even before he reads: he sees a title and a poem that typographically represents the title. It is a completed object, a

---

49. See the poems (such as "Byzantium") in which line length and rhyme patterns mirror the activity of the gyres.
50. See the examples given in Patrides, *The English Poems of George Herbert*, pp. 209–12.

foreign world, until he enters into it and moves through the lines, until the journey culminates in a return to the static object from which he began (the "wings"), now more truly understood because experienced by the reader himself. Wings are now known as an emblem for an event that is both the original resurrection event and that event recurring *now* in the reader, as he falls, dies, is buried, and rises, expanding again with Christ. The pattern of Christ becomes the poem's pattern, which in turn is transferred (ideally) into the reader: delight turns into sacrifice and then again to (aesthetic, spiritual) delight.

> Lord, who createdst man in wealth and store,
>   Though foolishly he lost the same,
>   Decaying more and more,
>   Till he became
>   Most poore:
>   With thee
>   O let me rise
>   As larks, harmoniously,
>   And sing this day thy victories:
> Then shall the fall further the flight in me.
>
>   My tender age in sorrow did beginne:
>   And still with sicknesses and shame
>   Thou didst so punish sinne,
>   That I became
>   Most thinne.
>   With thee
>   Let me combine
>   And feel this day thy victorie:
>   For, if I imp my wing on thine,
>   Affliction shall advance the flight in me.[51]
>
> (p. 43)

The key here (as earlier) is that a building completed on the

---

51. For editorial concerns arising over the printing of these poems, see the comments of J. Max Patrick in his essay "Critical Problems in Editing George Herbert's *The Temple*," in *The Editor as Critic and the Critic as Editor* by J. Max Patrick and Alan Roper (Los Angeles: University of California, William Andrews Clark Memorial Library, 1973), pp. 3–40.

page is invariably a sign of a building that is an event, a journey: the poetic equivalent of abandoning everything and following Christ. The successful construction of the poem, the fact of its existence, is itself the sign that affliction has indeed advanced the flight in the speaker; has, in fact, made the creation of these signs possible. Without the affliction (the narrowing down) and without Christ (who creates the expansion) the poem fails to exist, and there is in turn no sign of redemption, as if Easter had not happened.

We are reminded continually in Herbert that the Incarnation, the miracles, the healings, the crucifixion, and the resurrection are themselves all signs, pointing to the nature of the divine love for man.[52] The poem exists only because these signs existed first: this is part of what it means for the poem to "imp my wing on thine," or to "copie out" the "sweetnesse" of the divine act. As an individual man, and as a poet, he does not "fly" except by "combining" with Christ. The point of the poem, then, is not simply to exist as a physical sign of this truth but to exist as the labor whereby the reader himself experiences how this completed sign comes into existence.

"Easter Wings" is narrated in the present tense, as the speaker addresses his Lord in prayer "now" (as we saw similarly at the conclusion of "Deniall"). Again, as in "Deniall," the successful completion of the poem argues as an answer to prayer: grace has descended, allowing the poem to exist in its now completed, static form. It concludes with a satisfying roundness, or whole-

---

52. Stephen Happel ("Worship as a Grammar of Social Transformation," in *Proceedings*, ed. George Kilcourse [Philadelphia: Catholic Theological Society of America, 1987], vol. 42) writes: "Jesus' self-sacrificing love is the root-metaphor for Christians, the narrative which transforms. . . . The sacraments are . . . the memory of an unsettling life whose meanings do not easily confirm present prejudices. For the sake of the future, the sacramental narratives redirect our lives toward a new world." He then adds, following Ricoeur, "The sacraments can do this because they function the way metaphors do. They are a semantic impertinence; like the parables, they shock us into recognizing some new imaginative possibility, a world to be lived in by believers" (78). Happel in turn refers us to David Powers's *Unsearchable Riches: The Symbolic Nature of Liturgy* (New York: Pueblo, 1984), pp. 154–58.

ness, as "something understood" ("Prayer I"), suggesting that in the very moment of asking the poet is answered.

The man, like his own language, is whittled away to nothing: as a result of his own failure, and of the afflictions that followed on failure, he has become "most thinne." The journey appears to be at an end as the journeyer is about to disappear. "And yet," as Schwartz comments on the "Sacred Journey," "it may also happen that the people remain true to their calling even when their train, utterly spent, disintegrates. Now utterly without hope, they surrender even this, their sacred way, and commend themselves to the Lord without reserve." And in this letting go of one's desires, hopes for advancement, success, health, one finds the journey not abandoned but completed. As with Job, fullness returns and one is restored sevenfold. Only in this way can "the fall further the flight in me," making possible the return home:

> In this very instant the journey is over and God is at hand. Then, suddenly, it becomes evident that the Lord had already planned this outcome when he called the creature on its way, that he designed the whole way to lead to this very end and that from the very first this end was infused into the way to guide it. The last step was contained in the very first and each subsequent one drove the people on toward the end. And when the creature finally gives up reaching this goal—in the ultimate surrender even of this, his eternal hope and sacred chance—the goal has already been reached and God gives of himself abundantly. Here is altar.[53]

The poem takes its place in the created world, existing like all other objects both as entity unto itself and also, potentially, as sign, as way. No less than the *Pearl*-Poet, Herbert recognizes the necessity of the image, something one can see, but also recognizes the danger inherent in all images. In Augustine's terms, we can either use the created world as a means to a further end or simply enjoy creation's "sweetness" as an end in itself.[54] Indeed, it is

---

53. Schwartz, *Church Incarnate*, p. 134.
54. *On Christian Doctrine*, pp. 9–10. On Herbert's use of Augustine, see in particular Asals, *Equivocal Predications*, pp. 57–75, and Pahlka, *Saint Augustine's Meter*, throughout.

precisely this issue of sweetness that becomes crucial in Herbert; the sweetness of creation, and of his own creation, functions only as a sign to the sweetness of God, "readie penn'd," which "would make us blessed."⁵⁵ A poem like "Mattens," for instance, states both problem and solution:

> I cannot ope mine eyes,
> But thou art ready there to catch
> My morning-soul and sacrifice:
> Then we must needs for that day make a match.
>
> My God, what is a heart?
> Silver, or gold, or precious stone,
> Or starre, or rainbow, or a part
> Of all these things, or all of them in one?
>
> My God, what is a heart,
> That thou shouldst it so eye, and wooe,
> Powring upon it all thy art,
> As if that thou hadst nothing els to do?
>
> Indeed mans whole estate
> Amounts (and richly) to serve thee:
> He did not heav'n and earth create,
> Yet studies them, not him by whom they be.
>
> Teach me thy love to know;
> That this new light, which now I see,
> May both the work and workman show:
> Then by a sunne-beam I will climbe to thee.
>
> (pp. 62–63)

As so often, the poem ends in prayer, an acknowledgment of man's failure (he studies the gift, not the giver), and a request for the grace to use the creation as Augustine had argued he should, "so that by means of corporal . . . things we may comprehend the eternal. . . ." The awakening in the morning (Mattens) and the opening of the eyes at the poem's beginning become by the end figures themselves for spiritual truths (as we shall see

---

55. As we shall see, this word (*Sweet*) is itself a major motif in the poems at the end of *The Temple*.

again, more radically, in the opening of *Jerusalem*). The "new light" of the last stanza, then, is both the literal sunlight and the new understanding that has come by grace, an understanding experienced as "thy love," signified most profoundly in the incarnation and crucifixion. Again, the literal embodies the figure: it is not a question of turning away from sunlight in order to reach some other "light": "sun," of course, as always in Herbert, is likewise "Son": the sound parallel is itself a sign of the union between these two as the source of all life. Thus when he concludes that "by a sunne-beam I will climbe to thee," he means that through the sun and daylight he can see "Son." Yet in this seeing he acknowledges a demand, as the poem's opening reminds us: "I cannot ope mine eyes, / But thou art ready there to catch / My morning soul and my sacrifice. . . ." The "sunne-beam," then, is literal sunlight and also the beam of the Son's cross, by which alone we "climbe." To see the figurative in Herbert is to have one's eyes opened to the demand for sacrifice.

Clearly the poem asks the reader to do precisely what the narrator has done (or has had done unto him). The reader too must use the poem, look at the literal (the "sunne-beam," for example), and recognize the central spiritual truth, the divine love itself, played out by the Son. The perception of this truth is the point of the poem; it alone answers the question posed (twice) in the middle of the poem: "My God, what is a heart?" A heart ("mans whole estate") "Amounts . . . to serve thee." God, Herbert reminds us, pours his own art upon us—the beauty of the new day, for example—in order to woo us back. So too must we labor.

As in the parables, the poem ends with a call to action that is itself predicated on an earlier call, or prayer: action only follows the true understanding, the correct hearing and seeing of the Word. Works follow only from grace. We "climbe" only after having been shown the way from "sun" to "Son."

"Mattens" suggests that the poem, like the heart, is both nothing in the sight of God and everything. Nothing in its own right, the poem becomes potentially everything, as it leads us back home by turning us around, opening our eyes to the figure, and bidding us to climb. Changing the title of a poem that comes shortly after "Mattens" from "Poetry" to "The Quidditie" gives a clear indication of this dual nature of the poetic object, as "quidditie" itself, meaning among the Scholastics "the real nature or essence of a thing," came instead to mean almost the opposite: mere subtlety in argument, a quirk or quibble.[56] The poem is either, depending on the perspective of the viewer. This poem, for example, is cast entirely in negatives, until the final two lines, which reverse the entire field of action:

> My God, a verse is not a crown,
> No point of honour, or gay suit,
> No hawk, or banquet, or reknown,
> Nor a good sword, not yet a lute:
>
> It cannot vault, or dance, or play;
> It never was in *France* or *Spain*;
> Nor can it entertain the day
> With my great stable or demain:
>
> It is no office, art or news,
> Nor the Exchange, or busie Hall;
> But it is that which while I use
> I am with thee, and *most take all*.
> (pp. 69–70)

As we often find in Herbert, the denial of the worldly sphere is simultaneously an affirmation of the true place of the creation and of labor. It is in the denial of the poem as having earthly value that it has any value at all: only while he uses it, while he labors, "I am with thee, and most take all." In translating this secular proverb into the spiritual ("most take all"[57]), the poet gives a sign of the proper action of all art and beyond it of all work: taking the "secular" that is God's creation and transposing it to the "spiritual," as with the sun in "Mattens," which becomes, in

---

56. See Hutchinson, *Works of George Herbert*, p. 69, and the note on p. 500.
57. See the note on this line in Patrides, *English Poems*, p. 87.

the poem ("if we could but spell"), "Son." Only in this way can he "climbe to thee" and reveal the true function or worth of his own work: the poem as "Quidditie," as "essence."[58]

"The Rose" is even more outspoken in its apparent rejection of "this world of sugred lies"; immediately after "The Forerunners," it helps mark the transition into the final sequence of poems where the poet more radically cuts away all that is inessential and embraces "Death," "Doomsday," and "Judgement" in order to arrive at "Heaven" and "Love." The poem is also a fine commentary on Augustine's distinctions between use and enjoyment.

> First, there is no pleasure here:
>   Colour'd griefs indeed there are,
> Blushing woes, that look as cleare
>   As if they could beautie spare.
>
> (p. 177)

His example of a "colour'd grief" is the rose, which he proceeds to use in order to see beyond it, as the rose becomes the figure for all the world's apparent beauty:

> What is fairer than a rose?
>   What is sweeter? Yet it purgeth.
> Purgings enmitie disclose,
>   Enmitie forbearance urgeth.
>
> If then all that worldlings prize
>   Be contracted to a rose;
> Sweetly there indeed it lies,
>   But it biteth in the close.
>
> So this flower doth judge and sentence
>   Worldly joyes to be a scourge:
> For they all produce repentance,
>   And repentance is a purge.

58. The most obvious example of Herbert's taking the secular, in which man is attempting to enjoy God's creation (rather than using it), and changing it back to a figure for the spiritual, is in the two "Jordan" poems. Taylor, *Soul in Paraphrase*, p. 18–22.

Although there is a clear enough rejection of the world in the final stanza of this poem ("But I health, not physick choose"), it is also clear that much of the point of the poem is that if you do go by the way of the world, you still only reach your end by way of purgation or denial: the building you have erected will deny itself as a place of finality. So too the rose has a built-in safety device, denying our attempts to find rest in it. It reveals its own limits, points beyond itself, and in that way becomes a purgative that, itself a "worldly joy," judges these same joys.

Herbert here suggests that an intentional paradox lies at the center of the world (somewhat akin to the paradoxes found in the playing of "rest" in "The Pulley," where man finds "the rest" in the world but no "rest"). The rose attracts us, yet that same attraction leads potentially to repentance by way of purgation and thus to "health": the long way around to God, and usually the only way for us to go (though it is finally rejected here; toward the end of *The Temple*, even this rejection must come in the form of a figure).

Similarly with the poem, itself "The Rose." The aesthetic sweetness (mentioned in "The Forerunners," where again there is a rejection of "sweet phrases, lovely metaphors") draws us in, but it "biteth in the close," as, once again, delight is transformed as the poem too becomes purgative. We can rest in it only by denying its sharp point—what Augustine calls "abuse."[59]

Clearly the poet here is less interested in the poem as a figure leading directly to God ("rose" as the "mystical rose" of Dante) than as a figure leading by paradox to a denial of itself. Beauty, aesthetic delight, is most truly found in self-sacrifice. And if we recall that the church itself is often figured as a rose (as in "Church Rents"), we might also recall that the visible church as an institution is meant to be the bride of Christ, that is, a sign of the way of sacrifice, of self-denying love. "The Rose" in this light becomes a synecdoche for the entire collection of poems, Herbert's "Church," built simply as a means by which to climb.

59. *On Christian Doctrine*, p. 9.

The entire process becomes a slow purgation, a building that affirms its beauty by denying itself as an end. In that denial we find the building—in this case, the flower—completed:

> But I health, not physick choose:
>   Onely though I you oppose,
> Say that fairly I refuse,
>   For my answer is a rose.
>
> (p. 178)

As in Augustine, true sweetness for Herbert resides in the presence of God, known here and now through material form (beauty) but also still to come: "True beautie dwells on high: ours is a flame / But borrowed thence to light us thither" ("The Forerunners," p. 179).

* * *

"Love (III)," which immediately follows, is a variation on "Heaven" (as the titles would suggest). It is heaven seen as communion, with the Word now functioning as "Host." In it, in "Love," themes, images, are finalized, summed up. "Sweetness" is here, and dust, and sacrifice, and grace. This is "realized eschatology":[60]

> Love bade me welcome: yet my soul drew back,
>   Guiltie of dust and sinne.
> But quick-ey'd Love, observing me grow slack
>   From my first entrance in,
> Drew nearer to me, sweetly questioning,
>   If I lack'd anything.
>
> A guest, I answer'd, worthy to be here:
>   Love said, You shall be he.
> I the unkinde, ungrateful? Ah my deare,
>   I cannot look on thee.
> Love took my hand, and smiling did reply,
>   Who made the eyes but I?
>
> Truth Lord, but I have marr'd them: let my shame
>   Go where it doth deserve.

---

60. The phrase is that of C. H. Dodd; see *The Parables of the Kingdom* (1936; reprint New York: Charles Scribner's Sons, 1961), p. 164.

> And know you not, sayes Love, who bore the blame?
> My deare, then I will serve.
> You must sit down, sayes Love, and taste my meat:
> So I did sit and eat.
>
> (pp. 188–89)

The action of the poem, taking place in an eternal "now," a present tense leading to the finality of the past in the final lines, is a last remaking of the narrator, who enters with a lingering sense of being the wrong person in the wrong place. "You shall be he," Love says, and then acts on the soul to make him "A guest . . . worthy to be here." Love invites, questions, cajoles, leads, and finally serves, as piece by piece, yet tenderly, the soul is stripped of all that prevents its own will from existing within the will of God, until it is ready just to *be*. The duties of a guest are gratefulness; he must accept, without any sense of doing or making. Building is at an end: remade, we receive and eat. And the meal of course is the "Host" himself, Love, who now abides in us, is us, as we are stripped of all that separates us from him. "You shall be he" means becoming who we are.[61]

* * *

The altar constructed in the front of this temple finds its match in the conclusion, where the prayer is fulfilled: "thy sacrifice" has become "mine," and "this altar" "thine." The narrator within the poems is this persona who has "come to thy holy hill" only by way of a radical sacrifice, the building of an altar on the page and within the heart by means of an act akin to the stripping that takes place at the crucifixion. Only by offering everything—the heart itself, finally, as in "Love Unknown"—does love become known. An altar (or poem) built is at the same time a "stony heart" remade by the action of love, God's grace; and a remaking is a tearing down of the will. Herbert learns as Hamlet learns: "there's a divinity that shapes our ends, rough-hew them how we will."

The first altar that confronts us in *The Temple* is, as Schwartz

---

61. A similar emphasis on discovering (and becoming) "who one is" can be found in Shakespeare's late romances.

says, "the place where the people interrupt the course of their history and turn it to face the origin, the place of the first sacrifice which occurred in the very early morning." Yet the building also ends with an altar, which in Herbert is Love himself, welcoming us at the end of history:

> The road ends with the altar. . . . The altar is the place where the people cease their sacred wandering and hence it is the place of final sacrifice. It lies in purest, clearest light. Behind it the building is at an end; the building's movement has produced the goal.[62]

"Love (III)" is journey's end, as the narrator "sits and eats." He leaves behind him the outward, poetic construction as an embodiment of the transformation that the persona has undergone. The poems exist as the action of the transformed man, but they are also themselves the process of this transformation, because the change occurs in and through the labor, the strife of the building itself.

In the work of the poem, Augustine reminds us, word follows word, for the poem is part of the temporal order, caught in sequence, unlike the Word of God, and unlike the Trinity, which is simultaneously three and one. The Three

> are inseparable in their works, but it is the creation, so greatly dissimilar and corporeal, which constrains them to become separate in their manifestation, just as, with our words, which are of course corporeal sonorities, the Father and the Son and the Holy Spirit cannot be named except by fractions of duration proper to each, and clearly separated and occupied by the syllables of each word. Indeed, in the substance in which they subsist, the three are one . . . free of all temporal movement and of all intervals in space and time. But in my words, "Father," "Son," and "Holy Spirit" are separated, and it is impossible to name them together, and in my writing they occupy different spaces.[63]

---

62. Schwartz, *Church Incarnate*, p. 135.
63. Augustine, *De Trinitate* 4.xxi.30, quoted in Eugene Vance, "Saint Augustine: Language as Temporality," in *Mimesis*, ed. John Lyons and Stephen G. Nichols, Jr. (Hanover, N.H.: University Press of New England, 1982), pp. 23–24. Subsequent references to this essay are cited in the text.

Yet, although the actual poetic word is trapped within time, its ideal form manifests "an order that is not itself temporal." Meter is a universal form, recognized (in Augustine) as a divine sign and therefore sacramental.[64] Unlike the individual syllables of verse, the complete line is held simultaneously in the mind, just as the divine mind holds everything: "when the last syllable is spoken the previous ones are not heard at the same time, and yet along with the preceding ones it makes the form and metrical arrangement complete." It follows, then, as Vance argues, that "the art of poetry is an ideal that is distinct from the actual succession of sounds in the uttered poetic line" (30). He continues to quote Augustine:

> The art of verifying is not subject to change with time as if its beauty was made up of measured quantities. It possesses, at one and the same time, all the rules for making the verse which consists of successive syllables of which the later ones follow those which had come earlier. In spite of this the verse is beautiful as exhibiting the faint traces of beauty which the art of poetry keeps steadfast and unchangeably.[65]

The actual verse, then, Pahlka claims, is "an imitation of a sacrament, an incarnation of divine signs in the corporeal sounds of language" (200). By analogy, all human labor is an imitation of the sacramental act. This is the best we can do, following as well as we can in the footsteps of Christ. The sacrament itself occurs through the placing of the product of human labor—the bread, the wine—on the altar, where, through grace, our labor becomes the body of Christ, in which we then partake.[66]

So too does Herbert understand his own labor of verse making: "Poets are not able to make divine signs," Pahlka notes. "Herbert

64. Pahlka, *Saint Augustine's Meter*, p. 200.
65. Vance, "Saint Augustine," pp. 30–31, quoting Augustine, *De Vera Religione* xxii.42.
66. Compare Karl Rahner, who argues that "the Grace of God constitutes itself actively present in the sacraments by creating their expression, their historical tangibility in space and time, which is its own symbol." See "The Theology of the Symbol," in *Theological Investigations IV: More Recent Writings* (New York: Seabury, 1966, 1974), p. 242.

may write the words, but if they are accepted as a sacrifice on the altar and transformed into divine signs, that is not of his doing" (200).

Thus, Herbert reminds us, vocation is not what we do after we "find" ourselves: our work is our ongoing conversion. Our labor in this world is our dance with the divine. It is, figuratively (and literally for the priest) the liturgy that leads to sacrament, which is another way of saying that it is the striving we do in this world that leads us to our own cross, so that we too might be raised: both crucified and resurrected.[67] Our labor is the bread we bake, the vines we tend and pick, the grapes we press and ferment into wine. This is our gift, what we offer up as the work of our hands and hearts and minds. In this sense our labor, our profession is indeed who we are: what we profess in our daily acts is truly how we are known (thus: "you shall know them by their works").

For the poet of course, the labor is with the word, as it is as well, at least in part, for the priest. The poet's bread is the poem. This is the way he learns to copy Christ; through language he takes up his own cross, which specifically is the conflict, the contradictions inherent in human language when it attempts to rise to the infinite. Robert B. Shaw summarizes the poet's plight:

> What Herbert learns by hard trial is that by attempting to put his plight in words, the poet adds further strands to the web of contrarieties that ensnares him. Each word is potentially a sign of contradiction; language itself is the Christian poet's cross. It is an awesome affliction; at the same time it is one which he has chosen as the way to salvation.[68]

---

67. See Pahlka, *Saint Augustine's Meter*, p. 201: "It would be foolish to assert that the poems have exactly the same status as the Eucharist; the liturgy through which the sacrament is realized is probably a better parallel." See also Rahner, "Poetry and the Christian," in *Theological Investigations IV*, p. 362: the human word "really only attains the full realization of its being in the sacramental word, where it really becomes what God's grace made it as he uttered his eternal Word itself in the flesh of the Lord."

68. Robert B. Shaw, "George Herbert: The Word of God and the Words of Man," in *Ineffability: Naming the Unnameable from Dante to Beckett*, ed. Peter S. Hawkins and Anne Howland Schotter (New York: AMS, 1984), p. 92.

The poem is, in its form, distinct from the "art" or divine rhythm that exists in the ideal. We create a line of verse, and even an entire poem, one foot at a time, not truly knowing what we are about or where we are going. Only in the completed line or poem is there something approaching beauty, the "faint traces" described by Augustine. The whole is held in the mind in its completed form, giving us a glimpse at the divine order that is beyond time. And the poem, again, is an emblem of all human work, all human history. Vance writes: we labor in "a poem of history" that we "cannot read as a whole" (31). Our work is time bound; we cannot see the end toward which it reaches and toward which we labor. Yet in the line of verse there is at least a shadow of the end, a hint of the final form, of beauty, which contains and surpasses time.

The danger once again, of which Herbert is intensely aware, is preferring the moment of verse, the transitory corporeal sounds, to the ideal to which the sounds should lead us: to the Word of God, which exists without syllables. We must not (as Augustine warns) "prefer a verse to the art of versifying," as so many "love temporal things and do not look for the divine providence which is the maker and governor of time. Loving temporal things they do not want the things they love to pass away. They are just as absurd as anyone would be who, when a famous poem was being recited, wanted to hear one single syllable all the time."[69]

Ideally, such labor will itself approach ritual: this would mean the complete superimposing of our rhythm on the divine rhythm, which is finally also most truly our own: the rhythm by which and within which we live and move. Christ's life and sacrifice remain a model for this embodiment of the divine will. His life also affirms that body is an aspect of spirit, and not something "other" at all.[70] The body's rhythms, influenced so profoundly

---

69. Vance, "Saint Augustine," p. 31, quoting Augustine, *De Vera Religione* xxii.43.
70. See Rahner, "Theology of the Symbol," p. 247: "man. . . according to the clear doctrine of Thomism, is not composed of a soul and a body, but of a

by the universal rhythms of earth and sun, moon and stars, are a part of this underlying rhythm to which all things move and that all things are. Here in this embodied knowledge is where Yeats's dancer merges with her dance, and where in Eliot "we are the music while the music lasts." In all we do with our heart and bone and muscle, in complete coordination with our minds and spirits: here is where act becomes prayer, and the poet's rhythm merges with the divine. Here in this prayerful wrestling is our "Engine against th' Almighty" ("Prayer (I)"). In prayer "we take God Prisoner," sermonizes Donne, "and bring God to our conditions; and God is glad to be straitned by us in that siege."[71] In prayer, which is our daily labor to give over control of our lives to God, a rhyme is completed and "something understood" ("Prayer"). Here kingdom is known because experienced, embodied, lived. And here in our sacrificial labor is the unrealizable end of that labor, unrealizable because our steps never completely cohere with Christ's.[72]

So too for the reader: with building's completion, the reader can now walk in: he has reached not his end but his beginning. *The Temple*, like the parables and paradoxes of Jesus, points the sacrificial way that Jesus is and that the reader must also journey to become.

If *The Temple* has become a "eucharistic structure in its final poem,"[73] it is because in the Eucharist are gathered together all

---

soul and *materia prima*. . . . It follows at once that what we call body is nothing else than the actuality of the soul itself in the 'other' of *materia prima*, the 'otherness' produced by the soul itself, and hence its expression and symbol in the very sense which we have given to the term symbolic reality. . . . [t]he body is the symbol of the soul, in as much as it is formed as the self-realization of the soul. . . ."
71. Quoted from Donne's sermons by Patrides, *English Poems*, p. 70.
72. See Pahlka, *Saint Augustine's Meter*, pp. 207–8, in which the emphasis on the poet's surrendering of his will (and his failure to do so fully) is charted in the poet's meter.
73. Patrides, *English Poems*, claims, "In form as in content [*The Temple*] is itself an 'eucharist' . . . or 'thanksgiving,'" filled with images that remind us too of how truly embodied and earthy these poems are: "*altar, table, board, repast, banquet, feast, store, bread, meat, wine*, and especially *blood*, no less than the reiterated verbs *taste* and *eat*" (18). See too Chara Bloch's analysis of the Biblical sources for

the signs that matter to Herbert. As in *Pearl*, all the images circle around one center, which in Herbert can be called "Love," who is known by man only because of the sacrificial act of which the wine and bread are the sign and embodiment. *The Temple* in its turn is a sign of this same Love, built in the heart only by breaking down the old temple, the physical structure that appears deceptively to guarantee salvation and rest, when in fact it exists only as a result, as a sign of grace. The warning is perhaps clearest in "Sion:"

> Lord, with what glorie was thou serv'd of old,
> When Solomons temple stood and flourished!
>   Where most things were of purest gold;
>   The wood was all embellished
> With flowers and carvings, mysticall and rare:
> All show'd the builders, crav'd the seers care.
>
> Yet all this glorie, all this pomp and state
> Did not affect thee much, was not thy aim;
>   Something there was, that sow'd debate:
>   Wherefore thou quitt'st thy ancient claim:
> And now thy Architecture meets with sinne;
> For all thy frame and fabrick is within.
>
> There thou art struggling with a peevish heart,
> Which sometime crosseth thee, thou sometimes it:
>   The fight is hard on either part.
>   Great God doth fight, he doth submit.
> All Solomons sea of brasse and world of stone
> Is not so deare to thee as one good grone.
>
> And truly brasse and stones are heavie things,
> Tombes for the dead, not temples fit for thee:
>   But grones are quick, and full of wings,
>   And all their motions upward be;
> And ever as they mount, like larks they sing;
> The note is sad, yet musick for a King.
>
>   (pp. 106–7)

Herbert's use of the image of the feast in *Spelling the Word: George Herbert and the Bible* (Berkeley and Los Angeles: University of California Press, 1985), pp. 100–4.

"Grones are quick, and full of wings": the paradoxical faith in affliction, in the breaking down of the self, is accurately summed up here. Groans, sighs, and words—the flowing forth of spirit—make up this building, which is at the same time an act of surrender. In *Pearl* we saw a similar stripping away of the need to assert the self or will one's way home. We shall see it again, with variations of course, in Blake, in which an "unbuilding" is at the same time true building—of "Jerusalem" (and of *Jerusalem*). In Blake, although grace more or less disappears, sacrifice and surrender remain all-important, and these come only at the last moment, when all hope seems to be gone. Schwartz suggests, "That which is new in the world comes straight from God at the moment when it is no longer hoped for; this is the mystery of true and sacred failure."[74]

Such a failure is, I think, what we find in Herbert's building. It is never a question of worth or deserving, Herbert says; we *are* failures, we cannot will what we truly want, as St. Paul claimed; we cannot even decide to give ourselves up. Even surrender happens by grace. "I am not worthy of the least of all thy mercies," Herbert says with Jacob, who had "become two bands," split in half. Yet the mystery does happen, and the poems stand as visible signs of the invisible reality: the "delightful illumination of goodness and truth which simultaneously enlightens and gladdens the perceiver."[75]

Wrestling daily with our lives, Herbert claims, at some point we hear a whispering voice and realize that even this wrestling, this darkening affliction, is God-given, and in that awakening we find that night is over. We pass back across the Jordan, wounded by Love but newly named.[76] Though "broken in pieces all asunder" the poet yet prays that the struggle itself that breaks him

74. Schwartz, *Church Incarnate*, p. 231.
75. See Mazzeo, "St. Augustine's Rhetoric," p. 24.
76. John S. Dunne comments, expanding on the Jacob story, "Man comes out of the encounter with God lamed, blessed, and newly named. He walks in the light where before he walked in darkness, but he walks with a limp." *The Way of All the Earth: Experiments in Truth and Religion* (New York: Macmillan Publishing Co., 1972), p. 197.

may be put into service—as indeed it is, as the building of the poem itself testifies:

> Then shall those powers, which work for grief,
>   Enter thy pay,
>   And day by day
> Labour thy praise, and my relief;
>   With care and courage building me,
>   Till I reach heav'n, and much more, thee.
>   ("Affliction (IV)," p. 90)

4
Razing *Jerusalem*
Blake's Word as World

*What is the body? That shadow of a shadow
of your love, that somehow contains
the entire universe.*

*A man sleeps heavily,
though something blazes in him like the sun,
like a magnificent fringe sewn up under the hem.*
    Rumi, trans. by Coleman Barks

Thus far we have seen the goal of our poet (whether in *Pearl* or in *The Temple*) to lie in a radical reorienting of the reader's perception of the world, a reorientation we have equated with the parables of the New Testament, and more particularly with the life of Jesus, himself "the parable of God."[1] In the poem, as in the parable, our everyday world is ruptured by way of metaphor, revealing within or beneath or beyond (the "where" is by necessity undefined) a further home: the kingdom of God. Among many paradigms for this metaphorical destruction and subsequent imaginative construction is Jesus' statement in John's Gospel, foretelling the resurrection: "Destroy this temple and in three days I will raise it up" (2:19).

John has already informed us, "The Word was made flesh and dwelt among us" (1:14), "dwelt here" translating the Greek verb *skenoun*, more accurately translated as "tented" or "tabernacled."[2]

---

1. See Robert Funk, *Language, Hermeneutic, and the Word of God: The Problem of Language in the New Testament and Contemporary Theology* (New York: Harper & Row, 1966), p. 57; and Gerhard Ebeling, *The Nature of Faith*, trans. Ronald Gregor Smith (Philadelphia: Fortress Press, 1961), p. 190.
2. *The New Oxford Annotated Bible*, ed. Herbert G. May and Bruce M. Metzger

The creative and creating Word is now made fully human in Jesus, the Evangelist reports. All that follows from this, whether it is the Pauline temple of the holy spirit, the Augustinian City and sign, the *Pearl*-Poet's gem, or Herbert's own poetic building, is an approach to this truth.

Yet the approach is never complete. Tearing down the old temple and raising a new, metaphorical one in the form of a poem (or a parable) allow for the potential of disclosing kingdom, but this kingdom remains elusive. The poem as sign (in the Augustinian sense) points to; it does not contain or embody. Kingdom is, as Paul Ricoeur says of the symbol, "prelinguistic."[3] It is not contained in language but is something other, entering our fallen world only through the miracle of the Incarnation, on which event the Christian poems we have studied—like the sacraments themselves—base their claim to be vessels of grace. The poem may, like Dante's Virgil, lead the reader *to* the kingdom, but there always remains time left over, a last judgment still awaited, or simply some aspect of the self left unaltered by the experience. We recall, perhaps, St. Paul's own frustration with this fact, as he wrestled with this particular dilemma of the Christian conversion experience. A "new man" himself, with the "old" dead, he knew that he, with other followers of Christ, had become God's "temple" (1 Cor. 3:16). And yet both for himself and for those he led, advised, coaxed, and scolded, the problem persisted. Somehow the old man lingers on.

As suggested in the previous chapter, the problem here with the "new" is that linear time continues, suggesting that identity—that which we reach in those sacramental moments of bread breaking in Christ—falls continually back into nonidentity. As in life, so in language, which, at least for Augustine, cannot grasp "the literal truth of God's nature as pure presence. . . . We can-

---

(New York: Oxford University Press, 1973), p. 1286. For fuller analysis, see *The Jerome Biblical Commentary*, ed. Raymond E. Brown, Joseph A. Fritzmeyer, and Ronald E. Murphy (Englewood Cliffs, N.J.: Prentice Hall, 1958), p. 423.

3. See Ricoeur's *Interpretation Theory: Discourse and the Surplus of Meaning* (Fort Worth: Texas Christian University Press, 1976), pp. 57–63.

not speak truly (literally) about the world of changing phenomena because they are constituted by not-being. And since language itself is constituted by the not-being of time, we cannot speak truly of the one perfect Being." As Margaret Ferguson concludes, "This paradoxical dilemma underlies Augustine's sense that language is an obstacle between man and his desired union with God."[4]

Rarely (and I would suggest that metaphor is an exception) are we able to live within the paradox of simultaneous identity and nonidentity, just as, given our linguistic limitations, we must refer to the triune God as if He (?) were three separate entities engaged in three different activities: as if it were inevitable to distinguish "entity" from "act," Being from Doing. Although metaphor appears to suggest the possibility of finding "Kingdom" now in an identity of self and other, we continually fall out of this mode into the "not yet" of self versus other, the not yet of the temporal life and language, of human (and Biblical) history.

Thus, as we have seen, the Pearl Dreamer does become pearl in committing his life to his prince, but there is no mistaking the fact that—as in this definition of metaphor itself—a tension remains between the new nature born of the shattering and the old man, as Paul called him, who still lives on, apparently unaltered, the husk or body that we cannot do without as long as we remain in the physical realm. Thus, awakening in this context means returning to the old world (like Dante, Langland's Will, and the Pearl Dreamer), somehow remade, yet somehow still the same.

Or perhaps, as we found with Herbert, the remaking or conversion is more truly to be understood not as instantaneous but as our lifelong labor itself: conversion is the process of our daily labor, our ongoing wrestling with our angel, so that the self we become incorporates that old self: we are newly named like Jacob but forever crippled, and we are raised with Jesus but understand that this means both raised on a cross and resurrected. Even here we carry our wounds with us; in fact, we learn at last that it is

4. Margaret W. Ferguson, "Saint Augustine's Region of Unlikeness: The Crossing of Exile and Language," *Georgia Review* 29 (1975), pp. 853, 856.

precisely those wounds that make possible our passage. Our hands are pierced and stay pierced. They are the sign, a synecdoche of our offering, which is ultimately ourselves.

As with the man, so with the poem and the word itself: kingdom is glimpsed only by taking on flesh in the word, but that flesh must be pierced, wounded, burned away (to shift to one of Blake's metaphors); this alone makes possible the risen body. This is, in fact, the risen body, Albion to Blake, upon whom Los figuratively hammers and pounds throughout *Jerusalem*, just as Blake literally works on his metals within the city of London. Distinctions between literal and figurative collapse here, just as they do with the "risen body" of Jesus, which, although no longer "flesh," still bears the marks of the nails.

So too must Albion accept this crucifixion, Los's-Blake's nailing his body in order to make possible his rising. He must at last awaken to the fact that he was his own oppressor throughout his long, sad history. No longer blaming some external world and woman for his woes, he rises, throwing himself into the "Furnaces of affliction," finding, like Herbert, that this same affliction "furthers the flight," because it *is* flight.

Blake returns us directly to the passage from John with which we began (John 2:19). With this poet, however, the "where" of this new earth is precisely defined, because where is always here for Blake, just as when is always now. To look elsewhere for this home is always to fall: to split oneself into past, present, and future, into within and without. The dualism collapses in Blake's imaginative home.

But even here we must be cautious, for the tendency in Blake is to equate "imaginative" with "mental," suggesting to us simply one pole of the dualism: "outer" is eliminated as the fallen realm and "inner" is resurrected as the new Jerusalem. But this is to misread Blake on a crucial point. The beauty of *Jerusalem* itself as an object is the clearest example of what I mean: Blake after all was a manual laborer as much as a mental laborer. To attempt to split these two aspects of Blake's creative life is impossible, since each influences, works on, quarrels and struggles with the other, even in such simple ways as the battle to fit a lengthy line onto a limited metal plate—or fit the "illumination" in various plates with the text.[5]

Instead, Blake's mental warfare works with and within the world of images, revealing that what we see "around" us is not simply out there but also in here. It is neither out nor in for Blake: it is simply here and now. The self embraces, is that world on which it gazes. We awaken to ourselves and our home in and as the world.[6]

Annihilation of the tyrannical outer to allow for an emerging of the inner—that is, a recognition of the essential unity of these two contraries, and thus of our own intimate connection to the world—is the theme that "awakes" the poet as *Jerusalem* begins: "To open the Eternal Worlds, to open the Immortal Eyes of Man inwards into the Worlds of Thought. . ." (J 5:18–19; E 147).[7] This has been the theme of Blake's work as far back as "There Is No Natural Religion." "He who sees the Infinite in all things Sees God." The point of the Incarnation is to make this seeing possible. But "seeing God" for Blake means also seeing as God, for "we become what we behold" (J 30:54; E 177). "Therefore," Blake concludes, "God becomes as we are, that we may be as he is" (E 3).

Blake does not say here that the object ceases to be; what he does suggest, as so often, is that our prepositions fail to hold, or that our normal understanding of language fails to contain. In what sense can the infinite be seen "in" all things? What are

5. On this general argument, see W. J. T. Mitchell, "Visible Language: Blake's Wond'rous Art of Writing," in *Romanticism and Contemporary Criticism*, ed. Morris Eaves and Michael Fischer (Ithaca, N.Y.: Cornell University Press, 1986), pp. 46–95.
6. See Thomas R. Frosch, *The Awakening of Albion* (Ithaca, N.Y.: Cornell University Press, 1974), esp. pp. 31 and 61: "In Blake, to turn outwards is to turn away not from the inner but from a state of being in which a distinction between the two does not exist. . . . And when Blake calls the unfallen state "inner" or "within," he is not referring to mind or soul, but means, instead, that all things were once embraced by Albion's Edenic body" (p. 61).
7. All quotations from Blake, unless otherwise noted, are from *The Complete Poetry and Prose of William Blake*, ed. David V. Erdman (Berkeley and Los Angeles: University of California Press, 1982), referred to as E.

"Immortal Eyes"? Or even "Eternal Worlds"? What are the "things" in which we are invited to see the infinite? The grain of sand? The flower?

In *The Marriage of Heaven and Hell*, Blake's own act of engraving becomes a metaphor for the process by which the Word becomes as we are, "tenting" in the flesh in order to be seen, and seen through:

> When I came home; on the abyss of the five senses, where a flat sided steep frowns over the present world. I saw a mighty Devil folded in black clouds, hovering on the sides of the rock, with corroding fires he wrote the following sentence now perceived by the minds of men and read by them on earth.
> How do you know but ev'ry Bird that cuts the airy way
> Is an immense world of delight, clos'd by your senses five?
> (E 35)

The Devil, we know, is Blake. The sides of the rock are both the engraving plates and the human skull. The acid eats into the plate, cutting into the metal like the Bird that "cuts the airy way," removing all but that portion that is protected from the acid, protected by being the word that Blake has previously etched. The word then alone remains as rock or metal is burned away, so that we "on earth" may read. We read, as we just saw, of the Bird that "cuts the airy way," yet the Bird, we also know, is actually ("literally," as Northrop Frye likes to remind us[8]) the word on the page. The Bird is that word that cuts, like acid, like Jesus verbally razing the temple in John's Gospel. And it is also, like Jesus, that word that appears to rise (metaphorically, within the mind, as well as physically, on the plate) when all else is burned away. Truly seen, Blake affirms, that word reveals itself to us neither as a bird in a remote, indifferent sky, nor as a word that is simply a sign of that bird, but as "an immense world of delight" kept from us by our senses, by which we are somehow imprisoned. Instead we need imaginative wings that cut as they soar: wings that exist in a world where soaring *is* cutting.

8. *Anatomy of Criticism* (1957; reprint, New York: Atheneum, 1969), pp. 76–78, 87.

The word on the page before us, Blake suggests, is most fully that bird precisely as we grasp it as a metaphor; to understand, that is, "bird" not as a remote winged creature (or, worse, a sign on a page that points us to a "real bird" that remains remote) but as intimately involved with human life, and a true part of that life. Seen metaphorically, imaginatively, "natural objects are transformed into poetic percepts"[9] and are thus seen to contain a world, like Jesus, who was seen by a few to be not simply flesh but the creative Word existing potentially within and as us all, as Jesus himself proclaimed. Thus, each word for Blake, each "minute particular," is itself the Word, or all that exists.[10]

Seeing through a word, then, means (in one sense) burning away.[11] But the burning away of metal to reveal a previously hidden word is simply an analogy[12] for the metaphorical searing that takes place within the reader's mind. It is the latter that is of primary concern to Blake, as the opening of *Jerusalem* (quoted previously) most clearly suggests. Yet what that newly revealed word reveals is not some pre- or supralinguistic kingdom (Blake had little fondness for kings); it is instead that word itself as human. Or, Blake would just as easily say, the Word Himself, that "immense world of delight" that is the human mind, the imagination, or Jesus, who is "Manifested in his works of Art" (E 273), as we have just witnessed in this passage from *The Mar-*

9. Frosch, *Awakening of Albion*, p. 156.
10. What this passage also recalls to us is that nature, here represented by the bird, is a gift of the imagination. Nature in these lines, as elsewhere in much of Blake, is far from dead and oppressive. Instead, nature is a way back in because it is itself an expression of, even a definition of, the Divine Body. It is (in *Milton*) that "bright sandal formd immortal of precious stones and gold" (21:13; E 115). Mark Bracher rightly comments that instead of seeing the natural world "as a conglomeration of physical objects [Blake] now perceives it as something supporting his journeying—a form tailored to his needs ('a bright sandal') and composed of intrinsically valuable things ('precious stones and gold')." See *Being Form'd: Thinking Through Blake's Milton* (Barrytown, N.Y.: Station Hill Press, 1985), p. 115.
11. See *A Vision of the Last Judgement* (hereafter abbreviated as *VLJ*), E 566.
12. I use the word *analogy* here and subsequently in its Blakean sense, best defined by Northrop Frye in *Fearful Symmetry* (Princeton, N.J.: Princeton University Press, 1947), pp. 382–87. Frye finds analogy in Blake to be a "conception of the world of experience as a parody or inverted form of the imaginative world."

riage. In this sense "seeing through" the word means seeing "by means of": we see by means of Blake's metaphorical language just as we see by means of Jesus' language. It is a lens by means of which we discover that "immense world" within us, as us, in the ordinary: in the bird, the grain of sand.

* * *

When asked by Crabb Robinson whether Jesus was indeed the Son of God, Blake responded yes, of course, "and so am I and so are you."[13] It's easy to imagine Blake's giving a similar answer much earlier in his career; we need only think of "All Religions Are One" with his complete assurance "The Poetic Genius is the true Man, and that the body or outward form of Man is derived from the Poetic Genius" (E 1). And yet it is also true that much of the power we find in *Jerusalem* is due to the clear sense of struggle evident in the text. The letters and poems give poignant reminders of the darkness Blake labored in for years, and in particular as he was sculpting the great myth that culminates in *Milton* and *Jerusalem*. It is striking to realize from the Blake *Concordance* that key figures—and the concepts embodied in these figures—often appear for the first time in *The Four Zoas*. "Vala" of course is the most obvious example, but we suddenly find Blake's talking about "forgiveness" almost for the first time and turning increasingly to his own developing idea of the central place of Jesus in these poems.[14]

Jesus, sacrifice, and forgiveness join with Blake's earlier ideas regarding the Poetic Genius and Imagination by the time he gets to *Milton*. Here again "eternity" is not a place but a way of seeing that Blake now equates explicitly with sacrifice: "I come to Self Annihilation," Milton proclaims to his Spectre Satan; "Such are the Laws of Eternity that each shall mutually / Annihilate himself for others good, as I for thee" (M 38:34–36; E 139). The implication in this poem is that Blake himself has seen (or been)

---

13. G. E. Bentley, Jr., *Blake Records* (Oxford: Clarendon Press, 1969), p. 310.
14. "Forgiveness" comes up in Blake's Annotations to Lavater, but with a striking difference, as Jeanne Moskal reminded me. See E 589. Otherwise, this word is almost absent from the work before the *Zoas*.

this eternity, this Jesus who is both one man and a multitude; *Milton* is the poet's own story of his putting on this vision through the reconstruction of his great predecessor's labors and seeing them now preeminently as sacrificial. With its quiet conclusion in the Felpham garden, as Blake awakens from his swoon, it is equivalent to the journeys recorded in *Piers Plowman* or the *Pearl*,[15] except that for Blake *Milton* is just a prelude, setting the stage for the greater building yet to come:

Lo the Eternal Great Humanity...
Walks among all his awful Family seen in every face
As the breath of the Almighty. such are the Words of man to man
In the great Wars of Eternity, in fury of Poetic Inspiration,
To build the Universe stupendous: Mental Forms Creating
(M 30:15–20; E 129)

"To build the Universe" for Blake is nothing but a poetic act, as *Jerusalem* sets out to demonstrate. Jerusalem *is* this "fury of Poetic Inspiration . . . Mental Forms Creating." The poem is the Blakean equivalent of the Bible, which, as we learn in *The Laocoon*, is "the Great Code of Art," art itself being the manifestation of Jesus, the Divine Vision. *Jerusalem* as this manifestation is also the city-woman Jerusalem, defined as the "emanation" or "garment" of Jesus, the means by which men "in Eternity" converse.[16] As garment, she is associated with the natural world seen in reality as the bejeweled sandal (M 21:13; E 115). Yet in the fallen world, as Jesus' garment, this word-world is also the "Shadowy Female," or fallen time and space perceived as boundaries within which we are forced to operate. They are Kantian prisons

Written within and without in woven letters: and the Writing
Is the divine Revelation in the Litteral expression:
A garment of War, I heard it named the Woof of Six Thousand Years.
(M 42:13–15; E 143)

    15. Frye has already called attention to the close parallel of this moment with *Piers Plowman*; see *Fearful Symmetry*, p. 335. See also the brief references to both the *Pearl*-Poet and Herbert in Robert Gleckner's "Most Holy Forms of Thought: Some Observations on Blake and Language," *ELH* 41 (1974), pp. 560, 576.
    16. See *Jerusalem* (hereafter abbreviated as J) 88:3–11.

Leopold Damrosch complains that this is not the "true" word, that "it is still a garment," and that "Litteral" suggests its fallen state: "a garment of warfare in the world of history rather than of Eternity."

> The eternal vision may be communicated in symbols, but it is not itself reducible to material form. In Eden the garment will be needed no more. Poetic creation becomes literal as it is reduced to "expression" but in Eden expression will be immediate and intuitive rather than mediated and literal. Meanwhile we have to try and look through language and not with it. . . .[17]

But we must be careful here. "Seeing through" the language of the Bible (or of *Jerusalem*) does not mean seeing through a symbol to some undefined or unnameable other; what appears to be a "garment of war" in the fallen world is seen in Eternity too as "the Words of man to man / In the great Wars of Eternity." "Our wars are Wars of life, and wounds of love, with intellectual spears," Jesus reminds Albion;[18] thus it is not "war" that must be "seen through" (burned away) but our understanding or perception of war. Our first thought of "war" is likely to be physical combat, but works of art, Blake affirms, like the Bible, invite the reader to see metaphorically: that is, to see war, like everything else, as primarily imaginative labor, and thus to recognize the physical combat we now think of "literally" as war as a horrific parody of what individuals accomplish in Eden. Our fallen vision of warfare, Blake shows, is a destruction brought about by fallen repressive (and particularly sexual) conditions.

To see this truth about war, of course, is not something we can do with our corporeal eye; seeing itself has become a metaphorical activity. To see this is to understand that when we see by means of, we simultaneously see through or burn away a previously fixed perspective into which we were locked, like pris-

---

17. *Symbol and Truth in Blake's Myth* (Princeton, N.J.: Princeton University Press, 1980), p. 328.
18. J 34:14–17 (E 180); see also *Milton* 35:2 (E 135).

oners, by our senses. "Error," Blake says, "is Burnt up the Moment Men cease to behold it" (VLJ: E 565).

In the fallen world we see Jesus only by his taking on flesh, or, for Blake, becoming the visible word existing within the "stubborn structure" of language. He puts on this "garment of war" that is the Bible, containing within itself (Himself) all of fallen history, so that men may "see through." The garment is like the Bird in *The Marriage* (and the Bird, of course, is itself garment, a manifestation of the divine). If the reader does not enter into the images as Blake requests, the word will appear to his corporeal eye alone as a sign out there for a more real, and even more distant, physical object. As metaphor, it will appear to be nonsense, as Jesus' words appeared to the Pharisee Nicodemus.[19] If instead he sees by means of the metaphor, he sees what before appeared to be simply a physical, external object as simultaneously internal: internal and external collapse in the metaphor. Here is that "crossing over" that gives metaphor its name.

This union of mind and world in the artistic act is accurately portrayed by Ray Hart in his comments on Shelley's "Skylark." "Skylark is not a paraphrase of blithe Spirit, or *vice versa*. What Shelley saw he could only see through the skylark, yet what he saw was not the skylark ("bird thou never wert"). Indeed Shelley's vision was consummated in the 'carrying over,' the poem itself."[20]

In Blake's terms, the poem itself is the embodiment of that journey that metaphor is. And the paradigm of "poet" in Blake's world—at least in his world by the time of *Milton* and *Jerusalem*—is Jesus, Himself that poetic genius who constantly invites a similar crossing over, a death of sorts, from his auditors. The poem most fully embodying the metaphoric journeying is of course *Jerusalem*, viewed as the garment that allows for the meeting be-

19. John 1:19.
20. Ray L. Hart, *Unfinished Man and the Imagination* (New York: Herder and Herder, 1968), p. 239. See also Hart's own footnote to this: "The artist does not know in advance of representation but through representation."

tween two individuals, just as the word on the plate makes possible the meeting between the reader and Blake, ideally in "eternity," that mental landscape incorporating outer and inner that the poem as we read creates.[21]

So it is as well in *Jerusalem*'s words, by means of which we behold and thus become Jesus: by crossing over through the poem, the emanation or garment of the divine. *Jerusalem* leads us to "Heaven's gate, Built in Jerusalem's wall" (J 77; E 321). *Jerusalem* becomes Jerusalem as we enter into the poem's language and see our world from more than one perspective, see our world metaphorically, as neither inner nor outer but an expanded version of us. Vision, as Hart says, is consummated in the crossing over. This is the union between Jesus and Jerusalem, between the "divine vision" and its "garment" or manifestation—that object perceived as the embodiment of poetic genius, even as we speak of a "body of writing" or refer to Blake's writings as simply "Blake"—that is, as an aspect of the vision itself, and not something external to it. This consummation is true marriage. Here "skylark" is not just skylark but that "blithe spirit" or "immense world of delight" included in us as our own true expanded body or bounding line: who we are when we are most truly ourselves, which is everything. This for Blake is the equivalent of "putting on the Divine Vision" or seeing as Jesus.[22]

In discussing Blake's allusions in plate 86 of *Jerusalem*, Dan Miller suggests that Jerusalem as garment affirms both the ma-

---

21. Leslie Tannenbaum notes that in Blake, "the historical Jesus . . . is a type, a manifestation of the process known as Christ, the continual re-creation of God in human form. Internally, this process takes place continually in the human soul through the imitation of Christ, through the opening of the soul to the fires of divine inspiration." The object, Tannenbaum concludes, "is conversion of all the Lords people into prophets. . . . The reader is to become . . . a doer, not a hearer of the Word." See *Biblical Tradition in Blake's Early Prophecies: The Great Code of Art* (Princeton, N.J.: Princeton University Press, 1982), pp. 116, 122. Robert Gleckner has suggested (see note 15) that readers of Blake could benefit from reading Stanley Fish's arguments on Herbert in *Self Consuming Artifacts*; my own reading of Blake has indeed benefitted, I believe, from reading Fish, and from others in the "Reader Response" group of theorists.

22. See Hart, *Unfinished Man*, p. 254: "For every object grasped in imaginative symbol, there is a 'world' in which self and object are disclosed to each other in polysemous intercourse."

teriality of this vision and the impossibility of ever seeing it, or visualizing it in any literal fashion. Jerusalem as garment both covers and reveals: she reveals *because* she covers. The "figure" added to this female form is

> the "sublime ornament" that is an addition to Jerusalem's body yet also a revelation of it, a garment that covers the body in order to define it, wings that are both extensions of the body and the body's frame and outline, veils that enclose in order to disclose, flames that enfold themselves, and the allusive word itself, carried by Jerusalem upon herself as an inscription, an adornment, a garment.

Miller concludes, "Jerusalem is less a unified form than a dance of body and garment. . . ." In this state "everything is outline, and outline is a boundary so infinitely inflected that it presents us with insides and outsides—and with insides within insides, outsides around outsides."[23]

Blake's Jerusalem, then, like Ezekiel's chariot, is impossible to see, and yet she, like her covering, is described in great visual detail. So too do Blake's engraved words "insist on their physicality" even while they also defy the limits our senses place on the material manifestation. We feel we should be able to grasp this vision, yet we cannot, however much we attempt to frame it. Definitions abound, but they provide, paradoxically, no limits: "the eye finds no resting point, and the entire form never attains stability."[24]

Miller further suggests that Los's song on plate 86 functions in much the same way as Jerusalem's figural garment but through Biblical allusions. The text (both Los's and Blake's) is itself ornamented in much the same way as Jerusalem, a fact that should not surprise us, since the text *is* finally *Jerusalem*. Are these Biblical sources "outside" the body of the text? Are they garments that cover, or do they become the body by becoming incorpo-

---

23. Dan Miller, "Blake's Allusions: *Jerusalem* 86," in *New Orleans Review* (1986), pp. 30–31.
24. Miller, "Blake's Allusions," pp. 30–31. All other references to Miller are in the text.

rated within Blake's text? Is there ever a body, a "Jerusalem," without the allusions drawn from the "great code of art"?

The Word cannot be isolated from its garment, Blake suggests in his elaborately figured books. Word is simultaneously covering and revelation. Just as in Blake the fall and creation are simultaneous acts, so too must crucifixion and resurrection be the same. We fall into language in order to rise. We fall into the syntax that in part creates and in part mirrors our new splintered selves—with their limited notion of past present and future, of I versus other—but we have also fallen from language, from the Word that we are in our unity. And our way back to the Word is also through words: "[t]he fall into individual identity—into the little, self-defining eddy of free-floating anxiety and wrath that commences with our being drawn through the vagina—is a fall into language with its words and texts. The vortex both keeps us from the Paradise of the Word and also offers the medium (words, texts, pictures) that could, as Boehme suggested, draw us to it."[25]

Pierced into wood and elevated, Jesus as Word is, like Blake's own tortured text, the Risen One.

"The body becomes its own covering," Miller notes, "and the distinction between body and garment again grows doubtful" (31). Definitions, which so often in Blake are analogies and personifications bound together through the verb *to be*, such as those throughout *Jerusalem* ("Thou art my Pride & Self-righteousness . . . The blow of his Hammer is Justice. . ."), provide the verbal equivalence of the visual engraver's bounding lines, but the multiplicity and complexity of these definitions defy our attempt to erect insides and outsides to these boundaries.[26] Blake's point in

---

25. See Nelson Hilton, *Literal Imagination: Blake's Vision of Words* (Berkeley and Los Angeles: University of California Press, 1983), p. 226.

26. Blake's *Laocoön* is the most startling example of this complexity, as the engraving of this statue is overwhelmed with words that define, bound, and hem in what we see, all in an attempt to free us to the realization that "The eternal Body of Man is THE IMAGINATION" (E 273). For an extended treatment of this plate, see David E. James, "Blake's *Laocoon*: A Degree Zero of Literary Production," *PMLA* 98 (1983), pp. 226–34.

this is not to confuse but to reveal. Yet what is revealed is not some transcendental, allegorical existence somewhere other than in the text. The goal is to see at last that everything, even the reader, is included, bound figuratively, imaginatively, within Jerusalem/*Jerusalem*. As Miller concludes, "Blake's images characteristically summon the eternal less by serving as signs that point toward transcendental significances than by asserting their own elaborations and involutions" (31). We find in Blake Derridean playfulness, but without Derridean absence—or an absence that has been through the vortex of metaphorical, visionary language to find itself again as presence.[27]

Seeing through the word on the plate, or seeing through this garment is not, I again stress, to annihilate the garment; it is a perspective that is burned away as defining, fixing, separating inside and outside. As Ray Hart comments, "What active, symbolic imagination has first to step over . . . is its own corpse; i.e., itself in lifeless, reproductive mode."[28] Thus the eternal is in the corporeal (we can see "a world in a blade of grass"), but to say that the eternal is behind it or hidden is inaccurate: the failure is behind the eye, not within the object. "As a man is," Blake wrote to Dr. Trusler, "so he sees." When one sees through the fallen world or through the word, what in fact alters is one's own stance, or how one sees oneself: how one is. A vision dissolves in the activity of imagination, as Coleridge noted, but "[i]n the dissolving action of imagination the world is not destroyed or displaced but rather is allowed to appear in its primal rapport with the self. . . . Metaphor and symbol serve to carry over into consciousness the carrying over between things, and between things and the self, in their very being."[29]

27. See Mark Lussier, "'Vortext' as Philosopher's Stone: Blake's Textual Mirrors and the Transmutation of Audience," in *New Orleans Review* (1986), p. 50. I am not convinced that "Blake insists we move beyond that text" (since I'm not sure quite what this means) but do agree that although he "can seem very close to Derrida . . . Blake, as his textual objects make all too clear, is a poet of presence." For a thoughtful comparison of Blake and Derrida, see also the comments made by Mitchell after his "Visible Language" essay, pp. 88–90.
28. Hart, *Unfinished Man*, p. 243.
29. Ibid., pp. 246–47.

Blake's allusions to the Bible do not point us to anything other than Blake's own *Jerusalem*, because that text is the same place-state as the Jerusalem which exists in the Bible: Blake's book is coextensive, coinherent with the Bible. Allusions, then, are a form of dialogue (*dia-logos*) taking place within one diverse yet unified Self, as Blake suggests most fully at the end of *Jerusalem*, as the Eternals converse "in Visionary forms dramatic." This conversation is precisely what *Jerusalem* is and has been throughout: a dialogue from which nothing and no one is excluded. Here body and garment dance. So finely woven is the texture of the book that we cannot separate what are "Blake's" words and what are "outside" Blake or other than Blake. The words *are* Blake for us, just as "Blake" now carries within himself all that *Jerusalem* contains, which is everything. All the voices are one as the dancer embodies the dance.[30] If Imagination's first act is one of "disordering, dissolving, dissimulating the object of average, ossified sensibility," Blake constantly suggests that this dissolution or burning away is simultaneously re-creation, or, more accurately, revelation of what was already there. Crucifixion alone makes possible resurrection.

What we see with our "corporeal" eye, Blake suggests in an important passage in *Milton*, is simply "the hem of their garment," "they" being the "Visions of Eternity," which, appropriately enough for Blake, are themselves "human":

Thou seest the gorgeous clothed Flies that dance & sport in summer
Upon the sunny brooks & meadows: every one the dance
Knows in its intricate mazes of delight artful to weave. . .
These are the Children of Los; thou seest the Trees on mountains
The wind blows heavy, loud they thunder thro' the darksom sky
Uttering prophecies & speaking instructive words to the sons
Of men: These are the Sons of Los! These the Visions of Eternity

---

30. As Hart summarizes, "metaphor and symbol bring into consciousness . . . the 'interlacing of regions' out of which we have our being in the world. . . . Withal, symbolic imagination is not a merely demiurgic power, rearranging a dismembered body; what it achieves is ontological novelty, a fresh insertion of the self in being" (*Unfinished Man*, pp. 248–49).

But we see only as it were the hem of their garments
When with our vegetable eyes we view these wond'rous Visions
                    (M 26:2–12; E 123)

There is great power in the poetry here, a combination of the long lines, the simplicity and directness of the visual and auditory images, and the frequent heaviness of the stress, all of which suggest the sublimity of this scene: "the Trees on mountains / The wind blows heavy, loud they thunder. . . ." As so often in the Prophecies, Blake paints in broad powerful strokes, with no need to specify a particular scene or place. Certainly the point is that this place, and any such place (tree, mountain), is not to be particularized in terms of its geography but is instead to be viewed imaginatively; this does not mean to generalize or abstract a "mountain" but to create its own particular through the force of its art, in this case language. The strength of the lines increases as Blake continues to reconceive this landscape metaphorically, and through his intercourse with this view he allows us to consummate the same union. The wind now is not only a breeze; it utters prophecies and speaks "instructive words." Even more than Shelley and Wordsworth, both of whom use this same image of wind as inspiration, Blake means exactly what he says here: the metaphor of a speaking wind is to be heard as the literal truth. Here again is that poetic genius embodied in the landscape, *as* that landscape, and thus no longer external but perceived as part of who we are. All that we see comes from us and exists in turn as fresh encouragement and inspiration: "These are the Sons of Los!" Blake takes quite seriously what Wallace Stevens suggests only with irony: the poem does indeed take the place of the mountain.

Damrosch, misinterpreting this passage, suggests, "The hem of their garments" is all we can possibly see, given our fallen condition. Even "symbolic language" is "opaque," he claims: "it is all we have with which to communicate the truth of the epiphanic vision, but it is not enough."[31]

31. Leopold Damrosch, *Symbol and Truth in Blake's Myth* (Princeton, N.J.:

Yet surely when Blake says, "We see only . . ." we are to see the following line's adverbial clause as modifying this statement: "when *with* our vegetable eyes we view these wondrous Visions . . . we see only." We are asked, in the *Vision of the Last Judgment*, to see not with but through, as Damrosch himself often enough suggests. Blake in telling us of these visions clearly affirms that he himself has seen them by looking through: "to the Eyes of the Man of Imagination Nature is Imagination itself" (E 677). All the world is suddenly transformed, made human, a part of who we are. The dancing flies, the summer sun are children of Los, or products of our own creative imagination.

Damrosch, following Ricoeur's lead, argues that Blake (like the *Pearl*-Poet and Herbert) still awaits an Eden, reached "after an apocalypse of which our limited and temporary epiphanies are only premonitions. Symbols may lead us there, but Eden is greater than our symbols and can dispense with them" (73). But Eden for Blake is our symbols, is the manifestation of the Divine, which (or who) is a mode of perception and not a place. And it is available *now*. It might be argued that Blake, himself in the fallen world, "looks forward" to a time when, as he says in *Jerusalem*, "Time was finished!" for all men, but for the individual this is available in the here and now[32] (for there is no other time

---

Princeton University Press, 1980), pp. 72–73. Subsequent quotations from Damrosch appear in the text.

32. Lavater comments, "Whatever is visible is the vessel or veil of the invisible past, present, future—as man penetrates to this more, or perceives it less, he raises or depresses his dignity of being." Blake responds: "A Vision of the Eternal Now . . ." (E 592). For clarification of this point, see Frosch, *Awakening of Albion*, pp. 156–57, who distinguishes between Golgonooza and Jerusalem, seeing the former as the realm of fallen art in our world, where "natural objects are transformed into poetic percepts." Golgonooza, then, is "art within nature." In Eden, however, "the distinction of art and life vanishes" so that "what we now recognize as art disappears: when Albion enters the furnaces, Los drops out of the poem, consumed with all else in his Sublime Universe." Frosch can thus argue that for Blake too, "Art, *as we know it*, is thus not an end but a way" (pp. 173–76). The key words here, however, are "art *as we know it*." I would claim instead that it is not simply that Los disappears from the poem; instead the risen man recognizes Jesus as "the likeness & similitude of Los" (J 96:7; E 255). The labor of art then, embodied in Los, is not eliminated but revealed in its fullness as the creative activity of the Divine Man. Like Jesus, Los is both way and end, both gate and

and place than the here and now which is eternal and infinite), since the fallen world is itself simply a fallen perspective, a vision that has become fixed in our minds so thoroughly that we accept it as definitive. "I feel that a man may be happy in This World," Blake told Dr. Trusler. "And I know that This World Is a World of Imagination & Vision" (E 702). It is not a matter of waiting. There is nothing to wait for, for there is nothing at all ahead.

* * *

A closer look at Ricoeur's theory of symbol and metaphor, on which Damrosch relies for his interpretation, may help clarify, by way of opposition, Blake's own position on this issue. Ricoeur suggests a similar acceptance of this tensive, mortal state in his definition of symbol and metaphor, a split that we are incapable of overcoming because in the nature of the symbol, Ricoeur claims in his *Interpretation Theory*, there is something that does not pass fully into language. The symbol is, as I have suggested, "prelinguistic." This "something" is the "numinous element," the "Unconditioned."[33] "What asks to be brought to language in sym-

---

destination, for destination in Blake is itself labor: Jerusalem is not a place of rest but the state of ongoing activity. (Here of course we find Blake splitting from the allegorical model of Augustine (and de Man), where we remain imprisoned within time, and thus within signifiers that perpetually fall short of real presence.)

33. See Paul Ricoeur, "The Specificity of Language," *Semeia* 4 (1975), pp. 142–44. The terms are Kant's. In *The Rule of Metaphor*, trans. Robert Czerny (Toronto: University of Toronto Press, 1977), written within a few years of the *Interpretation Theory*, Ricoeur limits his discussion to metaphor, saying nothing of the symbol. But here, too, metaphor is "tensive" to Ricoeur, in that it "includes the 'is not' within the ontological vehemence of the metaphorical 'is'" (p. 255). In metaphor alone do we embrace both contradictory perspectives at once, thus finding in metaphor "the single moment that carries words and things beyond, *meta*" (p. 288). There is, according to Ricoeur here, no getting outside of metaphor, for there is nowhere else for us to stand. Quoting Derrida's conclusion that "each time there is the sun, metaphor has begun," Ricoeur adds, "metaphor has begun, for with the sun come the metaphors of light, of looking or glancing, of the eye" (p. 289). We are reminded, perhaps, of the opening of *Jerusalem*, in which sunlight is simultaneously "the Saviour . . . spreading his beams of love" (J 4:42; E 145). Yet Blake would argue with the notion that there is a "without" or "unconditioned," an "is not," outside language. Metaphorical language for Blake is, like the Augustinian God, a "perception" (or person) whose center is nowhere and whose circumference is everywhere. It is the "bounding outline" for the human-divine imagination, which is infinite in nature. Ricoeur, conversely, in another mid-1970s article, borrows Kant's concept of "limit" (*grenze*) to remind

bols, but which never passes over completely into language, is always something powerful, efficacious, forceful."[34] What we have called the kingdom is a symbol, in Ricoeur's sense, which, he claims, "does not correspond to a metaphor and, because of this fact, resists any linguistic, semantic, or logical transcription" (57).

The symbol, then, is something that corresponds to, or is bound to, the cosmos itself, within which "life is everywhere as a sacrality." The metaphor, on the other hand, "is a free invention of discourse" and exists only in language, unlike the symbol, which only comes "to language to the extent that the elements of the world themselves become transparent" (60–62). Both are necessary in Ricoeur's system, and the tension that appears to exist between the symbol and metaphor, as Ricoeur has here defined them, cannot be resolved simply by seeing through the metaphor to the symbol, which is, apparently, that portion of the metaphor that corresponds to the sacrality of the universe itself. Instead, the tension must continue to exist, because it is only in language (in metaphor, specifically) that the symbol becomes available for interpretation and in that way enters our lives. "Metaphor," Ricoeur concludes, "brings to language the

---

us that the "is like" of the figurative representation of the "unconditioned" "implies an 'is not'" (see "Specificity of Language," p. 143). This recalls Murray Krieger's use of Keats's phrase "waking dream" to explain what he calls "poetic presence and illusion." See note 42, as well as Krieger's *Poetic Presence and Illusion: Essays in Critical History and Theory* (Baltimore: Johns Hopkins University Press, 1979). For a fuller critique of the tensions in Ricoeur's own recent work, see Hazard Adams, *Philosophy of the Literary Symbolic*, chap. 12 (Tallahassee: University Presses of Florida, 1983).

34. Ricoeur, *Interpretation Theory*, p. 63. All subsequent quotations are from this text unless otherwise indicated. Janet Martin Soskice gives a brief but telling critique of Ricoeur's theory in *Metaphor and Religious Language* (Oxford: Clarendon Press, 1985), esp. pp. 86–90. Soskice comments, "Ricoeur's language implies that there is some definite, preexisting thing . . . that the metaphor is *about* and simply redescribes. . . . [But] the interesting thing about metaphor, or at least about some metaphors, is that they are used not to redescribe but to disclose for the first time." Her example is the attempt to describe, through metaphor, that Jesus is "the Son of God" or "the Lamb of God." See too, as suggested in the previous chapter, Stephen Happel's response to Ricoeur in "Worship as a Grammar of Social Transformation," in George Kilcourse, ed., *Proceedings* (Philadelphia: Catholic Theological Society of America, 1987), vol. 42, pp. 60–87. See note 45.

implicit semantics of the symbol." But "[m]etaphor is just the linguistic procedure—that bizarre form of predication—within which the symbolic power is deposited. The symbol remains a two-faced dimensional phenomenon to the extent that the semantic face refers back to the non-semantic one" (69).

But what precisely is this "nonsemantic" face to which Ricoeur refers? It is presumably the "sacred," which "permeates everything" in the universe and is "seen in the movement of the stars, the return of life to vegetation each year, and the alternation of birth and death. . ." (61). Yet to say that we see this is to say that the universe itself in some way signifies, through symbols, of course, which are themselves "bound within the sacred universe" and so are part and parcel of that universe. Without such symbols, we see nothing of significance, because "in the sacred universe the capacity to speak is founded upon the capacity of the cosmos to signify." It signifies, then, only through its own symbols, which adhere to a "logic of correspondences," through which we see. Yet, Ricoeur adds, this seeing of the correspondences between a temple and "some celestial model" is itself dependent upon human discourse:

> We might even say that it is always by means of discourse that this logic manifests itself for if no myth narrated how things came to be or if there were no rituals which re-enacted this process, the Sacred would remain unmanifested. (62)

Again it becomes clear that for Ricoeur, if the metaphor is dependent on the symbol, the symbol is equally dependent on the metaphor in order to enter into discourse, and thence through discourse, through the figurative to rise once again to the "conceptual" or "nonsemantic." His own summary is perhaps the best brief statement for this ongoing dialectic:

> First, the Spirit must become its 'other': a thing, a stone, an idol. Thanks to this "substantiation" of the Absolute we know that the Spirit is not far from us. It has the energy to let itself be known. It has indeed let itself be known. But, at the same time, it is the task of philosophy to show that this "alienation" (in the positive

sense of becoming an other) is the starting point of a process of self-overcoming. In this sense the death of idols paves the way from representation to concept. . . . It is against this background that Christianity is the "Manifested Religion." With it, *der Geist ist da*.[35]

In Blake, however, this revelation is itself a recognition that the symbol is not prelinguistic but is precisely and ultimately linguistic: is in fact itself metaphor. The "symbolic cosmos" to which Ricoeur refers (through Eliade),[36] which is made apparent only in language, must be seen, Blake insists, as purely metaphorical (in Ricoeur's own sense): that is, as a "free invention of discourse." It is a product of our own imagination, which is in Blake divine. Thus for Blake the imagination does not make fictions, as we normally define this term (the unreal); it makes what he defines as the real. Those trees on the mountain *are* the "sons of Los." In them we see their father, who is also us. Jesus *is* the imagination for Blake, the Word who is the source of words, like the sun that emanates light.

The only additional clarification needed is a reminder that for Blake word and discourse are themselves to be interpreted metaphorically. Edenic activity is conversation, Blake suggests, but "conversation" is, as Frosch puts it, "a community of human forms embracing through their activity." Labor in Eden is itself "a kind of speech, an utterance of the whole man."[37] Blake himself makes this clear enough in one of his rare descriptions of Edenic labor: "When in Eternity Man converses with Man they enter / Into each others Bosom (which are Universes of delight) / In mutual interchange . . ." (J 88:3–5; E 246). Thus this Word is the creative power in man, the fashioner of the universe we live and

---

35. Ricoeur, "The Specificity of Language," pp. 140–41. He distinguishes himself from Hegel by applying Kant's notion of "limit" (see note 33), which "implies not only and not even primarily that our knowledge *is* limited, has boundaries, but that the quest of the unconditioned *puts* limits on the claim of objective knowledge to become absolute. "Limit," Ricoeur concludes, "is not a fact but an act" (p. 142). "Limit" reminds us that the "is like" implies an "is not" (p. 143): an "act" of the mind that Blake would equate with a fall.

36. Ricoeur, *Interpretation Theory*, pp. 53, 60–63.

37. Frosch, *Awakening of Albion*, p. 173.

work and love within. In this sense that universe is a "free invention of discourse."

Blake's own best known explanation for this tension in our interpretation of language is another passage in *The Marriage of Heaven and Hell*:

> The ancient Poets animated all sensible objects with Gods or Geniuses, calling them by the names and adorning them with the properties of woods, rivers, mountains, lakes, cities, nations, and whatever their enlarged & numerous senses could perceive.
>
> And particularly they studied the genius of each city & country, placing it under its mental deity.
>
> Till a system was formed, which some took advantage of & enslav'd the vulgar by attempting to realize or abstract the mental deities from their objects: thus began Priesthood.
>
> Choosing forms of Worship from poetic tales.
>
> (pl. 11; E 38)

The passage is somewhat ambiguous, as it may refer to a prelapsarian state, yet could equally well point to a postlapsarian vision, a world that was already seen to be "out there," as in Ricoeur's symbolic universe. The "Ancient Poets," in such an interpretation, are the ones responsible for making us see the cosmos as symbolic, as filled with correspondences. They are the original (yet fallen) mythmakers out of whom a priesthood was formed, abstracting the "deities" from all "sensible objects" and subsequently pronouncing "that the Gods had ordered such things" (E 38).[38]

This tension between "poets" and "priests" is in Blake a neverending one: they are the two contraries described later in *The Marriage*, the prolific and the devourer, which will be seen again in the ongoing conversation between Los and Urizen. The reality that Ricoeur (like the *Pearl*-Poet and Herbert) sees as out there, the whirling stars and planets, is simply (Blake tells us) a problem of perspective. Understanding too often means standing under:

---

38. For an alternate reading of this passage, see Hazard Adams, "Blake, *Jerusalem*, and Symbolic Form," *Blake Studies* 7, (1975), p. 145.

standing at a center and looking up, so that everything appears to be "without." But from the circumference it is recognized as "within." And if Blake appears to take the latter perspective as definitive, it is only because from that perspective one can see that *everything* is a matter of perspective: it alters, depending on where you stand. At the center, Blake says (where he would undoubtedly place both the structuralists and most poststructuralists), it appears that you have no options. You are a prisoner of your own vision, caught within a whirling universe, and cannot find a way out, just as in language we appear to be caught within temporal and spatial fixities, as events happen out there, then, now, or tomorrow.

Such in Blake is the Fall: an event happening now even as we read and affirm (knowingly or not) what the syntax tells us is true about our reality: that it is unalterably defined by time and space and that either there is nothing else but this time and space, no sacred or Kantian *noumena*, or there is but it cannot be reached, except possibly through the grace of God descending from "above."

One problem with Urizen's point of view, then, is that what he sees he sees as fact. His perspective is the scientific (Cartesian, Newtonian) one; its descriptions are taken to be definitive. Yet scientific language, like poetic language, is in fact based on models. It is Los's task, then, to reveal these models as metaphors. It could easily be Los speaking in Colin Turbayne's *Myth of Metaphor*:

> I try to show that the metaphysics of mechanism can be dispensed with. The best way to do this is to show that it is only a metaphor; and the best way to show this is to invent a new metaphor. I therefore treat the events in nature as *if* they compose a language, in the belief that the world may be treated just as well, if not better, by making believe that it is a universal language instead of a giant clockwork.[39]

---

39. *The Myth of Metaphor* (1962; reprint, Columbia: University of South Carolina Press, 1970), p. 5. Compare Susan Handelman's comments in *The Slayers of Moses* (Albany: State University of New York Press, 1982). She suggests that

Blake's Word as World

Blake would recognize this strategy, but he would quarrel with our twentieth-century tendency to call this metaphor another "as if." Reality is for Blake precisely a universal language. If Turbayne sees this task as primarily destructive (if not deconstructive) and not as building, it is simply an indication that, like others, he sees language as its own "prison house," or itself a myth (and thus fictive) from which there is no escape.

Significantly enough, this work (which Murray Krieger calls "demystifying") is in Paul de Man's writings the work not of symbol but of allegory (and irony), which does not allow us the luxury of believing in an escape from our temporal fix. De Man writes:

> The prevalence of allegory always corresponds to the unveiling of an authentically temporal destiny. . . . This unveiling takes place in a subject that has sought refuge against the impact of time in a natural world to which, in truth, it bears no resemblance.[40]

The word as signifier reveals (in allegory) its own failure to contain its signified, which precedes it, de Man argues, and of which it is a repetition. Allegory, then, unlike the misleading symbol, "prevents the self from an illusory identification with the non-self, which is now fully, though painfully, recognized as a non-self." Allegory reveals the gap or void that exists perpetually between the word and that to which it (apparently) points:

> the failure of the attempt to conceive of a language that would be symbolical as well as allegorical, the suppression, in the allegorical, of the analogical and anagogical levels, is one of the ways in which this impossibility becomes manifest.[41]

Even Krieger, who struggles against this sense of defeat (in both de Man and Derrida, however playfully expressed), still

---

the Christian tradition, like the scientific, "literalizes the metaphor. . . . The birth of science was due in part to the separation of word, concept and thing in Greek thought, to a context where words could become mere empty signs pointing to concepts, with no life of their own" (p. 18).

40. "The Rhetoric of Temporality," in Paul de Man, *Blindness and Insight*, rev. ed. (1971; reprint, Minneapolis: University of Minnesota Press, 1983), p. 206.

41. De Man, *Blindness and Insight*, pp. 190–91.

concludes that at best our language is (in Keats's phrase) "a waking dream." The word contains its own signified, he claims, but (in metaphor at least) it simultaneously reveals its own failure to be for us the "real." Using Keats's "Nightingale," as I mentioned before, Krieger concludes,

> As in dream, the symbol creates for us a surrogate reality, claiming the completeness of an irreducible domain within its eccentric terms, although it also stimulates a wakefulness that undercuts its metaphoric extravagances and threatens to reduce symbol to allegory.[42]

The poem, although "demystifying" and thus "awake" to the illusion of the dream, nonetheless "contains also the vision of that incompleteness": it is itself a whole, a complete construction that reveals even in its completion the fact that it remains at best a "surrogate reality."[43]

Blake, however, sees that the work of deconstruction—Los's work of "giving a body to Falsehood that it may be cast off forever"—is itself a building operation, and not just of "Babylon," but also of "Jerusalem," our true if mythic home that, although linguistic in nature and thus our own imaginative creation, is at the same time infinite, eternal, divine, in part because "linguistic" is itself a metaphor for all imaginative human labor. The issue of secular versus religious collapses in Blake even as the split between signifier and signified, world and heaven, and man and God collapse within the divine Word, which is simultaneously the human.

Thus, it is not the poem that is the surrogate reality but that

---

42. "A Waking Dream" in *Allegory, Myth and Symbol*, ed. Morton Bloomfield (Cambridge, Mass.: Harvard University Press, 1982), pp. 21–22.

43. Krieger, "Waking Dream," p. 22. See also my comments in the introduction on these passages in Krieger. Related to this larger issue of the relationship between language and the reality of its constructions—which includes, ultimately, the self—see Stanley Corngold's introduction to *The Fate of the Self* (New York: Columbia University Press, 1986), esp. p. 3. Commenting on both Freud and Lacan, Corngold concludes that these two "do not assert that literature as a witness-bearer belongs to the unspeaking side of our more or less civilized personalities. For them . . . literature opens a way into our being. The entire jagged arc of poetic activity from writer to reader . . . is privileged evidence of the self."

Blake's Word as World

which we normally define as the real, the temporal that de Man claims we cannot escape. But de Man and Derrida, Blake would claim, are, like the sleeping Albion, victims of their own vision, a dream from which they refuse to awaken.

* * *

Ricoeur, as we have seen, would like to uphold the notion of a "sacred cosmos," a universe of correspondences (in Baudelaire's sense) that is at least momentarily revealed to us through metaphor. Thus, unlike the fallen Urizen (who wants to do without Los altogether), he recognizes that the mythmaking faculty is the necessary contrary for this cosmos to be perceived as sacred. Without the ability to perceive symbolically, we are left with a one-dimensional universe, with what Blake calls "single vision." We are left, as Urizen discovers, exploring dead rocks instead of a living, human world. And there is no way *out* because there is no way *in*. We are left instead with the "literal," which is either that whirling universe to which words as transparent signs point, or with the words themselves which, opaque, point to nothing (as in de Man).[44]

Within the metaphor, Ricoeur argues, the "literal sense has to be left behind so that the metaphorical sense can emerge." With this comes the "redescription of reality" made possible only through the tension that exists "at the level of the utterance." Thus, Ricoeur can finally ask:

> Must we not conclude then that metaphor implies a tensive use of language in order to uphold a tensive concept of reality? By this I mean that the tension is not simply between words, but within the very copula of the metaphorical utterance. "Nature is a temple where living pillars. . . ." Here "is" signifies both is and is not. The literal "is" is overturned by the absurdity and surmounted by a metaphorical "is" equivalent to "is like." Thus poetic language does not tell how things literally are, but what they are like.[45]

---

44. In his essay on Derrida's Rousseau in *Blindness and Insight* de Man concludes, "The metaphorical language which, in the fictional diachrony of the *Essai* is called 'premier' has no literal referent. Its only referent is 'le neant des choses humaines'" (p. 135).

45. Ricoeur, *Interpretation Theory*, p. 68. Happel questions this tendency in

The tension that Ricoeur sees here is akin, I think, to the tension found in the Blakean contraries and helps account for the fact that in *Jerusalem* the city is "continually building and continually decaying" (J 72; E 227). But for Blake it is not that (in the metaphorical statement) the literal "is" self-destructs to reveal a more real (if paradoxical) "is not" (as we found in *Pearl*, for example); instead in the metaphor both "is" and "is not" are equally real as simply two different ways of seeing: as Urizen and Los, in fact. In Blake, then, it is in fact poetic language that does tell "how things literally are," because things literally are literary (or linguistic).[46] Everything is a "free invention of discourse," the ongoing outpouring of the "Poetic Genius." All that we see, "even Tree Metal Earth & Stone" (J 99:1; E 258), becomes identified finally with Jerusalem, the emanation or "going forth" of the Divine Imagination. Thus, speech is the act of the divine mind that creates all it sees—and knows that it creates all it sees.

Words then in Blake are not either transparent or opaque; they are both. Seeing into does not annihilate the word as a mental image; it annihilates a perspective that was held to be the only real way of seeing. The words remain; the vision shifts and shifts again, from the opaque sign on the printed page to the mental image created by the sign, in this way continually "building and decaying," coming and going forth.

Los's advantage (which is the advantage of the poetic) is that he sees Urizen's struggle to swallow metaphor or to call it fictive as simply another metaphor, one of science, of mathematics, as Turbayne has suggested. Thus although art is merely one pole of the dialectic (the "prolific" in Blake's terms), from another perspective the artistic imagination can also be said to contain both sides of the dialectic within itself, insofar as it recognizes

---

Ricoeur to stress the "is not" of metaphor. For Ricoeur, he suggests, "the text reveals a virtual world, a possibility that is potentially present. . . . Metaphor always tells us how the world might be if. . . ; it does not speak a partial, heuristic judgement about the world's presence. The world both is and is not what metaphor says it is." He concludes that this leaves religious language "equally ambiguous and unresolved" (p. 76).

46. See Frye, *Anatomy of Criticism*, pp. 76–78.

its own opposite as its equivalent, as another form of myth, another vision. To see this is to see that Urizenic vision from a circumference: that is, to see it, like everything else, as a creation of our own imagination and thus contained within us.[47] This helps explain why, at the end of *Jerusalem*, the awakened Albion sees Jesus "in the similitude of Los, my friend." Los, like Jesus, is the imagination at work within the world (within Blake, and within us, as we read imaginatively), and it is the imagination that has perspective enough to see itself as one pole of an eternal dialectic, whereby one can see *either* "One Man" or a "multitude," depending on where one is standing.[48]

We are defining again the goal of *Jerusalem*: "To open the Eternal Worlds, to open the immortal Eyes / Of Man inwards" (J 5:18–20; E 147). As in *Pearl* and as in *The Temple*, the construction of the poem is intended to be read metaphorically for building or labor taking place within, recalling that for Blake this "within" encompasses not simply an isolated individual but all of London, all of England, within the totality which is humanity. Thus in Blake this "labouring in knowledge to build Jerusalem" (J 77; E 232) is not performed in order to create symbols or signifiers for some unknown, unnamable other, which we use (in Augustine's sense) only because we have no other way of arriving at a pre- or supralinguistic kingdom; instead the laboring in language is itself the building, for language, like building, is itself act: this ongoing activity *is* the "new earth." And so the words that compose this act of building are themselves permanent precisely as elements of discourse, again seeing "discourse" metaphorically: "Every Word and every Character was Human . . ." (J 98:35–36; E 258). What is burned up is the concept of an inhuman, external universe to which our words simply point. What is burned up is something, Blake says, that did not exist in the first place, except as a figment of the imagination and thus as part of us all the time.

    47. This concept of the "circumference" and "center" in Blake is clarified considerably in the lengthy chapter on Blake in Hazard Adams's study *The Philosophy of the Literary Symbolic*.
    48. See VLJ (E 556–57) and J 34:14–25 (E 180).

It is the external object as other that is annihilated. As separate: this is the perspective of the fall. To say that the world is all internal or contained by us is not to deny the existence of the world; it is to say that the world is in some sense (a metaphorical sense) both living and human, as it seems to be in myth, and in some poetry. Blake often uses his "illuminations" to convey this notion of the universe as a human place, most clearly, perhaps, in a plate such as *Jerusalem* 25, where we find the figure of a man with stars, moon and sun engraved onto his thighs, chest, and arm. These are not tattoos; instead this is myth. This man contains the universe. In turn the universe is seen as human.

And so this plate is the world. We hold it in our hands as an object; it is visible language, and yet is also clearly a sign of something that is human: that book is our body and the sun is a part of it. The word and image that make up the book, not something behind the word, remain. The visible word is the imagination's act, its manifestation. The world for Blake is Word that (or who) is itself the Divine Image: every particle of it, just as every page of *Jerusalem*, manifests this truth.

Thus the Last Judgment comes when our alienation from our world, and thus from ourselves, ends. And it comes not as a moment postponed to an unknown future; it is instead the "Eternal Now" that erupts (potentially) at any and every moment. There is no other world in Blake; instead there is only this world, seen imaginatively, as within us.

It is Blake who takes most radically the language of the New Testament, in which the kingdom is not simply in or behind Jesus' parables but is those parables because kingdom is itself the labor embodied in language, the language of poetry. Kingdom is the new earth, a perpetual act of self-giving. "Christianity is Art," Blake concluded; "God," "The Divine Body," "Jesus" and the "Eternal Body of Man" are all equated with "the imagination" which "manifests itself in his Works of Art" (E 273–75).

The question then becomes: Is such a "manifestation" necessarily a fall? Is there still a gap between this word and spirit, a

Blake's Word as World

gap that only silence can bridge?[49] The answer for Blake is clearly no, as long as we recall that manifestation does not imply a corporeal object existing as other than us. Art in Eternity (which is "now") is instead seen as the "bounding outline" or the "circumference" of vision that is Jesus, the Divine Imagination: the source of Art. Art, or the Word going forth, is that which makes apparent the nature of the fully human, which is "forgiveness of sins." In Eternity, which is where we are, art is Jerusalem, the city of the imagination, the light by which we see, "greet," and forgive one another:

In Great Eternity, every particular Form gives forth or Emanates
Its own peculiar Light, & the Form is the Divine Vision
And the Light is his Garment This is Jerusalem in every Man
A Tent & Tabernacle of Mutual Forgiveness Male & Female Clothings.
And Jerusalem is called Liberty among the Children of Albion.

(J 54:1–5; E 203)

The language is again inevitably metaphorical. Blake reminds us by speaking of "tents and tabernacles" that his own perspective is that of the Bible, the "Great Code of Art" (E 274). But as with any code, it must be "cracked," or seen (as Blake says) as "representing" or "signifying" (E 556; VLJ). But Blake is not offering us a theory of "substitution"[50] in which a palpable, opaque object stands for the unseen, abstract reality. In Blake the manifestation is not to be viewed as an external object ("corporeal vegetation") divorced from its source; it is the light that emanates from that sun that is itself light: that "place" where mass is energy. The manifestation is one form this energy takes, and it is through this form that we know and experience. Jerusalem is then a tabernacle, as Blake says; it is not only "like" one. Our mistake is that

---

49. See Robert Gleckner, "Romanticism and the Self-Annihilation of Language, in *Criticism* 18 (1976), pp. 173–89, where this point is affirmatively argued, insofar as the majority of the Romantics are concerned. See also Cyrus Hamlin's "The Temporality of Selfhood: Metaphor and Romantic Poetry," *New Literary History* 6 (1974), pp. 169–93.

50. See Ricoeur, *Rule of Metaphor*, pp. 173–87.

we think of the word as a copy of the real, external building, when in fact "tabernacle" is first an imaginative act that potentially includes everything within it. "Everything that lives is holy": every imaginative act is an opening to what in the fallen state appears as other. Just as inner and outer are contained within this space, so are sacred and secular.

* * *

Blake's revealed world is akin to what we think of as the dream world, where objects or images are recognized as metaphors, not existing somewhere other than the imagination but instead as its manifestation, part of the mind's ongoing labor: its mental warfare to maintain its own balance and health. They are real and living images, not just the "phantom[s] of the overheated brain," even though they are in part just that. We may now recall that Albion is asleep and dreaming throughout (or within) the text-world that is *Jerusalem*. As soon as he realizes this fact, acknowledging these things of darkness as his own, he can wake up, a metaphorical awakening that reverses our normal understanding, when we open our eyes and once again see the "natural" world outside us. Instead the true awakening would see that morning sun as living, human, and so part of the larger human life that embraces everything that is.

Jerusalem of course begins with precisely this small, personal revelation (to Blake himself), in this way picking up from the personal ending of *Milton*. In the earlier poem Blake clearly affirms that even as he returns to the "fallen world," as his "Soul returnd into its mortal state / To Resurrection & Judgment in the Vegetable Body," his vision of the eternal, and thus of the "natural" world as part of the greater human body, remains strong: "Immediately," he writes, "the Lark mounted . . . And Los & Enitharmon rose over the Hills of Surrey / Their clouds roll over London. . ." (M 42:26–32; E 143–44). There is nothing vague about this; we know precisely where we are both within geographical England (outside Blake's cottage in "Felphams Vale") and metaphorically (within Blake's vision of the universal humanity). We recognize clouds and sun, yet also see them as living members of our own greater body. Like Blake at this moment we move easily between the two perspectives, recognizing no incongruence between them.

So too with *Jerusalem*, which begins with the epic proclamation ("Of the sleep of Ulro! and of the passage through / Eternal Death! and of the awaking to Eternal Life"), which is immediately followed by the personal dimension of precisely that same universal story. If all of *Jerusalem* will tell of this great passage, climaxing with the universal awakening and apocalypse, then the poem will begin with the individual example of this same awakening (the individual being, of course, Blake himself):

This theme calls me in sleep night after night, & ev'ry morn
Awakes me at sun-rise, then I see the Saviour over me
Spreading his beams of love, & dictating the words of this mild song.

The parallel between the opening two lines, the epic invocation, and the following three is too close to be coincidental. In fact, the personal is again to be viewed as an aspect, a "particular" of the universal story that *Jerusalem* is, a reminder that for the reader, as for Blake, the particular is itself the whole. This is our story, Blake reminds us, the story of the human fall, journey, and rise encoded in the Bible. We too sleep "night after night," knowingly or not, with this "theme" calling us, and it is this same theme that "awakes" us at sunrise, because this fiction of a rising sun beyond us is the story within which our historical lives unfolds. And that sun is both what we recognize as sun—that ball of energy apparently rising outside our windows—and "the Saviour over me / Spreading his beams of love." Again we grasp simultaneously the specific stance of the individual living within fallen space and time, the artist-engraver William Blake, and the universal energy that we also are, which embraces all particulars. This of course is exactly what Blake hears from this human sun:

Awake! awake O sleeper of the land of shadows, wake! expand!
I am in you and you in me, mutual in love divine:
Fibres of love from man to man thro Albions pleasant land. . . .
I am not a God afar off, I am a brother and friend;

Within your bosoms I reside, and you reside in me:
Lo! we are One; forgiving all Evil; Not seeking recompense!
(J 4:1–20; E 146)

What we see in the dreaming state, then, is in fact the theme that tells us the truth about ourselves and the world: that everything we see is a portion of us. There is no falling away from the divine in the creation, as gnosticism often assumes, and no absence of light. We are made from that light and remain that light. Waking up is simply acknowledging the truth we find in our Los-given dreams, a truth that is not so much a piece of information as a way of seeing, speaking, and acting.[51]

* * *

It is easy to divorce this notion of the dream state (which serves Blake's purposes in both *Jerusalem* and *The Four Zoas*) from the political and historical situation within which Blake was writing, but to do so is to falsify both the works and the life of the man who created them. Clearly part of Blake's point is that to attempt to separate the various dimensions of human life—the political, the psychological, the spiritual, the artistic—is to split Zoas into fragmented corners of the universe we inhabit and is again to experience the splintered, subjective-objective world within which most of us spend the greater part of our lives. This is the dream world, and the repercussions in all areas are traced in *Jerusalem*.

Like the *Pearl*-Poet and (to a lesser extent) George Herbert, Blake lived through a time of remarkable historical changes. We cannot forget that Blake's class, the artisans, was at the forefront of change during this period;[52] nor can we forget that Blake was

---

51. See James Hillman, *Re-visioning Psychology* (New York: Harper & Row, 1975), pp. 48, 84–85, and 156–58, where Hillman acknowledges his debts to Vico and Vahinger in his own understanding of metaphor. This understanding of both metaphor and dream should be distinguished from *allegory*, a term that Blake generally uses derogatorily to refer to a delusive vision or perspective, or creation. Thus, "moral virtues are allegories and dissimulations" VLJ (E 563). See also VLJ (E 554); *Europe* 5:7 (E 62); *Song of Los* 6:17 (E 68); J 50:2 (E 197); and J 89:45 (E 249), and Tannenbaum's discussion of Blakean "sublime allegory," *Biblical Tradition*, pp. 86–123, esp. 107–8.

52. See E. P. Thompson, *The Making of the English Working Class* (1963; reprint, New York: Vintage, 1966), pp. 155–63. Subsequent quotations from this are

witness to, and directly involved in, the rise of industrialism in England in the first decades of the nineteenth century. E. P. Thompson summarizes the complaints of one laborer at this time: "the rise of a master-class without traditional authority or obligations: the growing distance between master and man . . . the loss of status and above all of independence for the worker, his reduction to total dependence on the master's instruments of production. . . ." Thompson concludes, "The worker has become an 'instrument,' or an entry among other items of cost" (202–3).

This exploitation becomes part of the dream world that *Jerusalem* is, in particular as it forms an aspect of the continual fragmentation of the society that Blake identifies potentially as one single man. And at the broken center of this fragmented unity is Los-Blake, the manual laborer at work in the furnaces ("storming, loud, thunderous & mighty / The Bellows & the Hammers move compell'd by Los's hand" (J 10:5–6; E 152)) along with his weaver-wife Enitharmon-Catherine. The individualized physical production of the glorious one-hundred-plate poem must itself be viewed as a revolutionary statement (then as now), since books were increasingly becoming mass-marketed items.[53] The leveling of the unique particular artifact to the assembly line product is a parody of Blakean democracy, in which we recognize the universal not by making everything outwardly the same and thus "equal" but through and in the unique particular. Without this individual, in fact, there is no way out of the limited self.

The poem in its entirety, like *The Temple* and *Pearl*, can be read and viewed simultaneously as a building project and as a pilgrimage, the journey taken by Los-Blake through London in particular, but through all of England-Albion more generally, as he seeks for the source of the nation's sorrows. Los's descent

---

cited in the text. See also, especially on this issue of Blake as artisan, Michael Ferber, *The Social Vision of William Blake* (Princeton, N.J.: Princeton University Press, 1985), pp. 34–39.

53. For a general discussion of the rise of a middle-class reading public and its effect on book publishing (and on authors) see A. S. Collins, *The Profession of Letters* (London: Routledge and Sons, 1928), esp. pp. 25–27, 40–44, and 89–92. See also Ferber, *Social Vision*, pp. 41–42.

through the "Door of Death for Albions sake Inspired" (E 144) in plate 1 recalls Jesus' harrowing of hell and also, as David Erdman notes, Diogenes' nighttime search for truth.⁵⁴ What Los finds is a body rent in fragments: politically, economically, psychologically, spiritually. Los's task is to awaken Albion to the interwoven character of his life: how all aspects of human existence emanate from one body, are all metaphors, "fibres" spun from the one whole we are. If Blake embraces the metaphorical nature of language to a greater extent than almost any other poet, the reason should be clear: here, Blake emphasizes, is the nature not just of language but of all life.

Consider, for example, the threads of money and economy, which for Blake are to be viewed as metaphors of exchange, the true commerce of life, because exchange *is* life in Blake. It is not then a question simply of "internalizing" the notion of money and economy; it is, however, crucial to Blake that we recognize the metaphorical basis for these activities, the way economics functions as an expression of exchange, forgiveness, and sacrifice within the single human family (the word *economy* after all is rooted in the common image of the household). When we lose sight of our own interconnectedness, we then develop into competitive economic—and ultimately military—states. The house or single structure we are in Eden splinters, and the "fibres of love" that are the means of our connection instead are viewed as means of binding, controlling, possessing, owning. These fibers themselves do not change; we change in our view of them and thus in our use of them.

To take one example: on plate 67 England's economic imperialism is cast into metaphorical terms so that we see the nature, the "Error" of such activities. Blake here roots imperialism, the parody of imaginative expansion, in both Druidic sacrifice (Salisbury Plain) and Baconian rationalism ("In Verulam the Polypus's Head") as England is "Shooting out Fibres round the Earth

---

54. See David Erdman, *Prophet Against Empire* (1954; reprint, Garden City, N.Y.: Anchor Books, 1969), p. 469. Subsequent quotations from this work are cited in the text.

... into Judea / To Sodom & Gomorrha: thence to India, China & Japan" (J 67:35–40; E 220). Geography too leaps into the metaphorical as Blake shifts from the representative fallen states of the Old Testament to the specific places of British economic conquest. The simple word *thence* indicates the relationship between these apparently disparate localities. The point of course is that the Biblical symbols of Sodom and Gomorrah are precisely and intimately associated with nineteenth-century British economic policy: a state of mind represented by Verulem and Salisbury Plain leads inexorably to the state represented by Sodom and Gomorrah and thence to the exploitation of the people and resources of a land considered "other" and inferior. Blake had personal reasons, certainly, to insist toward the end of his life, "Christianity is Art & not Money / Money is its Curse" (E 274), but he was also speaking from accurate observation, standing within a nation that in the name of Christianity was exploiting other nations and people for economic gain.

As Nelson Hilton notes, the metaphor of money as the "sinews of war" or "the nerves of worldly power" speaks the precise truth.[55] Money too is a means of conversing and thus connecting, but unlike art it tends to polarize and divide individuals into classes. Money is the analogy of a living system that unites us as one body.

* * *

Blake's concern in *Jerusalem* with economy is underscored by his increasing recognition of the importance of labor and laboring within the body of England. This is one reason that *Jerusalem* is the sweatiest of all poems in the language, including anything we might find in Whitman or Ginsberg. Los's struggle at the furnaces is cast precisely and poignantly in terms of hard manual labor. The fact that this labor metaphorically represents Blake's engravings and is constantly cast in terms of metaphor ("I took the sighs & tears . . . / I lifted them into my furnaces . . .") is of course the point: mental, emotional anguish is transformed in

---

55. Hilton, *Literal Imagination*, p. 96.

the physical labor of engraving and coloring; here there is no separation between outer and inner. Instead the two are united in the ongoing productive activity of Los. The art that he begets from that vision of a world revolving around us is the child who transforms this vision. Out of his own woundedness is born the Christ, the Minute Particular who is Himself all creation. If, then, the temple is etymologically the "enclosed space," this art reveals that the holy is the hole, the wound through which we enter that space where we know and become the holy. We are that enclosed space exactly when we are most fully open. Our temple is Christ on the cross, and not Christ as something other, as one more building or "shell" to separate those inside and those left without, but Christ as us, as all. This, Christ declares, is what it is to be whole: to be a hole, a wound, an opening through which creation continually comes.

Blake-Los must work with our perspective of the fallen world to transform our sense of that world, breaking up the "mundane shell," that false tabernacle that closes us off:

> Every Emanative joy forbidden as a Crime:
> And the Emanations buried alive in the earth with pomp of religion:
> Inspiration deny'd; Genius forbidden by laws of punishment:
> I saw terrified; I took the sighs & tears, & bitter groans:
> I lifted them into my Furnaces; to form the spiritual sword.
> That lays open the hidden heart: I drew forth the pang
> Of sorrow red hot: I workd it on my resolute anvil:
>
> (J 9:14–20; E 152)

These lines work on us as we feel the true burden of this song. The "outer" burden or load we carry on our backs is metaphorically, imaginatively, the same as the "inner" emotional burden: for example, the duty or responsibility Blake takes on himself in creating his song ("Trembling I sit day and night . . . I rest not from my great task!"). Thus the song's burden, its refrain, is also this physical-psychological-spiritual weight. And of course the song's burden is the transformation of that terrible weight, those sighs and tears and groans now transformed into art, which in turn transforms us. This, as Blake repeatedly reminds us, is the theme, the refrain, the burden that awakens him and must awaken us.

When Blake stepped out from his doorway in the early decades of the nineteenth century he saw the dark forest that London's streets had become. He saw clearly the corroding results of an increasingly alienated vision: man set against man in economic competition; woman set against woman—and against man—in sexual strife and deceit; and all of humanity set against a passive, yet oppressive nature, which in turn was remote from an increasingly abstract and alien God whose home was no longer on earth, and no longer even in the stars, but in the void between—and then, finally, nowhere at all.

One particular result of this vision was the further alienation, as Marx noted so powerfully a few decades later, of the worker from his work: "the fact that labour is *external* to the worker, i.e., does not belong to his essential being. . . ."[56] Thus, as David Punter notes, in Blake it is not simply an increase in a subjective vision that is sought; "rather, it is the separation of internal and external worlds which is itself criticized" (542).

Los-Blake perceives very quickly, therefore, in *Jerusalem*, in part because the ground has already been laid in *Milton* and *The Zoas*, that the task must be to transform Urizenic labor, represented most fully in the building of the Mundane Shell, because "the Urizenic version of perception is inseparable from Urizenic labour; the restriction of the senses . . . is . . . an essential accompaniment to the creation of a race of men 'suitable' to the operation of a growing industrial economy" (Punter 547). In Blake, the growth of the factories and mills and the loss of work that exists as a true extension of the laborer are inevitable results of the "single vision" of Newton and Locke.

So too, then, is it necessary for Los's labor to be corrosive, furious, destructive; this is in part Blake's own genuine rage

---

56. David Punter, "Blake: Creative and Uncreative Labour," *Studies in Romanticism* 16 (1977), p. 544. See Marx, *Early Writings*, trans. R. Livingstone and G. Benton (Harmondsworth: Penguin, 1975), p. 326. Subsequent quotations from Punter are cited in the text.

transformed into art, but it is also a recognition that given the conditions of England, the artist's labor is destined to be hard prophetic labor, cast along the same lines as the labor of Jeremiah and Isaiah. Continually as *Jerusalem* advances Blake reveals, explains, defines, all the while pounding furiously within his furnaces: these acts are exactly the same. Wounded himself, Blake finds himself by acknowledging the wound and in that way using it. This process of opening and expansion begins with his own Spectre, which is his own place of greatest vulnerability. He acknowledges this dark angel, wrestling in furious labour with what is now unveiled as his own "Pride & Self-righteousness" (J 8:30; E 151). He puts his own terror to work in the furnaces (J 8:39), this in turn leading to and making possible the building of Golgonooza "in London" (J 10:17; E 153).[57] It is often forgotten that Los's famous statement—"I must Create a System, or be enslav'd by another Mans"—follows immediately upon this first mention of Golgonooza; the context suggests that Los's creation of a "System" is the equivalent of his building Golgonooza, the city viewed as our own human creation, the extension of us, with wires, Blakean fibers, running everywhere through it connecting us. The present-day city (and world!) is an extraordinarily accurate parody of Blake's own vision of the "fibres of love" connecting us all in the city of art.

The system Los creates, then, is Golgonooza: the city is ongoing creative and connecting labor. What is a system but this whole made up of interconnected parts, a single body? Blake reclaims the word from the rationalists: Paley's *Natural Theology* in 1802 declares, "The universe itself is . . . a system; each part either depending upon other parts, or being connected with other parts by some common law of motion"; Locke one hundred years earlier saw the sun as the center of a great system; his is one of

---

57. Surely this relationship between Blake-Los and his Spectre is the equivalent of all we have read and seen of the mad doctor or scientist who has as an assistant a smaller, deformed human, someone who, as in the 1931 *Frankenstein*, must be carefully guarded and supervised: a "shadow" (to use Jung's term) who is necessary for the creative birth. The failure to acknowledge this servant truly often leads to disaster. This is, of course, Prospero and Caliban as well.

the first citations in the OED for what we commonly refer to still as our own solar system: "a group of heavenly bodies connected by their mutual attractive forces and moving in orbits about a centre or central body. . . ."[58] Perhaps Blake knew that the word's own underlying metaphor is to a musical "system," the series of notes that sound together to make up a whole; our own more abstract notion of system derives ultimately from an artistic grounding. "System" is first and foremost Los's work, then, and it is work of connecting, forging, and weaving together through art, through image, through the body, and not through the abstract logic that leaves us with a vision of an external "solar system" as the sole defining perspective of our lives. The latter Blake sees clearly enough a few plates later:

> I turn my eyes to the Schools & Universities of Europe
> And there behold the Loom of Locke whose Woof rages dire
> Washd by the Water-wheels of Newton. black the cloth
> In heavy wreathes folds over every Nation; cruel Works
> Of many Wheels I view, wheel without wheel, with cogs tyrannic
> Moving by compulsion each other: not as those in Eden: which
> Wheel within Wheel in freedom revolve in harmony & peace.
> (J 15:14–20; E 159)

This weaving covers the nations like the night: because it *is* night Blake here depicts, night as perceived within a Newtonian perspective, these "heavenly bodies" that the OED describes "moved by compulsion," locked into wheels. Here again is the analogy to the Blakean system, the system turned inside out: not "wheel within wheel in freedom" revolving but "wheel without wheel." Not everything contained in the single body but everything external, separate, connected only at the turning cog. So it is that Los has said, "I will not Reason & Compare: my business is to Create" (J 10:21; E 153).

58. *Oxford English Dictionary*, *system*, definition I.1, I, 2. This understanding of Los's "system" perhaps suggests that Logos is also better translated as "system" than "word," as Hazard Adams also suggests, if for different reasons. See "Synecdoche and Method" in *Critical Paths: Blake and the Argument of Method*, ed. Dan Miller, Mark Bracher, and Donald Ault (Durham, N.C.: Duke University Press, 1987), p. 49.

* * *

We will recall now that as *Jerusalem* begins Los is entering the dark body of Albion in an attempt to explore and expose the nightmare that keeps us all split asunder. This occurs, of course, and climaxes properly enough at the end of the poem with the revelation of "Religion hid in War, a Dragon red & hidden Harlot" (J 89:53; E 249). We see here too the culmination of Los's laboring in metaphor, inviting us to see the true nature of the fallen universe that we have built for ourselves as a precise parody of Jerusalem. As Frosch has noted, the problem we have is that the parody is so closely related to the real thing: our love for Vala, that beautiful external world, approximates the love we have for Jerusalem, for Vala is Jerusalem turned inside out. We grow confused. If Blake is saying to Albion, "Expand," he means what he says, because England is the diminished form of Albion who is intended to encompass the globe and the universe as a whole. He is Blake's version of Everyman, just as the body of Ireland is Joyce's. The parody of this expansion, of course, is imperialism, which culminates in a further parody of Blake's intentions, the notion that "the sun never sets on the British Empire." Imperialism is economic expansion, expanding boundaries through possession and finally, inevitably, military power that protects those broadened boundaries. In the revelation of this dragon, Blake reveals that England is fast becoming its own enemy and devourer: it has created itself as Antichrist.

It is not, however, that England has simply become literal-minded, for economic expansion remains a metaphor; it is instead that England has placed its faith within the wrong metaphor and even fails to see that it is a metaphor. It has misinterpreted "expansion" because it has misinterpreted the nature of unity (and ultimately misinterpreted the metaphors, the wounds of Christ). The parody created is a unified economic, religious, and military England that encompasses the globe.[59] This is an imaginative vision, certainly, but one based on an extremely limited concep-

---

59. See Frosch, *Awakening of Albion*, p. 85.

tion of "unity": based, that is, on Urizen-Jehovah-George III's hierarchical conception wherein you expand by devouring others until everything is apparently contained within you. The "Covering Cherub," Blake's other name for this Antichrist, is an apt metaphor for the process here described because this is a vision that does cover and that does, as the Biblical Covering Cherub did, block the passage back to Eden. Its goal is complete consumption, closing everything within itself like a black hole until all is night. It is the parody of Christ, whose wounds suggest His openness to all.

Increasingly as the poem builds we hear Los's crying out "at his Anvil in the horrible darkness weeping!" (J 91:31; E 251), and yet still calling out what he sees in that dark, for this is the one way that the artist can reveal the vision that underlies the metaphors by which we work and live. Preeminently we must learn to see the fruits of our own labors again not as commodities to be bought and sold in order to increase our own power and wealth but instead as living creations, sons and daughters, part of the whole that we are, and in particular as that ongoing imaginative act of love that by opening outward binds us all together.

Our own labor, then, is our partner: we take the burden, the wound, whatever cross we carry, and make of it a new burden, a song: our "emanation," known ultimately as Jerusalem, who is this ongoing activity and conversation. And the burden that is born(e) from this labor is the world we create and are. It is in this sense that Blake might say that we are truly married to our work.[60]

Thus it is fitting that revelation becomes complete as Los and Enitharmon are reunited, a sign of the reconnection of male-female, inner-outer, and laborer-work. Enitharmon fears the annihilation of her separate, independent existence, but Los explains that he too in a sense will end: "Sexes must vanish & cease

---

60. See *bher 1 in the appendix to *The American Heritage Dictionary of the English Language*, ed. William Morris (Boston: Houghton Mifflin, 1973), p. 1509. The root of *burden* suggests carrying, including the bearing of children (*bairn*) and, presumably, the carrying of a tune.

/ To be, when Albion arises from his dread repose" (J 92:13–14; E 252). Then, after one final attempt by Enitharmon to establish a separate dominion in the name of this false mother (nature, church, and country), Los proclaims again to all on which he has labored:

Fear not my Sons this Waking Death. he is become One with me
Behold him here! We shall not die! we shall be united in Jesus.
Will you suffer this Satan this Body of Doubt that Seems but Is Not
To occupy the very threshold of Eternal Life. if Bacon, Newton, Locke,
Deny a Conscience in Man & the Communion of Saints & Angels
Contemning the Divine Vision & Fruition, Worshipping the Deus
Of the Heathen, The God of This World, & the Goddess Nature
Mystery Babylon the Great, The Druid Dragon & hidden Harlot
Is it not that Signal of the Morning which was told us in the Beginning
(J 93:18–26; E 253–54)

The beginning referred to here is, in part at least, the beginning of this very poem, with its own rising sun, heralding the metaphorical new day and life: a new vision of life based on the essential unity of the human and the universe. This reminder of the poem's genesis is also a reminder that this revelation is available at any moment in the poem; such is the nature of metaphorical particulars that can bring about an opening at any time, in any place. With the text before us—or below us or more truly, Blake would hope, with the text finally digested, contained within us—we are like the Eternals Blake describes at the end of the poem who, containing all, can choose times and spaces to enter; can choose any point in the "text" to enter, finding there an immersion in a particular time, in a precise place, but knowing that this time and place are the mind's own creation, and not something one is trapped within. This is what Blake means by the "liberty both of body & mind." We are not trapped in the particular; the moment, the object, is not a wheel linked by cogs to another wheel outside it; instead that moment in time and space is the hole, the wound through which we enter and become eternity. Eternity is always there, inside the moment that is truly inside us. "Eternity is in love with the productions of time," Blake says; these moments *are* the productions of time: the children born of this love affair. Here again is the Blakean "wheel within wheel," all time and space contained within any given particular. This is what it means to converse "together in Visionary forms dramatic . . . in Visions / In new Expanses, creating exemplars of Memory and of Intellect / Creating Space, Creating Time according to the wonders Divine / Of Human Imagination, throughout all the Three Regions immense / Of Childhood, Manhood & Old Age & the all tremendous unfathomable Non Ens" (J 98:28–33; E 257–58).

Blake is again describing artistic labor, which stands as always as the paradigm of all labor. *Jerusalem* is his own example of what he has just described, even as his own poem is approaching its end. In its apparently odd, even tortuous form we have seen Blake's conversing. Creating his own "exemplars of Memory and of Intellect," Blake has engaged us in conversation, an exchange (as the word *conversation* implies) and not a monologue. Recalling that the root of the word also suggests turning, there is a sense too that Blake's labor has been both a "conversing" as in turning around, a "conversion" process, and the turning that those wheels within wheels do.

There is no end to this art: no goal, no finishing point, except its own ongoing creative labor. A poem finishes, and yet, as we sense in *The Pearl* as well, and in Herbert's *Temple*, with its conclusion at the feast, there is a sense in which it does not finish, cannot finish, because once entered into the poem has gone beyond the bounds of time and space or contains those boundaries within itself. For the *Pearl*-Poet and Herbert, the "unfinished" sense is resolved only through Jesus and the sacraments, to which both poets lead us. For Blake, however, the sacraments are themselves the imaginative acts of "Throwing off Error . . . continually & receiving Truth . . . continually" (VLJ; E 562). This of course describes the action of Blake's own poem, so that at least for Blake, his own poem truly is the sacrament that will lead us in. We see this as we find ourselves with those at poem's end who "walked / To & fro in Eternity as One Man reflecting each in each & clearly seen / And seeing" (J 98:38–40; E 258).

"The outward ceremony is Antichrist," Blake argued (E 274), precisely as it is seen as outward: here again is the analogy or parody of the true act of (self) sacrifice with which *Jerusalem* climaxes. The sacred is not experienced through the observation of remote acts but through taking that apparently external into oneself, not only literally in the Eucharist but through an imaginative act, an opening up, a crucifying of one's small "Selfhood." This amounts to a transformation of vision that art makes possible and that is art's great function. This is why for Blake "Christianity is Art" (E 274).

On a universal level, this imaginative transformation and simultaneous sacrifice are Albion's grand act at the conclusion of the poem, as he acknowledges the outcast world as his own, recognizing finally that all the world's damage has been caused by "the Visions of my deadly Sleep of Six Thousand Years . . . I know it is my Self" (J 96:11–13; E 255). Psychologically, this can be seen as recognizing one's own Shadow for what it is, recognizing all that we fear, all that we attempt to kill or buy off as portions of ourselves that we project outward;[61] on a political level it is acknowledging the disenfranchised, the poor, the prisoner: all whom we think of as "other." And certainly Blake's genius asks us to see again the coincidence of these perspectives; the psychological shadow is simultaneously the political shadow, as it is also reinforced by a scientific and economic worldview that allows us in apparent good conscience to accept the outcast as inevitable, as the way things naturally and divinely are. Albion

---

61. See Carl Jung, *Aion: Researches into the Phenomenology of the Self*, rev. ed., trans. R. F. C. Hull (1959; reprint, Princeton, N.J.: Princeton University Press, 1979), pp. 8–11. To the conscious mind, Jung notes, "one meets with projections, one does not make them." The key shift, as it is for Albion, is to recognize that one indeed has made them. Until then, Jung continues, "[t]he effect of projection is to isolate the subject from the environment, since instead of a real relation to it there is now only an illusory one. . . . In the last analysis . . . they lead to an autoerotic or autistic condition in which one dreams a world whose reality remains forever unattainable" (p. 9).

awakens at last to this trick that he has perpetrated on himself and in awakening steps outside that perspective, turns around, goes through the vortex—and undergoes his own last judgment.

* * *

We have returned again to the goal of *Jerusalem*. It is complicated, however, because in a fallen world an artist is forced to work with the error engraved on individuals by the fall itself, the narrowing of vision to self versus other. Here is the wound that must be opened and raised up on the wood of the cross and book: the vision of a world in competition and not communion, not conversation.

Blake knew well enough that most men "when the Sun rises . . . see a round Disk of fire somewhat like a Guinea" and not "an Innumerable company of the Heavenly Host crying Holy Holy Holy" (E 566); and it is not that Blake himself could not see the Guinea sun: it is that other men can see nothing but and are unwilling to accept the fact that *that* vision (as the simile slyly suggests) is itself imaginative, a creation of the mind like everything else. Thus, the Error is not so much that "single vision" as it is the mistaking of the single vision for the real, or for Jesus as an external, cyclical dying God (or Orc in Blake's myth).

Similarly with the poem itself. For Blake, *Jerusalem* is "Jerusalem": the poem as the city and as the woman is also the poem as the manifestation of Jesus, the verbal light by which we see the divine. Yet as an external form, as an object which we perceive as outside ourselves, *Jerusalem* (like anything else) is potentially Babylon—or Babel. Like anything else, it is something we make or build according to how we see, and if we see just one way, we build (or read, or interpret, or abstract *from* it, like a "devourer")[62] according to that way. The trouble with this, of course, as Blake takes great pains to remind us, is that as we see we also become. What we build as we read is who we are, our vision of ourselves.

It is in this way that Albion discovers that "turning his back"

---

62. See Adams, "Blake, *Jerusalem*, and Symbolic Form," p. 152.

on the Divine Vision "into the Wastes of Moral Law" is the equivalent of building Babylon "in the Waste, founded in Human desolation" (J 24:24–25; E 169). To induce Albion (and so us) to see this equivalence is the purpose of Los's continual labor. A misconception regarding the nature of things leads to a misconception (or misperception) regarding the nature of language and thus of reality (or vice versa). Once the fall has taken place and Albion is asleep, he sees (egotistically) all reality as "revolving around" himself. The metaphorical, dreamlike truth of this statement becomes a literal truth as the vision of the fallen universe, with its whirling stars above, is created. In Blake, the literal truth of our sleep *is* the metaphorical truth.

The poet, then, is forced to work backward, with Blake's own engraving process being a sign of this truth, as suggested at the beginning. He must put his words "out there," engraved on metal and stamped onto paper, so that Albion (in us) can see. But like the acid that eats away the surface of the plate, the metaphorical language of the poet similarly works its way inward, revealing to the reader that what he thought was out there is in fact within. We cross over, with Blake's metaphorical art the bridge. Albion, we come to see, is not a character existing in our external world, performing various acts (including dying several times); all act, no matter how distant, is part of who we are and has repercussions on us.[63] Blake never lets us forget this. Even his narrative, although forced by the "stubborn structure of language" to speak in spatial and temporal terms, everywhere asks us to see "spaces" and "times" as imaginative options and thus not as enclosing prisons. We find, for example, in an early revelation of the Spectre to Los in *Jerusalem*, precisely this demand to see better:

Los opend the Furnaces in fear. the Spectre saw to Babel & Shinar
Across all Europe & Asia. he saw the tortures of the Victims.

63. A clear example of this interconnectedness is Blake's "London," in which "the youthful Harlots curse / Blasts the new-born Infants tear / And blights with plagues the Marriage hearse" (E 27).

He saw now from the outside what he before saw & felt from within
He saw that Los was the sole, uncontrolld Lord of the Furnaces. . . .
(J 8:23–26; E 151)

Seeing begins with the literal, the literary or artistic, as the Spectre stares into Los's "furnaces," where the imagination labors, and sees in Los's text the tortures of his own victims in the fallen world. This seeing leads to a movement out from his center, which in turn leads to insight: seeing then becomes metaphorical, imaginative, as what the Spectre sees is clearly internal. To see or understand that "Los was Lord" is a different sort of seeing from seeing "to Babel & Shinar," yet the verb remains the same. And in Blake, finally, these visionary acts *are* the same, as places themselves become recognized simultaneously as metaphorical states.

Donald Ault has observed:

> One of Blake's central purposes in constructing anti-Newtonian narrative was to create in his readers an experience of the bankruptcy of the kinds of assumptions about the interconnections in knowledge, perceptions, and reality which were embedded in the doctrine of *prisca sapientia*—the "ancient wisdom" which was believed by Newton and his contemporaries to have been revealed to Moses and to have been passed through the Hermetic Tablet and philosophers like Epicurus and the atomists.[64]

In Blake's narrative, we learn that, as with this movement from sight to insight, everything exists as analogy, or as an external form cast into the furnaces of Blake's language to be redeemed from that form. Thus, the metaphorical act from one perspective is incarnational: like the "tent and tabernacle of forgiveness," all words viewed metaphorically embody Jesus, since Jesus is not so much the object of sight as he is imaginative or polyvalent seeing (or we might say that the way of seeing defines the object of sight). Given the fallen state, however, the word must first exist

---

64. "Incommensurability and Interconnection in Blake's Anti-Newtonian Text," *Studies in Romanticism* 16 (1977), pp. 277–78.

on the page before us, must be made present to the corporeal eye, before it can be seen by the imaginative and thus "annihilated" as that which is separate. It is then burned away as a perspective that defines us. The word, like Jesus (or *as* Jesus), must "assume flesh, and dwell among us." It must, in Blake's terms, "take on the Satanic Body" (J 90:38; E 250), which is itself the analogy, the outward form, or the Babel printed on the page before us.

This error of an apparently separate world (or word) must be seen to be revealed, and this seeing begins with the corporeal eye. We grasp the book with the hand, enter its word on "Wings of thought" as we recognize the metaphor, and in that recognition grasp metaphorically, imaginatively: the two acts of grasping become one as that book now lives and dwells within us, and we within it. We can still split the metaphorical act into inner and outer, into spiritual and physical, or into figurative and literal, but no longer need do so and no longer need treat one as "real" and the other as a "phantom." We cross over, experiencing in the act a form of death, a letting go of our separate self. Coleridge, we recall, noted that imagination "dissolves, dissipates, in order to reunite"; Ray Hart glosses this action:

> What active imagination dissolves is the "givenness" of the delineated object with respect to the focalized limits of its putative self-presentation. It wrests the "thing" out of its customary context, taken for granted by the perceiver or reasoner, and puts it in an alien (to everyday mentality) context that is however its natural habitat. . . . In the dissolving action of imagination the world is not destroyed or displaced but rather is allowed to appear in its primal rapport with the self.[65]

Incarnation, then, is simultaneously crucifixion, as the Word is pinned to a fallen, dead tree (or printed into paper). It is in this sense that the Word "offers itself up"; it is available, that is, to be "seen through." But for Blake, we recall, to see through the word also means to see by means of: it is not the word that

---

65. Hart, *Unfinished Man*, p. 246.

moves but the mind. Jesus or the metaphoric language is there so that we may "become what we behold."

A reader of the New Testament, like the reader of *Jerusalem*, can reject this metaphorical language, can "turn his back on the Divine Vision" like Albion and call it "a Phantom of the overheated brain" (J 4:24; E 146), or he can enter into it as he would a house or temple or city, finding within it[66] that "immense world of delight," which he simultaneously recognizes as existing within himself, or as himself, since it is a creation of his own imagination. At this point, as we have just seen, a "last judgement" passes over him. He recognizes in the outward, separate form (Jesus or the word on the page) a reality or word that is the true definition, boundary, or circumference for himself or herself. That apparently external object, the work of William Blake, is found to be our own, to be us. Inner and outer vanish except as imaginative categories, like "spaces" and "times."

So that which is offered up, we discover, is also raised up: resurrected. Yet the visible language, each word, existing in a powerful physical state on the plate of Blake's text, does not disappear into an "allegorical abode where existence hath never come" (*Europe* 5:7; E 62); the word is the image and remains that image. We enter into it as Blake requests of us and find that it has also entered us: "I am in you and you in me, mutual in love divine" (J 4:7; E 146). The word is the end of the golden string that leads us into Jerusalem, a place and poem with no copyright, no owner.[67]

Once again the "temple" is seen metaphorically, less a place than a way of being and doing. Rather than being "too absurd and obscure," as the leading eighteenth-century rhetoricians claimed,[68] the metaphorical language of the Bible is itself the

---

66. See VLJ (E 560).
67. For another treatment of this notion of "entering into" Blake's texts but from a Lacanian perspective, see Mark Bracher's "Rouzing the Faculties: Lacanian Psychoanalysis and the Marriage of Heaven and Hell in the Reader," in Dan Miller, ed., *Critical Paths*, pp. 168–203.
68. See Victor Harris, "Allegory to Analogy in the Interpretation of Scriptures," *Philological Quarterly* 45 (1966), esp. pp. 17–22. Scripture, Bolingbroke

thread that leads us through the gates, because metaphor demands an interpretation that connects and brings to life what before was divided and dead. "Metaphor and symbol," Hart argues, "serve to carry over into consciousness the carrying over between things, and between things and the self, in their very being."[69]

Blake will deny that this imaginative truth is in any sense disembodied, vague, or undefinable by language. Nothing is stripped away from the world, no husk is removed; it is instead another way of seeing that has been revealed to us. The word is left not just on the page but in the mind, clear and definite. It has still a "bounding outline," a form unique to itself (as in the words *tree, rock, water*), and in its form it remains a manifestation or representation of "what eternally exists": of Jesus, the Logos. What these words refer to—tree, for example, or earth—is not an external object but that object as a living part of the human world. Tree is tree still but it is tree as an aspect of us, a part of all that we are, growing, blossoming, decaying.

Yeats thought of Blake as a literalist of the imagination, and he was right. This literalness is part of the point of the beauty of Blake's physical creation, the hard physical labor of the engraver, painter, book maker. We *see* words in Blake; each word as word is itself art, while also being part of a larger whole that, taken together, is a single identity called by Blake "Jerusalem," itself (herself) the embodiment of the "Divine Imagination." The image the actual word casts is real in Blake; it is its own self always, maintaining its own identity through its firm, bounding lines. Even so, that identity constantly changes in shape; one

---

complained in 1752, is "too absurd and obscure to provide a credible basis for religion." Matthew Tindal, two decades earlier (in 1732), stated, "Happy is the man, who is so far at least directed by the law of reason, and the religion of nature as to suffer no mysteries—no Allegories, no Hyperboles, no Metaphors, Types, Parables—to confound his understanding." Harris summarizes, "The irreducible, figural mystery, by which nature and spirit were joined . . . was patronized as a pleasant fable . . . or simply dismissed" (p. 22). See also Michael McCanles, "The Literal and the Metaphorical: Dialectic or Interchange," *PMLA* 91 (1976), pp. 279–80.

69. Hart, *Unfinished Man*, p. 247.

could almost say that any single use of a word in Blake is different from any other use of that word, since each is uniquely, manually drawn. Yet identity remains. Our words, Blake says (twice), are

> All Human Forms identified even Tree Metal Earth & Stone. all Human Forms identified, living going forth & returning wearied Into the Planetary lives of Years Months Days & Hours reposing And then Awaking into his Bosom in the Life of Immortality.
>
> (J 99:1–4; E 258)

As an apparently external construction, existing on the plates before us, Blake's book offers itself up like Jesus, the Divine Word who took on the "Satanic Body" in order to reveal that separate corporeal self as Satanic, as error. The poem from this perspective (as we saw with *Pearl* and *The Temple*) is intended to be broken down as a separate external form, a temple or "enclosed space" that encloses by excluding, and restored (like Jesus' metaphorical temple) as part of the reader through the imaginative expansive act of reading. This is Blake's crucifixion and resurrection, his sacraments and his last judgment, which "passes upon that Individual . . . whenever [he] Rejects Error & Embraces Truth" (E 562).

Yet one aspect of this truth is that this tension between alternative visions is itself eternal. Urizen himself is not annihilated or sent down to a fiery hell, and when the "fourfold Man" is reunited and "Milton & Shakspear & Chaucer" appear triumphantly in the "innumerable Chariots of the Almighty," that other demonic triumvirate, "Bacon & Newton & Locke," is likewise along for the ride (J 98:9; E 257). It is not silence and peace that reign eternally in the kingdom but, as one would expect of a bustling city, "intellectual War" and "Hunting,"[70] as individuals spend their days in a conversation in which "every Word & every Character was Human. . ." (J 98:35–36; E 258). The failure exists, as I have suggested, only when one vision takes itself as definitive, thereby splitting itself off from the unity that sees all perspectives as equally real.

70. *Four Zoas* IX, p. 139:9 (E 407); see also M 35:2–7 (E 135).

This ongoing dialectic between ways of seeing is one reason why it is not just in the fallen world that the city is "continually building, continually decaying" (J 72; E 227). The contraries are eternal, and so there must be a continual supply of food for thought as well as an endless supply of Devourers: each aspect, of course, being one element in the warfare that goes on in Blake's eternity. It is the warfare or tension, as Ricoeur says, that is inherent in the metaphor itself, an ongoing creation of the Divine Imagination that is read by Urizen in one way and by Urthona (or Los) in another. Both are simply aspects of Albion, and thus both are contained in a larger unity, a truth that Los alone can see in the fallen world, which is why he is praised for "keeping the Divine vision in times of trouble."

But in the fallen world, and especially in Blake's time, as in our own, Urizen's perspective threatens to become the sole defining one. He claims that the figurative is the fictive and the fictive unreal. Los and Blake see this differently and labor to make the reader to see differently. That is, they choose to include Urizen's perspective in a larger whole that remains fluid and permanently in tension. Blake thereby sees reality rather as John McPhee sees the continual rise and fall of land masses: the earth's apparent stability is simply a matter of limited perspective.

5
Conclusion
Toward the End of the Image

Not 'common speech'
a dead level
but the uncommon speech of paradise,
tongue in which oracles
speak to beggars and pilgrims:

not illusion but what Whitman called
'the path
between reality and the soul,'
a language
excelling itself to be itself,

speech akin to the light
with which at day's end and day's
renewal, mountains
sing to each other across the cold valleys.
    Denise Levertov, "A Common Ground"*

It is "the death of the soul," Augustine warns in the third book of *On Christian Doctrine*, to take literally what is intended as a sign.

> He who follows the letter takes figurative expressions as though they were literal and does not refer the things signified to anything else. . . . There is a miserable servitude of the spirit in this habit of taking signs for things, so that one is not able to raise the eye of the mind above things that are corporal and created to drink in eternal light.[1]

---

*Denise Levertov: *Poems 1960–1967*. Copyright © 1961 by Denise Levertov Goodman. Reprinted by permission of New Directions Pub. Corp.

1. Saint Augustine, *On Christian Doctrine*, trans. D. W. Robertson, Jr. (New

Conclusion

The Hebrews in particular, Augustine continues, did take "signs of spiritual things for the things themselves," confusing the earthly temple and city of Jerusalem, and the sacrifices conducted there, all of which are temporal, for the presence of God himself. Yet he also believes that they were being led in this way, like children, led, of course, to Jesus, "who condemned" the earthly sign as a way to induce his listeners to hear the word as figurative. They must see in temple, and in Jerusalem itself, a sign of a divine reality that he himself embodied, a love "greater than the temple" (Matt. 12:6), a love and kingdom that demanded not just attendance at Sabbath and sacrifice of a burnt offering but a complete remaking of a life. This love defined itself as sacrifice.

Augustine writes that in the first Church at Jerusalem a few heard this sacrificial word: "they sold everything they had and placed the proceeds 'before the feet of the Apostles' (Acts 4:35) . . . dedicating themselves to God as a new temple whose earthly image, which is the old temple, they were serving" (p. 85).

The new church, Augustine later claims, "is itself the land of the blessed, 'the land of the living.'" Yet this too is figurative: it is a city or land within each individual, possessed partially now, as she lives in the midst of the earthly city, to be gained fully at the end of time, in the "future age when there shall be a 'new heaven and a new earth' in which the unjust will not be able to dwell (p. 111)."[2]

Language, in which Augustine struggles to explain literal and figurative meanings, is itself sign. Human speech is like the Word of God, who comes into the world, "uttered forth" by God, so that all men might see, and seeing, believe. The sign exists "so that by means of corporal and temporal things we may comprehend the eternal and spiritual."[3]

York: Bobbs-Merrill, 1958), p. 84. All subsequent quotations are from this edition, unless otherwise noted.

2. See also *The City of God*, trans. L. Marcus Dods (New York: Modern Library, 1950), pp. 479–80.

3. On Augustine's theory of language as sign, see also Tzvetan Todorov,

End of the Image

Yet a sense of tension remains, given the fact that the ineffable cannot possibly be spoken by us; only God can utter the Divine Word, which is profoundly different from the words we speak, caught as they are within linear time. God's action is conducted within a timeless present, toward which we strive. Augustine comments:

> Have we spoken or announced anything worthy of God? Rather I feel that I have done nothing but wish to speak: if I have spoken I have not said what I wished to say. Whence do I know this, except because God is ineffable? If what I said were ineffable, it would not be said. And for this reason God should not be said to be ineffable, for when this is said something is said. And a contradiction in terms is created, since if that is ineffable which cannot be spoken, then that is not ineffable which can be called ineffable. This contradiction is to be passed over in silence rather than resolved verbally. (pp. 10–11)

In our world, we have no choice but to continue to labor in the vineyards, using the tools, including language, bestowed on us by God at the creation. Acting within the dimensions of time and space, which are the dimensions of nonidentity (each moment distinct from another, each place and person distinct), we strive to overcome these limits by means of the labor that is itself caught within the limits. As Eliot said, "Only through time/time is conquered." Of course for Eliot the paradigm for this overcoming of time is Jesus, who enters time to conquer time. Incarnate, His word and act share the properties of our words and acts. Yet as the embodiment of eternity, Jesus transcends those limits even as He lives and dies within them. He is raised from the dead, meaning, in this context, that who He is cannot be confined within the boundaries of nonidentity imposed by linear time and space. And he promises to us this same resurrection.

Theories of the Symbol (Ithaca, N.Y.: Cornell University Press, 1982), pp. 42–44. On Augustine's Greek dualism here—splitting language and the real, letter and spirit—and on his misinterpretation of Judaism, see Susan Handelman's *The Slayers of Moses: The Emergence of Rabbinic Interpretation in Modern Literary Theory* (Albany: State University of New York Press, 1982), esp. pp. 107–20.

To take one example: the parable of the pearl, as Paul Ricoeur comments, contains three verbs, "representing three 'moments'":

> He *found* a pearl of great price,
> He went *to sell* all that he had,
> He *bought* the pearl.

These moments, appearing in language as separate in time (and space), still bring into language "the time of the kingdom," represented here as "a sudden event, a reversal of all past experience, an engagement with others in a new future of action and history."[4] The parable exists inevitably within our fallen temporality, and yet through the temporal process it raises the possibility of illumination, including the simultaneity of these three distinct moments.

Out of time comes the timeless, as out of human history comes apocalypse, spelling the end, both goal and accomplishment, of human history.

As with any good book, the end of the Bible comes appropriately in the final chapter, with John's *Revelations*. Yet there are hints, foreshadowings, throughout, as there are of course in Blake's work, that revelation for any individual can come on any ordinary day, in any ordinary place. There is no need to wait one's turn, or stand in line, for the very notion of line, as *Pearl* reminds us, is faulty. When a line creates an infinite circle we are already home.

"The kingdom is like . . ." the parables often begin, and then a story is told. The story is secular, mundane, yet it contains elements that shock, surprise, and disorient the listener, in order, Ricoeur argues, to reorient. It attempts, that is, to make this kingdom *happen* to the listener, as if kingdom were not so much a place as an event, and an event, furthermore, that does not merely cause a turning about, or a new way of seeing, but is itself that turn.

Yet critics like Ricoeur, and more recently Sallie McFague,

---

4. Paul Ricoeur, "The 'Kingdom' in the Parables of Jesus," *Anglican Theological Review* 63 (1981), p. 168.

End of the Image

would in other respects agree with Augustine's definition of language as sign. Kingdom of God, they would argue, both "is" and "is not" in our language. The metaphorical, imaginative leap required by the paradox of the metaphor (and of the parables as a whole) indicates that the "is not" implied in the figure indicates that our language indirectly suggests a way of seeing (and of being) in the world defined in the Gospels as kingdom. Again, as in Augustine, to identify the ineffable with this literal image or any other image is finally idolatrous. Thus it must also be said that there is nothing magical about such images. Saying kingdom is no guarantee of the divine presence.

The point, it appears, is that the divine is not contained and is never containable within the bounds of time and space. It is in this sense that the kingdom is not in our language. Yet the divine manifests itself through, or by means of, the act of our language, through the labor we engage in each day. This is the meaning of sacrament and reveals sacrament as the end of human work.

Sacrament too is metaphor: the offering up we do ritually on Sunday simply reminds us of the goal of all our labor. In this there should be nothing inherently different about these rituals. *All* acts are potentially sacramental. Changing a child's diaper in the deep of the night, packing her lunch for school a few years later: here too God can be found. These too are means of offering ourselves up.

Pray without ceasing, Paul tell us; every act is prayer, is real presence.

It follows that nothing is left behind in this understanding of metaphor. Just as sacrament is made possible through the physical labor we offer up—bread, wine—so too is metaphor dependent on the "literal" that grounds it, just as this literal depends on the figurative for the "crossing over" to occur: the leap into connection.[5]

Metaphor by its nature is an event, albeit an imaginative one:

5. See Michael McCanles, "The Literal and the Metaphorical: Dialectic or Interchange," *PMLA* 91 (1976), p. 285.

it exists as an act of the mind, a paradoxical coupling of two distinct objects (words) creating a moment of simultaneity: "a miracle of rare device," as Coleridge describes Kubla Khan's "sunny pleasure dome with caves of ice." For a moment in time we find ourselves out of time, existing in an imaginative wonderland that feels like paradise. However, metaphor also reminds us constantly that it creates not a place of residency but a way of being. As act it embodies the new earth, even as it defies our attempts to make ourselves at home.

In *Metaphorical Theology* Sallie McFague comments that even Jesus himself must be seen not just as "parable of God" but as "metaphor of God." Jesus' own task, she claims, was iconoclastic: as sign he teaches that the old way of thinking about kingdom *was* idolatrous. "Is it possible," she asks, "to say that the heart of the drama of Jesus' life and death is the tension that it manifests between accepted ways of relating to God and to others *and* a new way that does not so much tell us about but *is* in all his words and deeds?" She then adds:

> Are his life and especially his death extravagant and radical, a shock and a scandal which, when encountered seriously, call into question the comfortable homes that our myths have built for us? Is Jesus himself the whisper that our presumed security rests on an earthquake fault and that only a radically different kind of security, one based on utter trust in God, will provide us with houses, albeit never "solid" ones, in which to live?[6]

We are to "look through" the story of Jesus, she concludes, in order to see and know this new way of being in the world, a new way that we identify with kingdom. This new way of seeing, and thus of being, which is made available through Jesus, is what is meant by a "believer."

6. Sallie McFague, *Metaphorical Theology: Models of God in Religious Language* (Philadelphia: Fortress Press, 1982), p. 51. Subsequent quotations are cited in the text. McFague extends these ideas in her more recent study, *Models of God: Theology for an Ecological, Nuclear Age* (Philadelphia: Fortress Press, 1987). On this question of idolatry, see also Paul Tillich's *Dynamics of Faith* (New York: Harper Colophon Books, 1957), pp. 51–52. "Faith," Tillich claims, "if it takes its symbols literally, becomes idolatrous! It calls something ultimate which is less than ultimate."

End of the Image

To be a human being is to interpret, to think of "this" as "that" . . . to think metaphorically. To be a believer is to follow the way of the parables, and Jesus as parable, to live with the tension between the kingdom and the world, never identifying the one with the other while aware of the transformation of the world by the kingdom. (65)

Kingdom, then, is a way of seeing. "A deeply metaphorical perspective such as that based on parable demands a way of being in the world characterized by a high degree of tension, relativity, iconoclasm, and change."[7]

Jesus' story is itself metaphorical, McFague claims, and thus intentionally iconoclastic. All attempts to identify him with the expected Davidic Messiah who would reign in the earthly Jerusalem are rejected by his acts, by his words, and finally by the sign of the cross. *Here* is your kingdom, the signs all say. Follow this figurative road to this figurative place. It is apparently this spiritual laboring that is, as Blake wrote, "to build Jerusalem."[8]

Kingdom, then, or this "new earth," has indeed come among us, full of grace and truth, and yet any attempt to locate it fails. No wonder that so many have felt that the greatest respect we can pay the divine is to be silent. Silence is a way of saying that kingdom, finally, is none of our doing. Silence is the great letting

---

7. McFague, *Metaphorical Theology*, p. 65. It is interesting to compare this analysis of the role of language in how we "see" and thus exist in the world to that of Jonathan Edwards, who also claimed, "The will follows perception's view of things rather than things themselves." The incarnation is the pivotal point in human history because for the first time man could "see" God, that is, perceive a new way of being in the world. And this new perception is made available, of course, through the Bible: the "Word of God." See Perry Miller, *Jonathan Edwards* (1949; reprint, New York: Meridian Books, 1959), p. 257, and also James Carse, *Jonathan Edwards and the Visibility of God* (New York: Charles Scribner's Sons, 1967), esp. pp. 93–94.

8. McFague's clam that Jesus is a "metaphor" has some affinity with Blake's argument against worshipping the dead Jesus on the cross. Such a belief may lead to the notion of an "atonement" that happens magically simply by saying that "Jesus died for the sins of the world." Instead, Jesus is to be seen as the ultimate sign of the way of God's own being and love, a sacrificial love that demands a reversal of our normal, self-centered vision of life. Thus Blake would agree with McFague's implication that the sacraments, like Jesus, are to be seen metaphorically. However, for Blake this metaphorical vision is itself "Divine Vision." Blake denies McFague's (and Ricoeur's, and Tillich's) "is not."

go into the boundaryless god, where conversation is not limited by the inability of speech to say more than one thing at a time. God's silence, after all, is not silent; it is instead the failure of our ears to hear.

Yet how many of us can spend a life in the labor of silence? Instead we must find our home in the continual "cross-biasing" that George Herbert endures, or like the dizzying, paradoxical conversations suffered by the dreaming *Pearl*-narrator and Albion. That, at least, is how kingdom must appear to us, for our logic "is a logic of equality, of equivalence," in which laws attempt to balance the crime with the punishment. But "the logic of God, the logic of Jesus, is quite another matter," Ricoeur claims. "This other logic is one of excess, of superabundance."[9] We have all been asleep, dreaming, these stories and poems tell us, mistaking figure for the literal, mistaking love for law (as Paul suggests), and thus misinterpreting our lives. It is metaphor's task to arouse us, for what needs reorienting is our imagination. Ricoeur again comments:

> Our will is our capacity to follow without hesitation the once chosen way, to obey without resistance the once-known law. Our imagination is the power to open us to new possibilities, to discover another way of seeing, or acceding to a new rule in receiving the instruction of the exception. As Ray Hart suggests in *Unfinished Man and the Imagination*, while the will is the intention to a specific project, the imagination is the intention of dominant direction. It is at the level of dominant direction that we are overtaken by the disorienting logic of Jesus.[10]

Kingdom, this logic teaches us, is like a story, which in turn is a way of being in the world. The parable stories illustrate the narrative that is also the Gospel as a whole: the story of Jesus, culminating in the cross and resurrection. This metaphorical (and literal) journey, this construction and destruction, leading to a startling and unexpected *rebuilding*, is what kingdom is: the new

---

9. Paul Ricoeur, "The Logic of Jesus, the Logic of God," *Anglican Theological Review* 62 (1979), p. 27.
10. Ricoeur, "Logic of Jesus," p. 39.

earth, where the divine dwells with us, or perhaps where the divine dwells *through* us, not fixed in any particular mountain or building yet available everywhere.[11] The infinite is, and now, as we participate in it.

The "Biblical Poetics" that I have been tracing is modeled on this paradoxical understanding, an understanding made available through metaphor. Metaphor here too is iconoclastic; it undermines its own image's apparent solidity, shattering the visible language in order to suggest that the signified is knowable, unnameable (as in *Pearl* or *The Temple*) or to reveal that "what is above is within," as in Blake, in which all reality is seen as imaginative.

Thus metaphors (and these poems) function like the Eucharist, another self-sacrificing sign, revealing in its nature as sign that it is intended to be broken. Again, the literal breaking is to be understood as a figure for one's own life. The Eucharist *is* Eucharist only through this interpretive breaking, to which the literal breaking of the bread by the priest points. The Eucharist (and thus the cross) is the goal, the destination of metaphor.

"Just as art leads us into a new world gradually through its participative structures," Stephen Happel writes, "so sacrament is not only a contrasting, overturning metaphor for our daily lives. They seduce us by their sights and sounds into participation; they confirm what is good, building upon it, and they overturn what is idolatrous and narcissist."[12] So indeed is the *Pearl* Dreamer "seduced . . . into participation" and led ultimately by

---

11. Belden Lane comments on the striking contrast between the Navajo sense that a particular place (near the southwest corner of Colorado) is inherently sacred and the Hebrew sense that "entry to a sacred place is always a matter of one's dynamic and ethical relationship to Yahweh alone. There is no unchangeable quality of holiness seen to reside statically in any given place." We may long for this, "but on gaining possession of the sanctuary we come quickly to presume upon its guaranteed mystery—only then to be driven from it in search of yet another place, another center of meaning." See *Landscapes of the Sacred: Geography and Narrative in American Spirituality* (New York: Paulist Press, 1988), pp. 128, 131.

12. "Worship as a Grammar of Social Transformation," in George Kilcourse, ed., *Proceedings* (Philadelphia: Catholic Theological Society of America, 1987), vol. 42, p. 85. The following quotations from Happel are from this essay.

this seduction to the sacraments, meaning not simply observing but participating, becoming that pearl, that round wafer, by offering up all he has and is. And so too does Herbert seduce, turning "delight into sacrifice," leading us again at last to the table where we become, as Happel says, "the world we would like to be." Happel concludes that

> participation in the Christian sacraments allows us to live, however gradually, however momentarily, the linguistic history we would like to make for ourselves. . . . [B]y taking up the symbolic presence of the life, death and resurrection of Christ in a ritual fashion, we become that history that we and God make for the world. (87)

In this poetic tradition it is not enough to say that "the way of the Cross" is metaphorical; metaphor *is* the way whereby the sign is intentionally broken in order to reveal the sign's true meaning, which is that breaking. The signifier here points to a signified not simply silent, nor simply absent, as is so often assumed by contemporary theorists. Here the signifier points to the cross, to Jesus, who is, the tradition claims, both signifier and signified, both way and truth. In his words and life he embodies kingdom, for kingdom is this wounded way of being, a way that we too are called to become.[13]

To see through this "parable of God" is to see by means of this sign, which says: I am not the sort of king you expected, and my kingdom is not the kingdom you think you are seeking. Thus the cryptic sayings and acts demand interpretation. They are signs referring continually to Jesus himself, who in turn is the sign of God, also demanding interpretation and also in this way denying any idolatrous reduction. He asks, Can you see by

---

13. As we have seen, McFague, following suggestions in Tillich (and following Ricoeur's theory of metaphor), qualifies this traditional understanding of Jesus *as* God, as both signifier and signified. In "metaphorical theology," she writes, "*no* finite thought, product or creature can be identified with God and this includes Jesus of Nazareth, who as parable of God both 'is and is not' God." Jesus *is* God, McFague suggests, in the same way that any metaphor speaks a figurative truth: "they point to a real, and assumed similarity between the metaphors and that to which they refer." Thus Jesus "tells us actually and concretely (though, of course, indirectly) about God's relationship to us" (*Metaphorical Theology*, p. 19).

means of me? Which means, Can you *be* by means of me? For it is not enough, as Albion learns, simply to understand this metaphorical principle in language, or even in Christ, as though it were still something other than us. We too are intended as metaphors. Our own lives must be broken on whatever cross we carry—and we all carry a cross.

But of course it is easier to forget. To awaken to the burden of our wounds is to be thrown again into this death, this panic and fear of our utter isolation, for this isolation, caused by our self-consciousness, is at heart the burden we carry. And yet this burden is also the way to glory: by living with our homelessness, living *inside* of it, we find that homelessness becomes our home: the Son of Man has nowhere to lay his head, and yet all the world is His. Claiming nothing, open to all, He contains, is all. And in this same vulnerability we too find our own rebirth: out of the hole, the wound that pierces us, we rise. All of our work lies in living inside this opening until, as Blake shows in *The Marriage*, what appeared as hell to us in our confinement is now conceived as heaven on earth. What felt like death is life.

* * *

Metaphor combines apparent disparities, and in doing so, critics claim, it alters us by changing the way we see. It is illogical in its defiance of apparent boundaries; if it is claimed as true, it is a truth of the imagination, and not of the world we normally see, in which a poem does not take the place of a mountain. Perhaps, after all, this imaginative truth is simply a "shrinking from / The weight of primary noon" as Wallace Stevens told us. Perhaps it is a "waking dream," and, as Paul de Man writes of Rousseau's metaphors, "that what Rousseau calls 'truth' designates, neither the adequation of language to reality, nor the essence of things shining through the opacity of words, but rather the suspicion that human specificity may be rooted in linguistic deceit."[14]

---

14. Paul de Man, "Theory of Metaphor in Rousseau's Second Discourse," in *Romanticism: Vistas, Instances, Continuities*, ed. David Thorburn and Geoffrey Hartman (Ithaca, N.Y.: Cornell University Press, 1973), p. 110.

Yet that we continue to be haunted by metaphor's gift, and perhaps never before as haunted as now, appears certain. De Man comments in a succinct footnote, "What is at stake is not the existence of an ethical, psychological, or theological discourse but their authority in terms of truth or falsehood." In philosophy, psychology, theology, and in literary theory (fields that are increasingly learning to cross-fertilize) individuals continue to explore this already well covered terrain, seeking to understand what figurative language is and does, seeking to ascertain its "truth or falsehood," the nature of its referentiality.[15]

Those who favor the assumption that metaphorical language does indeed tell us something new (and true) about our universe might well take heart from developments in the traditional sciences. A universe that once appeared to be stable, discrete, and accountable in rational, nonmetaphorical prose suddenly looks quite protean indeed, so that increasingly the paradoxical, the illogical, and the fantastic appear to be telling us the truth of our existence.[16]

Werner Heisenberg writes, in *Physics and Philosophy*, "The ontology of materialism rested upon the illusion that the kind of existence, the direct 'actuality' of the world around us, can be extrapolated into the atomic range. This extrapolation is impossible, however." It follows from this, Heisenberg claims, that if we wish to speak about this atomic range, we must find a different sort of language, different, that is, from the logical, Newtonian discourse:

> In the experiments about atomic events we have to do with things and facts, with phenomena that are just as real as any phenomena

---

15. De Man, "Theory of Metaphor," p. 112. This of course is nothing new; the skeptical position of de Man and others can be seen as a new variation of nominalism, whereby "the existence of the universal consists in an act of the understanding and it exists only as such. It owes its existence simply to the intellect: there is no universal reality corresponding to the concept." See Frederick Copleston, *A History of Philosophy*, vol. 3, part 1 (1953; reprint, Garden City, N.Y.: Image Books, 1963), p. 69.

16. It is also true of course, that these same "facts"—the "fact" of entropy, for example—can be used to justify a less than optimistic interpretation of life's

in daily life. But the atoms or the elementary particles themselves are not as real; they form a world of potentialities or possibilities rather than one of things or facts.

At the least we can say that in modern physics, new models, new metaphors, are needed, for "one had learned that the old concepts fit nature only inaccurately."[17]

Perhaps our metaphors and symbols, like these atomic particles, are "potentialities or possibilities," not "real," yet forcing us by their presence to reexamine what we mean by real. Perhaps it is as Blake once argued: everything possible to be believed is an image of truth.[18] Newton's image is vision, Blake wishes to remind us; it is metaphor. Its failure is its own inability to recognize this. Thus the poet's own use of metaphor forces us into a re-vision of our world, whereby what we thought of as disparate, isolated, and disconnected turns out to be otherwise.

Perhaps our metaphors are akin to the way one child explained myth: stories that are not true on the outside but are true on the inside.

* * *

What has been most thoroughly disconnected by Blake's time is subject and object, inside and outside, self and other. We are fallen creatures still, homeless and wandering, trying to build ourselves a home in or out of the world. Various artistic attempts at this are chronicled in a recent exhibit entitled "The Spiritual in Art: Abstract Painting, 1890–1985."[19] Looking at the development of Kandinsky, Mondrian, and others, one is struck by the slow disintegration of the world in their work. In painting after painting they approach and then reach abstraction, yet when seen chronologically it is clear that what was there in Mon-

---

ultimate direction, as a writer such as Thomas Pynchon suggests (in *Gravity's Rainbow*, for example, where entropy is a controlling metaphor).

17. Werner Heisenberg, *Physics and Philosophy: The Revolution in Modern Science* (1958; reprint, New York: Harper Torchbook, 1962), pp. 145, 186, 143.

18. *The Marriage of Heaven and Hell*, plate 8, in *The Complete Poetry and Prose of William Blake*, ed. David V. Erdman (Berkeley and Los Angeles: University of California Press, 1982), p. 37.

19. I saw this exhibit at the Museum of Contemporary Art in Chicago, May 1987.

drian's cubes, in Kandinsky's wild splashes of color and form, was nature still, but nature exploded, seen thoroughly into and through. What comes with abstraction is a sense of release and power, as if here the atom had first been unlocked and exploded. Looking at a series of Mondrian paintings one sees quite clearly how it was not sufficient to paint the landscape; the painter sees form and color purified, or stripped bare, until we arrive at last at geometry: cubes of color on a rectangular board. Here is your world, Mondrian says, meaning nothing disrespectful at all. Spirit is line, color, image. He has stood in another place and looked with other eyes.

Abstraction at last ends where Augustine ends—in silence. But whether this is the silence of God that speaks in a finer tone, silence like the blinding, blank white that yet includes all colors, or whether this is the silence of ultimate absence, Ahab's malevolent all-colorless atheism, depends perhaps on the point of view. Do we find in the desert nothing or everything?

Image remains, of course, as long as color and line remain, but we are clearly near the end of image here, as we are in such minimalist works in music as Steve Reich's lovely *Desert Music*, or in the haunting, Kafkaesque detective novels of Paul Auster.[20] Here, as we reach toward the next millennium, Blake's great conversation among the eternals seems to be approaching something closer to a steady electrical hum, like the sound we might hear in telephone wires were our ears acute enough to catch it.

20. See especially the first two volumes of his New York Trilogy, *The City of Glass* and *Ghosts* (Los Angeles: Sun & Moon Press, 1985, 1986), and, more recently, *Moon Palace* (New York: Viking, 1989). In one long scene from this novel, Auster portrays a famous artist who has disappeared in the desert and is in fact living in an abandoned cave, where he returns to his art, using up the few canvasses remaining to him and finally painting his masterpiece on the walls of the cave itself, only to leave it half finished when he runs out of paint. "No longer afraid of the emptiness around him . . . now he was able to feel its indifference as something that belonged to him, as much as he belonged to the silent power of those gigantic spaces himself." This is a world in which signs and names apparently have meaning but where the meaning is endlessly ambiguous, so multiple and complex as to defy meaning—and thus where it becomes impossible to decipher any ultimate meaning. It is a world where we are all orphans (like the novel's narrator), all homeless, and where we are subsequently free to shed identities and take on new ones at will.

End of the Image

Language, image, always by necessity audible, visible, appears to want to become invisible, to move toward silence.

This is understandable enough; part of the point of this book is to demonstrate how long a tradition this attempt to say the unsayable is, and how glorious such attempts can be even when apparently frustrated by the limitations of our languages. There is always that in us that wants to break free, explode the words, the images, and reach some preverbal heart, a Kristevan *chora* in which once again we are connected to the mother.[21] Floating, yet held: that sensation that comes in Kandinsky's work, in Chagall's, and later in Rothko's and others', as if here we really have seen through natural form to the elemental rhythms and shapes that make up our universe. We are with Eliot in his Quartets, dancing at the still point of the turning world, and with Yeats, who saw his own dancers spinning themselves into the vortex, free for a moment just to be the image they have created.

But I must admit: after hours among such images, viewing the Kandinskys and Mondrians, the Klees and Munchs, I am always happy to glance out to the street and see that Chicago is still there; the sun shines still on Ontario Street. I am ready to be back. I feel at such times as if I have been orbiting the planet, or been so far inside it that it ceases to be recognizable. These artists have metamorphized the world back into its basic particles of energy and light: a powerful experience, certainly, but one that leaves me eager to return. Like Dorothy, I had not known Kansas could look so good or the world so much like home.

All of this is a way of asking, What becomes of the earth in that moment when we pass through Jerusalem's gates? It is like pearls, the dreamer says, a city of gold and grace. It is like sitting and feeding, another sighs; it is wine and bread. Or it is endless talk, argument, debate, a final one claims, in which human words

---

21. Kristeva writes: "The *chora*, as rupture and articulations (rhythm), precedes evidence, verisimilitude, spatiality, and temporality. . . . The *chora* precedes and underlies figuration. . . . [Plato] calls this receptacle or *chora* nourishing and maternal, not yet unified in an ordered whole because deity is absent from it." *Revolution in Poetic Language* (New York: Columbia University Press, 1984), p. 26.

whirl, shine, change shapes and times. But each of these writers, with all of their differences, seems to agree with the parables: transformed, the world still has something significantly human about it. It is our home and in it our images finally can be all they really are: signs no more but the real thing.

If Blake could argue with twentieth-century artists (and perhaps he does), it might be with this loss of the human dimension to the divine. This loss recalls the importance of visible language, words that roll off the tongue like wine, that hit the ear like music. It is there whenever we hold a well-bound, thoughtfully constructed book, not just a "text" but a real living book, like the ones Blake made, one by one, engraving, coloring, printing, and all. Here is earth transformed but earth still, the way it comes to us in our dreams, with all the resonance and richness of those images that, when looked at closely enough, are seen to be pieces of us, aspects of our lives. Even the other people in the dream are finally us, as we are as well in theirs. Everything counts; every image means and is part of the whole that ultimately we are.[22]

"Mark my words well," Blake says repeatedly, with a verb craftily chosen, "they are for your eternal salvation." The mark, the engraver's physical labor, is to be repeated figuratively (and perhaps literally) by us. We mark these words with our own pens, engraving the image on our minds, and they save us by reconnecting us with all that appears to be other. Yet there is nothing otherworldly about this in Blake, and so little of the mystical. Blake's engagement with the political and social world of England and Europe was intense and ongoing; his search for transformative metaphors was a result of his engagement.

He would agree, I suspect, with a contemporary writer like

---

22. James Hillman writes: "Within the metaphorical perspective . . . nothing is more sure than the soul's own activity following its wayward inertia from insight to insight. . . . Thus the soul finds psyche everywhere, recognizes itself in all things, all things providing psychological reflection." See *Re-Visioning Psychology* (New York: Harper & Row, 1975), p. 154.

Carolyn Forché, who claims, "All language . . . is political; vision is always ideologically charged. . . . We are responsible for the quality of our vision; we have the say in the shaping of our sensibility. In the many thousand daily choices we make, we create ourselves and the voice with which we speak and work."[23] Forché's is a poetry of witness, as was Blake's, as was Jeremiah's. She formed that voice and vision by opening herself imaginatively to the world: by reading, observing, and living in places like El Salvador and working with individuals like Archbishop Oscar Romero. The way she sees and thus writes inevitably is altered by these experiences. Forché acknowledges the great difficulties of such a prophetic stance by quoting Neruda: "The blood of the children / flowed out onto the streets / like . . . like the blood of the children." Political reality swallows the transformative force of metaphor. Yet the power of Neruda's lines rises from its own acknowledged failure to transform: we see and are awed by hearing the silence in the voice of the poet as he struggles to get across, to connect, to speak the horror in such a way that we find ourselves together in community again, imaginatively healed of this act.

All we see is ourself, Blake reminds. The myths in that sense get it right: every object is populated; everything has soul, is soul. We might think that for writers like Forché and Blake the "natural" world is simply left behind. But is it really so far from the world Forché describes, or from Blake's world, to the one described by Barry Lopez, who discusses the close interrelationship between wolf and Indian? Lopez too asks us to rethink our understanding of metaphor:

> The sense of being Wolf that came over a Pawnee scout was not the automatic result of putting on a wolf skin. The wolf skin was an accouterment, an outward sign to the man himself and others who might see him that he was calling on his wolf power. It is hard for the Western mind to grasp this and to take seriously the

---

23. "El Salvador: An Aide-Memoire," *Granta* 8 (1983), p. 235.

notion that an Indian at times could be Wolf, could actually participate in the animal's spirit, but this is what happened. It wasn't being like a wolf; it was having the mind set: Wolf.[24]

Here too is an entering in with the world so intense that the individual takes on, becomes that other, and sees it at last as one's own self. Here taking care of the other becomes an act of self-preservation, since self embraces everything we see. Mythic living has no relation to leaving the world. Blake's goal, Thomas Vogler has written, "is not to escape 'Albions land: / Which is this earth of vegetation on which now I write' (*Milton* 14.40–41) but to experience it as a home, to be at home in it—which means to be creative, to be an artist, to labor in a material medium."[25]

What Vogler suggests, at least to my mind, is that we must reconnect with the earth in us, to see her not as other, not as deathly matter but as the embodiment of all our metaphors. We must see her, that is, as Jerusalem: the manifestation, the body, of Christ. "Mark my words well," we recall the poet's telling us; it is here or nowhere that we make our mark and find our salvation. Thus the manual laborer in Blake would agree at least in this with the manual laborer in Wendell Berry:

> The soul, in its loneliness, hopes only for "salvation." And yet what is the burden of the Bible if not a sense of the mutuality of influence, rising out of an essential unity, among soul and body and community and world? . . . The world is certainly thought of as a place of spiritual trial, but it is also the confluence of soul and body, word and flesh, where thoughts must become deeds, where goodness is to be enacted. This is the great meeting place, the narrow passage where spirit and flesh, word and world, pass into

---

24. *Of Wolves and Men* (New York: Scribner's Sons, 1978), p. 112. There is nothing naive or sentimental about this imaginative leap by the Indian, according to Lopez; the Indian may well kill the wolf, but in doing so he knows who it is he has killed; he sees that death as part of himself: he takes the wolf within him metaphorically and literally in the form of food. Lopez writes: "The death is mutually agreeable. The meat it produces has power, as though consecrated" (p. 95).
25. "Re: Naming MILTON," in Nelson Hilton and Thomas A. Vogler, eds., *Unnamed Forms: Blake and Textuality* (Berkeley and Los Angeles: University of California Press, 1986), p. 175.

End of the Image

each other. The Bible's aim, as I read it, is not the freeing of the spirit from the world. It is the handbook of their interaction.[26]

Earth is, in all of her loveliness, us. She is the stuff of our dreams, and in her we are at home, remembering always that home is imaginative activity, our own ongoing metamorphosis.[27]

* * *

Metaphor's meaning is akin to what the biologist Lewis Thomas calls a "biomythology." The "meaning of the stories" of bacteria, *Myxotricha paradoxa*, and other microorganisms "may be basically the same as the meaning of medieval bestiary," he claims, wherein two different species are "unnaturally" joined: the unicorn, the griffin, the sphinx. "There is a tendency for living things to join up, establish linkages, live inside each other, return to earlier arrangements, get along, whenever possible. This is the way of the world."[28]

Metaphor so often in the texts we have studied has the shape of a dream, as though the essence of metaphor were dream, or the essence of dream were metaphor: each refers to the other, appears to have its origin in the other. Each appears to teach that "Wrongness now means singleness. The constructs of right and wrong imply an either/or world, not the polysemous, polyvalent one of dreams and images. When we realize the inherent multiplicity of meaning in the image itself, we cannot force the dream into any single truth."[29]

Metaphor, we have seen, implies a break, a rupture, in the way we see ourselves in our world. Expressed broadly enough, it can even be argued that poetry, or poetic language (as Julia Kristeva defines this term), "confronts order at its most funda-

---

26. Wendell Berry, "The Body and the Earth," reprinted (from *The Unsettling of America*) in *Recollected Essays 1965-1980* (San Francisco: North Point Press, 1981), pp. 284-85.
27. Of course in Blake if earth is not us she is Vala, that illusion for the male of an external feminine form, and thus alluring, haunting, and forever unattainable.
28. *Lives of a Cell: Notes of a Biology Watcher* (New York: Viking Press, 1974), p. 126.
29. James Hillman, "Further Notes on Images," *Spring* (1978), p. 156.

mental level: the logic of language and the principle of the State."[30] Yet once overturned, what becomes of the world of the Law and the Temple? What, even, of the body, that flesh that Paul and Augustine so dearly wished to leave behind? Are the things of the earth good only as food for thought, images in dreams? Think of wolves hunting over snow, or the sight of an hawk over an island. Whales, bears, all those creatures that seem more than our words could ever suggest, and are more than our dreams of them, are, in fact, the coinhabitants of this world. Where do they all go when the dream ends and the world awakens from its ancient slumber?

But this is to reach the end of speculation, the place where world becomes a matter of pure wonder. It might just be that we are asking the wrong question entirely, seeing the problem in the wrong way. Our own vision is limited by our human circumstances; hard enough for most us to imagine truly life in a small town in Nicaragua or in the deserts of Africa; harder still to imagine how other creatures see this world. We know that death comes into the physical world; all objects break down, change, become something other, but we have little idea of what this means, except that as a metaphor it says (truly) how one thing passes and another becomes: sacrifice, metamorphosis, is the way of the world, and not just the physical, transitory world but the one that goes on eternally, the one that time does not contain but that goes on within and beyond time. So death itself is finally a metaphor as well and must be grasped, known, and loved not only as a single event, the "end of life," but as the necessary eternal act of giving over of the self, a never-ending opening of arms to embrace the other as ourselves, to contain and be contained.

Does the animal know the world this way? Have salmon any imagination? How apparently futile its final upstream struggle simply to spawn and die. From one perspective it is all vain, as Ecclesiastes says. And yet at our best we work as the salmon

---

30. *The Revolution in Poetic Language*, p. 80.

work, perhaps sensing that our daily tasks transform us, for better or worse, in minute invisible ways, alchemically. Day by day as we labor over words and figures, over bread or stone or clay, something goes on within us as well because our own work is the "point of contact between the outer and inner world." "It almost seems," Michael Donner writes, "that one couldn't say where the tool ends and where 'myself' begins."[31] Work is the place of meeting, even when we work alone.

At our best, these poets claim, we work from our own wounds, finding in them the source of our gifts. In great pain and joy we offer up the burden we carry in whatever form we can, whatever shapes our particular gifts tend to take. The gift, we have found, only matters as far as it is *us*, a true piece of who we are in our brokenness. It is and must be ourselves we offer: we are homeless, and it is this very truth we offer to the world again and again.

Yet in this letting go of all that holds us up we find ourselves at home. And perhaps we find at such moments that we no longer pray to Christ but pray *as* Christ. As Christ we pray without ceasing because labor itself has become prayer, a continual giving birth out of our own ceaseless death. Utterly present to the world at such moments, our labor is both inevitably in time and yet beyond time: a moment, as Blake wrote, that Satan cannot find. Timelessly present and total, we know ourselves as temple.

* * *

This is what Rilke calls "emerging at last from the violent insight," an emergence which leads him to "sing out jubilation and praise to assenting angels," not in spite of the great longing at the center of his life but *through* it. This is his work, this longing. Out of the wound comes song. He offers it up, lives within it as though it were sacred space, finding that

> where there had been
> just a makeshift hut to receive the music,

---

31. Michael Donner, "The Hand and the Tool," in *A Way of Working: The Spiritual Dimension of Craft*, ed. D. M. Dooling (1979; reprint, New York: Parabola Books, 1986), pp. 32–33.

> a shelter nailed up out of their darkest longing,
> with an entryway that shuddered in the wind—
> you built a temple deep inside their hearing.[32]

These "hours of pain," Rilke claims, "are really / our winter-enduring foliage . . . not only a season in time—, but are place and settlement, foundation and soil and home."[33] If we never face our essential homelessness we can never find ourselves at home. It is impossible to face life by turning our backs on death, Rilke explains. Instead we face life by facing death: seeing through death, by means of death, and so living that death. Only in this way do our labors become sacraments, temples "deep inside." Giving ourselves over to this crucial truth of life—how profoundly love is built on sacrifice and surrender—we find that "[w]e live in eternity while we live in time."[34]

There is no proof, yet we believe that something endures within and beyond the mortal act. To call this something "heaven" or "paradise" says so little to most of our ears, yet how much better can any of us do? We turn the soil in the spring, mark out the words with the engraver or computer keyboard, knowing that our labor is not the isolated act but has repercussions everywhere, both in the world apparently "out there" and in the world known by (self) consciousness as "in here." And maybe at some point we see the fallacy of this artificial separation of realms. One works on the land as one works on oneself. Blake's work inside Albion is simultaneously his laboring on his own body, his own mind and spirit, the nightmares and wounds his Spectre brings him, *and* it is his work on the body of England.

---

32. From *The Sonnets to Orpheus*, (I,1), in *The Selected Poetry of Rainer Maria Rilke*, trans. Stephen Mitchell. Copyright © 1982 by Stephen Mitchell. Reprinted by permission of Random House, Inc.

33. From *Duino Elegies* ("The Tenth Elegy"), in Mitchell, p. 205. Rilke wrote in a letter on February 17, 1914: "Sister, the sacrifice! The sacrifice is in the world. What is sacrifice? I believe it is nothing other than the boundless, no longer limitable resolve of a human being to reach his purest inner potential." See *Rilke and Benvenuta: An Intimate Correspondence*, trans. Joel Agee (New York: Fromm, 1987), p. 80.

34. Wendell Berry, *Standing By Words* (San Francisco: North Point Press, 1983), p. 90. Berry then adds, "It is only by imagination that we know this."

This is truly, as Wendell Berry notes, "to *live* in my subject, and to learn that living in one's subject is not at all the same as 'having' a subject. To live in the place that is one's subject is to pass through the surface. The simplifications of distance and mere observation are thus destroyed."[35]

Blake does not have a subject, in Berry's terms; he lives in his subject, knowing that land and city as part of who he is. And he comes to this knowledge precisely in his labor. He gets his hands on the world through his work and marries it to himself, loving the burden and the children it becomes:

> Thou seest the Constellations in the deep & wondrous Night
> They rise in order and continue their immortal courses
> Upon the mountains & in vales with harp & heavenly song
> With flute & clarion; with cups & measures filld with foaming wine.
> Glittring the streams reflect the Vision of beatitude,
> And the calm Ocean joys beneath & smooths his awful waves!
> These are the Sons of Los, & these the Labourers of the Vintage
> (M 25:66–26:1; E 123)

* * *

José Faur notes that in Jewish Biblical tradition, "Creation itself is . . . described as the writing of God":

> "In thy book," says the Psalmist to God, "all my members shall be written" (Ps. 139: 16); i.e., he shall become an integral part of creation, the Book of God. The Rabbis too, refer to "the letters with which the heaven and earth were created" (*Berakhot* 55a). We must therefore conclude, with Judah ha-Levi (ca. 1075–1141), that in Jewish thought "the writings of God are His creations and the words of God His writings." "Writing" is creation itself.[36]

The task of the reader of God's writing, Faur adds, is not to discover or unveil a static, Platonic truth (*aletheia*); instead the

---

35. "The Making of a Marginal Farm," in *Recollected Essays*, p. 337. José Faur suggests the final extension of these ideas by quoting Maxim Gorki, who "wrote that there are two classes of people, those who follow God and those who make God. Literary theology implies the latter." See Faur's essay, "God as a Writer: Omnipresence and the Art of Dissimulation" in *Religion and Intellectual Life* 6 (1989), p. 40.

36. Faur, "God as a Writer," p. 34.

reader too acts "as a writer and becomes finally the text itself." Through the labor of interpretation the student becomes Torah and so embodies the ongoing divine creation, as, for Blake, the reader enters and becomes Jerusalem "on wings of thought." The prison of time and space is indeed finished, yet creation is not, for Logos itself "is *dynamic* and creative; it does not depend on an ulterior order. Rather it establishes the order of things."[37] "We discover," M. C. Richards writes, "that what is being created is a single being: its apparent lives and deaths only the appearances of its metamorphosis."[38]

Perhaps the best that can be said is that although no outer form is final, something, an identity, does persist. "In Eternity one Thing never Changes into another Thing," Blake writes; "Each Identity is Eternal." Yet that identity can be seen in numerous ways, depending upon the perspective: "when distant they appear as One Man but as you approach they appear Multitudes of Nations" (VLJ; E 556–57). To the question, which is it, One or Multitude, Blake would of course say: both. Again, although "the Oak dies as well as the Lettuce. . . . Its Eternal Image & Individuality never dies. but renews by its seed." This cycle of renewal, Blake argues, is exactly how the truth of these Eternal identities has been maintained among us: "just [so] the Imaginative Image returns [by] the seed of Contemplative Thought" (VLJ; E 555–56). Here again the physical is an analogy for the mental world, where "All Things are comprehended in their Eternal Forms in the Divine body of the Saviour the True Vine of Eternity." Does the seed wonder where its own form goes when it bursts from its case and blossoms? Is blossom the goal, or is seed? Perhaps the world's form is filled eternally with an endless sacrifice, this coming and going, so that there is no end to this conversation.

37. Ibid., pp. 33–34. He distinguishes between the Logos of Plato, in which "the truth is already there," and that of Philo. "For the Hebrews," he states, "the truth cannot be 'dis-covered.' It demands a fundamental process of decoding and interpretation whereby the reader acts as a writer and becomes finally the text itself."

38. M. C. Richards, *Centering in Pottery, Poetry, and the Person* (Middletown, Conn: Wesleyan University Press, 1962), p. 29.

6
Epilogue

Silence remaind & every one resumd his Human Majesty
And many conversed on these things as they labour at the furrow
Saying: It is better to prevent misery, than to release from misery
It is better to prevent error, than to forgive the criminal:
Labour well the Minute Particulars, attend to the Little-ones:
And those who are in misery cannot long remain so long
If we do but our duty: labour well the teeming Earth.
                                      Jerusalem 55:47–53; E 205

All of this enormous work done by "The labourer of ages in the Valleys of Despair!" (J 83:52; E 242) is necessary, Blake says, because of the Urizen always within us who seeks "for a joy without pain, / For a solid without fluctuation." It was this same failure of vision that was responsible for the perspective maintained by the priests of the Pentateuch, a vision that located the divine in "one command, one joy, one desire, / One curse, one weight, one measure / One king, one God, one Law."[1] It is a vision that, nervous about centering the spiritual life on a potentially anarchic internal shift, where "The sacrifices of God are a broken spirit . . . and a contrite heart," tags onto the Psalm two extra verses for "clarification": "Do good in thy pleasure unto Zion: build thou the walls of Jerusalem. Then shalt thou be pleased with the sacrifices of righteousness, with burnt offering and whole burnt offering: then shall they offer bullocks upon thine altar" (Ps. 51:18–19).

But this vision will not do for the true Jerusalem, John says; there is "no temple therein: for the Lord God Almighty and the Lamb are the temple of it," and there is no need for sun and

---

1. Blake, *The Book of Urizen* 4:9–10, 38–40; E 71–72.

moon, "for the glory of God did lighten it, and the Lamb is the light thereof." In metaphor too does the *Pearl* Dreamer see it: "The self god was her lombe-lyghte, / The Lombe her lantyrne, wythouten drede" (1046–47). It is the city of the Lamb who, as in Herbert, serves up himself, and in that symbolic sacrifice becomes the light by which we see and act.

All metaphor, this language, and as such our way of saying all we cannot say. There is no temple, but light remains, and something recognizably human, understanding human in the broadest possible way in order to include all that the world holds. Place here is seen as act, what we call love, forgiveness, charity, which can only occur between individuals in relationship with each other. This is Jerusalem, Blake concurs, and is built in that "shift of the center of living" that Abraham Heschel describes, "from self-consciousness to self-surrender."[2] Because in that shift, Blake claims, in his own version of a sacramental theology, all that we now know of earth, "even Tree Metal Earth & Stone," will be identified as "Human Forms," utterances, we might say, of the Divine Logos, of whom all of us are members. Altars, temples, gems, and cities are all human forms, part of an age-old conversation. What we now know as bread and wine is, like all else, a part of our dream, a version of the living bread and wine that exists as a word uttered in Eternity, "living going forth and returning wearied . . . reposing / And then Awakening into his Bosom in the life of Immortality" (J 99:1–4; E 258). These are all forms of forgiveness, the Word continually going forth. The light that shines from them comes from the city of our dreams, into which we awaken when we throw ourselves into the source of their radiance, shining through our fallen forms. Like Albion, we must disappear into the poem we have dreamed.

2. Heschel, "Prayer as Discipline," in *The Insecurity of Freedom: Essays on Human Existence* (New York: Farrar, Straus & Giroux, 1966), p. 255.

"The End of the Song of Jerusalem"
Plate 99 from Blake's *Jerusalem*; reproduced by Courtesy of the Trustees of the British Museum.

Bibliography

Adams, Hazard. "Blake, Jerusalem, and Symbolic Form." *Blake Studies* 7 (1975): 143–66.
———. *Philosophy of the Literary Symbolic.* Tallahassee: University Presses of Florida, 1983.
Altizer, Thomas J. J. *Descent into Hell: A Study of the Radical Reversal of the Christian Consciousness.* New York: Seabury Press, 1979.
———. *History as Apocalypse.* Albany: State University of New York Press, 1985.
———. *Total Presence: The Language of Jesus and the Language of Today.* New York: Seabury Press, 1980.
Andrew, Malcolm, and Ronald Waldron, eds. *The Poems of the Pearl Manuscript.* Berkeley: University of California Press, 1979.
Asals, Heather A. R. *Equivocal Predications: George Herbert's Way to God.* Toronto: University of Toronto Press, 1981.
Auerbach, Erich. *Scenes from the Drama of European Literature.* New York: Meridian Books, 1959.
———. *Literary Language and Its Public In Late Latin Antiquity and in the Middle Ages.* New York: Pantheon Books, Bollingen Series LXXIV, 1965.
Augustine, Saint. *The City of God.* Trans. Marcus Dods. New York: Modern Library, 1950.
———. *On Christian Doctrine.* Trans. D. W. Robertson. New York: Bobbs-Merrill, 1958.
Ault, Donald. "Incommensurability and Interconnection in Blake's Anti-Newtonian Text." *Studies in Romanticism* 16 (1977): 277–303.
———. *Visionary Physics: Blake's Response to Newton.* Chicago: University of Chicago Press, 1974.
Auster, Paul. *The City of Glass.* Los Angeles: Sun & Moon Press, 1985.
———. *Ghosts.* Los Angeles: Sun & Moon Press, 1986.
———. *Moon Palace.* New York: Viking Press, 1989.
Becker, Ernst. *The Denial of Death.* New York: Free Press, 1973.
Bentley, G. E., Jr. *Blake Records.* Oxford: Clarendon Press, 1969.
Berman, Morris. *Coming to Our Senses: Body and Spirit in the Hidden History of the West.* New York: Simon and Schuster, 1989.
Berry, Wendell. *Recollected Essays 1965–1980.* San Francisco: North Point Press, 1981.
———. *Standing by Words.* San Francisco: North Point Press, 1983.

Blake, William. *The Complete Poetry and Prose of William Blake*. Rev. ed. Ed. David V. Erdman. Berkeley: University of California Press, 1982.
Blenkner, Louis. "The Theological Structure of *Pearl*." *Traditio* 24 (1968): 43–75.
Bloch, Chara. *Spelling the Word: George Herbert and the Bible*. Berkeley: University of California Press, 1985.
Bonaventura, Saint. *The Mind's Road to God*. Trans. George Boas. New York: Bobbs-Merrill, 1953.
Bracher, Mark. *Being Form'd: Thinking through Blake's Milton*. Barrytown, N.Y.: Station Hill Press, 1985.
Brown, Raymond E., Joseph A. Fitzmeyer, and Ronald E. Murphy, eds. *The Jerome Biblical Commentary*. Englewood Cliffs, N.J.: Prentice Hall, 1958.
Carr, Stephen Leo. "Visionary Syntax: Nontyrannical Coherence in Blake's Visual Art." *Eighteenth Century* 22 (1981): 222–48.
———. "William Blake's Print-Making Process in *Jerusalem*." *ELH* 47 (1980): 520–41.
Carruthers, Mary J., and Elizabeth D. Kirk, eds. *Acts of Interpretation: The Text in Its Contexts 700–1600*. Norman, Okla.: Pilgrim Books, 1982.
Carse, James. *Jonathan Edwards and the Visibility of God*. New York: Charles Scribner's Sons, 1967.
Chang, Chung-yuan. *Creativity and Taoism: A Study of Chinese Philosophy, Art and Poetry*. New York: Harper & Row, 1970.
Charles, Amy. *A Life of George Herbert*. Ithaca, N.Y.: Cornell University Press, 1977.
Collis, A. S. *The Profession of Letters*. London: Routledge and Sons, 1928.
Copleston, Frederick. *A History of Philosophy*. Vol. 3, pt. 1. 1953. Reprint. Garden City, N.Y.: Image Books, 1963.
Corngold, Stanley. *The Fate of the Self*. New York: Columbia University Press, 1986.
Countryman, L. William. *Dirt, Greed and Sex: Sexual Ethics in the New Testament and Their Implications for Today*. Philadelphia: Fortress Press, 1988.
Crawford, John R. *The Pearl*. San Francisco: Grabhorn-Hayem, 1967.
Damrosch, Leopold. *Symbol and Truth in Blake's Myth*. Princeton, N.J.: Princeton University Press, 1980.
Davenport, W. A. *The Art of the Gawain-Poet*. London: University of London/Athlone Press, 1978.
De Man, Paul. *Blindness and Insight*. 1971. Rev. ed. Minneapolis: University of Minnesota Press, 1983.
Derrida, Jacques. *Margins of Philosophy*. Trans. Alan Bass. Chicago: University of Chicago Press, 1982.
———. *Writing and Difference*. Trans. Alan Bass. Chicago: University of Chicago Press, 1978.
Dodd, C. H. *The Parables of the Kingdom*. New York: Charles Scribner's Sons, 1961.

Dooling, D. M., ed. *A Way of Working: The Spiritual Dimension of Craft.* 1979. Reprint. New York: Parabola Books, 1986.

Dougherty, James. *The Five Square City: The City in the Religious Imagination.* Notre Dame, Ind.: University of Notre Dame Press, 1980.

Dunne, John S. *The Way of All the Earth: Experiments in Truth and Religion.* New York: Macmillan Publishing Co., 1972.

Eaves, Morris. *William Blake's Theory of Art.* Princeton, N.J.: Princeton University Press, 1982.

Ebeling, Gerhard. *The Nature of Faith.* Trans. Ronald Gregor Smith. Philadelphia: Fortress Press, 1961.

Eliot, T. S. *Four Quartets.* London: Faber and Faber, 1944.

Ellul, Jacques. *The Meaning of the City.* Trans. Dennis Pardee. Grand Rapids, Mich.: William B. Eerdmans Publishing Co., 1970.

Emert, Joyce Rogers. "Pearl and the Incarnate Word: A Study in the Sacramental Nature of Symbolism." Ph.D. diss., University of New Mexico, 1969.

Endicott, Annabel M. "The Structure of George Herbert's *Temple*: A Reconsideration." *University of Toronto Quarterly* 34 (1965): 226–37.

Erdman, David. *Prophet Against Empire.* 1954. Reprint. Garden City, N.Y.: Anchor Books, 1969.

Faur, José. "God as a Writer: Omnipresence and the Art of Dissimulation." *Religion & Intellectual Life* 6 (1989): 31–43.

———. *Golden Doves with Silver Dots: Semiotics and Textuality in Rabbinic Tradition.* Bloomington: Indiana University Press, 1986.

Ferber, Michael. *The Social Vision of William Blake.* Princeton, N.J.: Princeton University Press, 1985.

Ferguson, Margaret W. "Saint Augustine's Region of Unlikeness: The Crossing of Exile and Language." *Georgia Review* 29 (1975): 842–64.

Field, Rosalind. "The Heavenly Jerusalem in *Pearl.*" *Modern Language Review* 81 (1986): 7–17.

Fish, Stanley. *The Living Temple: George Herbert and Catechizing.* Berkeley and Los Angeles: University of California Press, 1972.

———. *Self-Consuming Artifacts: The Experience of Seventeenth Century Literature.* Berkeley: University of California Press, 1972.

Forché, Carolyn. "El Salvador: An Aide-Memoire." *Granta* 8 (1983): 221–37.

Foucault, Michel. "Dream, Imagination, and Existence." Trans. Forrest Williams. *Dream and Existence*, a Special Issue from the *Review of Existential Psychology and Psychiatry* 19 (1984–85).

Freccero, John, ed. *Dante: A Collection of Critical Essays.* Englewood Cliffs, N.J.: Prentice-Hall, 1965.

———. "The Fig Tree and the Laurel: Petrarch's Poetics." *Diacritics* 5 (1975): 34–40.

Frosch, Thomas R. *The Awakening of Albion.* Ithaca, N.Y.: Cornell University Press, 1974.

Frye, Northrop. *Anatomy of Criticism.* 1957. Reprint. New York: Atheneum, 1969.

———. *Fearful Symmetry*. Princeton, N.J.: Princeton University Press, 1947.

Funk, Robert. *Language, Hermeneutic and the Word of God: The Problem of Language in the New Testament and Contemporary Theology*. New York: Harper & Row, 1966.

Gatta, John, Jr. "Transformation Symbolism and the Liturgy of the Mass in Pearl." *Modern Philology* 71 (1973–74): 243–56.

Gleckner, Robert. "Most Holy Forms of Thought: Some Observations on Blake and Language." *ELH* 41 (1974): 555–77.

———. "Romanticism and the Self-Annihilation of Language." *Criticism* 18 (1976): 173–89.

Gordon, E. V., ed. *Pearl*. Oxford: Clarendon Press, 1953.

Halewood, William. *The Poetry of Grace: Reformation Themes and Structures in English Seventeenth Century Poetry*. New Haven: Yale University Press, 1970.

Hamlin, Cyrus. "The Temporality of Selfhood: Metaphor and Romantic Poetry." *New Literary History* 6 (1974): 169–93.

Handelman, Susan A. *The Slayers of Moses: The Emergence of Rabbinic Interpretation in Modern Literary Theory*. Albany: State University of New York Press, 1982.

Happel, Stephen. "Worship as a Grammar of Social Transformation." In *Proceedings*, ed. George Kilcourse. Philadelphia: Catholic Theological Society of America, 1987. Vol. 42, 60–87.

Harman, Barbara Leah. *Costly Monuments: Representations of the Self in George Herbert's Poetry*. Cambridge, Mass.: Harvard University Press, 1982.

———. "The Fiction of Coherence: George Herbert's 'The Collar.'" *PMLA* 93 (1978): 865–77.

———. "George Herbert's Affliction (I): The Limits of Representation." *ELH* 44 (1977): 267–85.

Harris, Victor. "Allegory to Analogy in the Interpretation of Scriptures." *Philological Quarterly* 45 (1966): 1–23.

Hart, Ray L. *Unfinished Man and the Imagination*. New York: Herder and Herder, 1968.

Hattingberg, Magda von, ed., and Joel Agee, trans. *Rilke and Benvenuta: An Intimate Correspondence*. New York: Fromm, 1987.

Hawkins, Peter S., and Anne Howland Schotter, eds. *Ineffability: Naming the Unnameable from Dante to Beckett*. New York: AMS, 1984.

Heisenberg, Werner. *Physics and Philosophy: The Revolution in Modern Science*. 1958. Reprint. New York: Harper Torchbook, 1962.

Herbert, George. *The English Poems of George Herbert*. Ed. C. A. Patrides. London: J. M. Dent, 1974.

———. *The Works of George Herbert*. Ed. F. E. Hutchinson. Oxford: Clarendon Press, 1941.

Herrstrom, David Sten. "Blake's Transformations of Ezekiel's Cherubim Vision in Jerusalem." *Blake: An Illustrated Quarterly* 15 (1981): 64–77.

Bibliography

Heschel, Abraham. *The Insecurity of Freedom: Essays on Human Existence*. New York: Farrar, Straus & Giroux, 1966.
Hill, Christopher. *The Century of Revolution: 1603-1714*. Edinburgh: Thomas Nelson, 1961.
Hill, John. "Middle English Poets and the Word: Notes Toward an Appraisal of Linguistic Consciousness." *Criticism* 16 (1974): 153-69.
Hillman, James. *Re-visioning Psychology*. New York: Harper & Row, 1975.
Hilton, Nelson. *Literal Imagination: Blake's Vision of Words*. Berkeley and Los Angeles: University of California Press, 1983.
Hilton, Nelson, and Thomas A. Vogler, eds. *Unnamed Forms: Blake and Textuality*. Berkeley and Los Angeles: University of California Press, 1986.
Hugh of St. Victor. *On the Sacraments of the Christian Faith (De Sacramentis)*. Trans. Roy De Ferrari. Cambridge, Mass.: Medieval Academy of America, 1951.
James, David E. "Blake's *Laocoon*: A Degree Zero of Literary Production." *PMLA* 98 (1983): 226-34.
Jantzen, Grace. *God's World, God's Body*. Philadelphia: Westminster Press, 1984.
Johnson, Mark. *The Body in the Mind: The Bodily Basis of Meaning, Imagination and Reason*. Chicago: University of Chicago Press, 1987.
Jung, Carl. *Aion: Researches into the Phenomenology of the Self*. Trans. R. F. C. Hull. 1959. Rev. ed. Princeton, N.J.: Princeton University Press, 1979.
―――. *Psychology and Religion: West and East*. 2d Ed. Vol. 11 of the *Collected Works of C. G. Jung*. Trans. R. F. C. Hull. Princeton, N.J.: Princeton University Press, 1969.
Jungmann, Joseph A. *The Mass of the Roman Rite*. New York: Benziger Brothers, 1951.
Kean, P. M. *The Pearl: An Interpretation*. New York: Barnes and Noble, 1967.
Kerrigan, Will. "Ritual Man: On the Outside of Herbert's Poetry." *Psychiatry* 48 (1985): 69-82.
Klauser, Theodore. *A Short History of the Western Liturgy*. London: Oxford University Press, 1969.
Klemm, David E. "'This is My Body': Hermeneutics and Eucharistic Language." *Anglican Theological Review* 64 (1982): 293-310.
Krieger, Murray. "A Waking Dream." In *Allegory, Myth and Symbol*, ed. Morton Bloomfield. Cambridge, Mass.: Harvard University Press, 1982, 1-22.
―――. *Poetic Presence and Illusion: Essays in Critical History and Theory*. Baltimore: Johns Hopkins University Press, 1979.
Kristeva, Julia. *Revolution of Poetic Language*. New York: Columbia University Press, 1977.
Lane, Belden. *Landscapes of the Sacred: Geography and Narrative in American Spirituality*. New York: Paulist Press, 1988.

Larson, Kay. *New Work New York*. Lawrence, Kans.: Spencer Museum of Art, 1988.
Lewalski, Barbara Kiefer. *Protestant Poetics and the Seventeenth Century Religious Lyric*. Princeton, N.J.: Princeton University Press, 1979.
Lussier, Mark. "'Vortex' as Philosopher's Stone: Blake's Textual Mirrors and the Transmutation of Audience." *New Orleans Review* 13 (1986): 40–50.
Martin, F. David. *Art and the Religious Experience: The "Language" of the Sacred*. Lewisburg, Pa.: Bucknell University Press, 1972.
Martz, Louis. *The Poetry of Meditation: A Study in English Religious Literature of the Seventeenth Century*. New Haven: Yale University Press, 1954.
Marx, Karl. *Early Writings*. Trans. R. Livingstone and G. Benton. Harmondsworth: Penguin, 1975.
Mazzeo, Joseph Anthony. *Renaissance and Seventeenth Century Studies*. New York: Columbia University Press, 1964.
McCanles, Michael. "The Literal and the Metaphorical: Dialectic or Interchange." *PMLA* 91 (1976): 279–90.
McCloskey, Mark, and Paul Murphy, trans. and eds. *The Latin Poetry of George Herbert: A Bilingual Edition*. Athens: Ohio University Press, 1965.
McClung, William Alexander. *The Architecture of Paradise: Survivals of Eden and Jerusalem*. Berkeley and Los Angeles: University of California Press, 1983.
McFague, Sallie. *Metaphorical Theology: Models of God in Religious Language*. Philadelphia: Fortress Press, 1982.
———. *Models of God: Theology for an Ecological, Nuclear Age*. New York: Paulist Press, 1987.
Merton, Thomas. *Bread in the Wilderness*. New York: New Directions, 1953.
Miller, Dan. "Blake's Allusions: *Jerusalem* 86." *New Orleans Review* 13 (1986): 22–33.
Miller, Dan, Mark Bracher, and Donald Ault, eds. *Critical Paths: Blake and the Argument of Method*, Durham, N.C.: Duke University Press, 1987.
Miller, Perry. *Jonathan Edwards*. 1949. Reprint. New York: Meridian Books, 1959.
Milroy, James. "*Pearl*: The Verbal Texture and the Linguistic Theme." *Neophilologus* 55 (1971): 195–208.
Mitchell, W. J. T. "Visible Language: Blake's Wond'rous Art of Writing." In *Romanticism and Contemporary Criticism*, ed. Morris Eaves and Michael Fischer. Ithaca, N.Y.: Cornell University Press, 1986, 46–95.
Mott, Michael. *The Seven Mountains of Thomas Merton*. Boston: Houghton Mifflin, 1984.
Mukarovsky, Jan. *The Word and Verbal Art*. Ed. and trans. John Burbank and Peter Steiner. New Haven: Yale University Press, 1977.

Muscatine, Charles. *Poetry and Crisis in the Age of Chaucer*. Notre Dame, Ind.: University of Notre Dame Press, 1972.
Nasr, Seyyed Hossein. Interview with Jeffrey P. Zaleski. *Parabola* XIII (Spring 1988): 24–35.
Nelson, Cary. *The Incarnate Word*. Urbana: University of Illinois Press, 1973.
Nolan, Barbara. *The Gothic Visionary Perspective*. Princeton, N.J.: Princeton University Press, 1977.
Nuttall, A. D. *Overheard by God: Fiction and Prayer in Herbert, Milton, Dante and St. John*. London: Methuen, 1980.
Otto, Rudolf. *The Idea of the Holy*. Trans. John Harvey. New York: Oxford University Press, 1923.
Pahlka, William. *Saint Augustine's Meter and George Herbert's Will*. Kent, Ohio: Kent State University Press, 1987.
Patrick, J. Max, and Alan Roper. *The Editor as Critic and the Critic as Editor*. Los Angeles: University of California, William Andrew Clark Memorial Library, 1973.
Paz, Octavio. *The Bow and the Lyre*. Trans. Ruth L. C. Simms. Austin: University of Texas Press, 1973.
Perrin, Norman. *Rediscovering The Teaching of Jesus*. New York: Harper & Row, 1967.
Petroff, Elizabeth. "Landscape in *Pearl*: The Transformation of Nature." *Chaucer Review* 16 (1981): 181–93.
Pettit, Norman. *The Heart Prepared: Grace and Conversion in Puritan Spiritual Life*. New Haven: Yale University Press, 1966.
Power, David N. *Unsearchable Riches: The Symbolic Nature of Liturgy*. New York: Pueblo, 1984.
Powers, Joseph M. *Eucharistic Theology*. New York: Seabury Press, 1967.
Punter, David. "Blake: Creative and Uncreative Labour." *Studies in Romanticism* 16 (1977): 535–61.
Ragland-Sullivan, Ellie. *Jacques Lacan and the Philosophy of Psychoanalysis*. Urbana: University of Illinois Press, 1986.
Rahner, Karl. *Theological Investigations IV: More Recent Writings*. Trans. Kevin Smyth. New York: Seabury Press, 1974.
Richards, M. C. *Centering in Pottery, Poetry, and the Person*. Middletown, Conn: Wesleyan University Press, 1962.
Ricoeur, Paul. *Interpretation Theory: Discourse and the Surplus of Meaning*. Fort Worth: Texas Christian University Press, 1976.
———. "The 'Kingdom' in the Parables of Jesus." *Anglican Theological Review* 63 (1981): 165–69.
———. "The Logic of Jesus, the Logic of God." *Anglican Theological Review* 62 (1979): 37–41.
———. *The Rule of Metaphor*. Trans. Robert Czerny. Toronto: University of Toronto Press, 1977.
———. "The Specificity of Language." *Semia* 4 (1975): 107–45.
Rilke, Rainer Maria. *The Selected Poetry of Rainer Maria Rilke*. Ed. and trans. Stephen Mitchell. New York: Random House, 1984.

Roudiez, Leon. "Readable/Writable/Visible." *Visible Language* 12 (1978): 231–44.
Rubey, Daniel. "The Poet and the Christian Community: Herbert's Affliction Poems and the Structure of *The Temple*." *Studies in English Literature* 20 (1980): 105–23.
Sacks, Sheldon, ed. *On Metaphor*. Chicago: University of Chicago Press, 1979.
Schwartz, Rudolph. *The Church Incarnate: The Sacred Function of Christian Architecture*. Chicago: Regnery Co., 1958.
Shaviro, Stephen. "'Striving with Systems': Blake and the Politics of Difference." *Boundary 2*, no. 10 (1982): 229–50.
Skillens, John E. "Revisionism and Renaissance Poets." *Christian Scholar's Review* 18 (1988): 81–86.
Soskice, Janet Martin. *Metaphor and Religious Language*. Oxford: Clarendon Press, 1985.
Spearing, A. C. *The Gawain-Poet: A Critical Study*. Cambridge: Cambridge University Press, 1968.
Staudt, Kathleen Henderson. "The Text as Material and Sign: Poetry and Incarnation in William Blake, Arthur Rimbaud, and David Jones." *Modern Language Studies* 14 (1984): 13–30.
Stein, Arnold. *George Herbert's Lyrics*. Baltimore: Johns Hopkins University Press, 1968.
Stevens, Wallace. *The Collected Poems of Wallace Stevens*. New York: Alfred A. Knopf, 1954.
Summers, Joseph. *George Herbert: His Religion and Art*. Cambridge, Mass.: Harvard University Press, 1954.
Tannenbaum, Leslie. *Biblical Tradition in Blake's Early Prophecies: The Great Code of Art*. Princeton, N.J.: Princeton University Press, 1982.
Taylor, Mark. *The Soul in Paraphrase: George Herbert's Poetics*. The Hague: Mouton, 1974.
Thomas, Lewis. *Lives of a Cell: Notes of a Biology Watcher*. New York: Viking Press, 1974.
Thompson, E. P. *The Making of the English Working Class*. 1963. Reprint. New York: Vintage, 1966.
Thorburn, David, and Geoffrey Hartman, eds. *Romanticism: Vistas, Instances, Continuities*. Ithaca, N.Y.: Cornell University Press, 1973.
Tillich, Paul. *Dynamics of Faith*. New York: Harper Colophon Books, 1957.
Todd, Richard. *The Opacity of Signs: Acts of Interpretation in George Herbert's The Temple*. Columbia: University of Missouri Press, 1986.
Todorov, Tzvetan. *Theories of the Symbol*. Ithaca, N.Y.: Cornell University Press, 1982.
Tolliver, Harold. "Herbert's Interim and Final Places." *Studies in English Literature* 24 (1984): 105–20.
Tompkins, Jane P. *Reader-Response Criticism: From Formalism to Post-Structuralism*. Baltimore: Johns Hopkins University Press, 1980.

Turbayne, Colin. *The Myth of Metaphor*. 1962. Reprint. Columbia: University of South Carolina Press, 1970.

Tuve, Rosemund. *A Reading of George Herbert*. London: Faber and Faber, 1952.

Vance, Eugene. "Saint Augustine: Language as Temporality." In *Mimesis*. Ed. John D. Lyons and Stephen G. Nichols, Jr. Hanover, N.H.: University Press of New England, 1982, 20–35.

Vendler, Helen. *The Poetry of George Herbert*. Cambridge, Mass.: Harvard University Press, 1975.

Via, Dan. *The Parables*. Philadelphia: Fortress Press, 1967.

Watts, Ann Chalmers. "*Pearl*, Inexpressibility, and Poems of Human Loss." *PMLA* 99 (1984): 26–40.

Wilson, Edward. "Word Play and the Interpretation of *Pearl*." *Medium Ævum* 40 (1971): 116–34.

Yanagi, Soetsu. *The Unknown Craftsman: A Japanese Insight into Beauty*. Adapted by Bernard Leach. New York: Kodansha International Ltd., 1972.

Zukav, Gary. *The Dancing Wu Li Masters: An Overview of the New Physics*. New York: William Morrow, 1979.

Index

Adams, Hazard, 21n, 24n, 142n, 145n, 151n, 163n, 169n
Agee, Joel, 198n
Allegory, 147, 156n, 173
Altizer, Thomas J. J., 5, 7
Andrew, Malcolm, 29n, 57, 62n
Andrewes, Lancelot, 87n
Aristotle, 15n
Asals, Heather A. R., 81n, 82, 107n
Athanasius, 66n
Auerbach, Erich, 49, 51–52n, 55n, 85
Augustine, Saint, 14–16, 21, 24n, 62n, 74, 76, 79, 93, 107–8, 111–13, 115–18, 121, 124–25, 141n, 177–79, 181, 190
Ault, Donald, 171
Auster, Paul, 190

Babel, 6, 8, 70, 75, 86, 100, 169, 173
Becker, Ernst, 17n
Beckett, Samuel, 25
Bentley, G. E., 130n
Berman, Morris, 4n
Berry, Wendell, 194–95, 198–99
Blake, Catherine, 157
Blake, William, 2, 8, 20, *123–176*, 183–85, 187, 189–90, 192–95, 197–202
  Topics: Albion, 126, 151, 154, 169–71, 187, 202; building, 151, 157, 169–70; Covering Cherub, 165; dream, 154–57; economy, 158–59; Enitharmon, 157, 165; eucharist, 23, 168; figurative/literal language, 126, 131–33, 136, 139, 141–46; forgiveness, 130, 153, 158; garment, 131–37; Golgonooza, 140–41n; imagination, 144, 152–53; incarnation, 21, 23–24, 32, 42, 59; Jerusalem (city/woman), 131–32, 134–36, 148, 150, 153, 165, 169; Jesus, 129–30, 133–36, 151, 153, 160, 169, 171–72; kingdom (of heaven), 124, 126, 129, 152; labor, 125, 126, 144, 151, 159–61, 165–67, 174, 194, 199, 201; Los, 126, 140–41, 145–46, 148–51, 156–58, 161–63, 164–66, 170, 176; metaphor, 126, 128–130, 132–33, 141–46, 158–60, 164, 170–76; nature, 129n, 131, 195n; sacrifice, 125–26, 168–69; Selfhood, 12, 168; Spectre, 162; system, 162–63; Urizen, 145–46, 149–51, 165, 175–76
  Works: *All Religions Are One*, 130; *The Book of Urizen*, 201; *Europe*, 156n, 173; *The Four Zoas*, 130, 156, 161, 175; *Jerusalem*, 16, 109, 121, 126–27, 130–38, 140, 150–76, 202; *Laocoon*, 131, 136n, 152; "London," 170n; *The Marriage of Heaven and Hell*, 128, 145–46, 187, 189; *Milton*, 130–31, 133, 138–40, 154, 161; *Song of Los*, 156n; *There Is No Natural Religion*, 127; "A Vision of the Last Judgement," 23–24, 129, 133, 140, 151n, 153, 156n, 173
Blenkner, Louis, 59n
Bloch, Chara, 119–20n
Body, 3–8, 17–18, 20, 30, 118, 126, 136; as a temple, 12
Bohm, David, 20n
Bonaventura, Saint, 28, 36n, 48, 51
Borroff, Marie, 63–64
Bracher, Mark, 129n, 173n
Building, 2, 6–7, 9, 12, 15, 24–25. *See also* under Blake, Herbert, and *Pearl*, building

Burgesse, Robert, 87

Carse, James, 183n
Chagall, Marc, 191
Chang, Chung-yuan, 9
Charles, Amy, 74n
Coleridge, Samuel Taylor, 137–38, 172
Collins, A. S., 157n
Copleston, Frederick, 188n
Corngold, Stanley, 17–18n, 148n
Countryman, L. William, 14n
Crawford, John R., 36

Damrosch, Leopold, 132, 139–41
Dante, 21, 33, 48, 112, 124–25
Davenport, W. A., 31n, 35n, 37, 52n, 53, 55n
De Man, Paul, 21–22, 26, 141n, 147–49, 187–88
Derrida, Jacques, 4, 17n, 22, 25, 137, 141n, 147–49
Descartes, René, 4
Dodd, C. H., 54, 62, 113
Donne, John, 119
Donner, Michael, 197
Dougherty, James, 13
Dualism, 3–4, 7, 14, 17–18, 30, 41, 118–19, 126, 179n
Dunne, John S., 121

Eaves, Morris, 127n
Ebeling, Gerhard, 123n
Edwards, Jonathon, 183n
Eliot, T. S., 63n, 119, 179
Ellul, Jacques, 14n
Emert, Joyce Rogers, 28n, 33n, 49, 55n, 66n
Endicott, Annabel M., 87n
Erdman, David V., 127n, 158, 189n
Eucharist, 5, 12, 14, 29, 185. *See also* under Blake, Herbert, *Pearl*, eucharist. *See also* Sacrament

Faur, José, 25, 199–200
Ferber, Michael, 157n
Ferguson, Margaret W., 15n, 125
Field, Rosalind, 63n
Figura, 49
Figurative language, 2–3, 18–20, 45, 49, 58–59, 69, 126, 131–33, 136, 139, 141–46, 188. *See also* under Blake, *Pearl*, figurative language
Finkelstein, David, 18–20
Fischer, Michael, 127n
Fish, Stanley, 78n, 81n, 83n, 84n, 87n, 89n, 134
Forché, Carolyn, 193
Foucault, Michel, 16–18
Freccero, John, 15n, 33
Frosch, Thomas R., 127n, 140–41n, 144, 164
Frye, Northrop, 11n, 128, 129n, 131n, 150n
Funk, Robert, 10, 31, 55, 62, 64, 86, 123

Gadamer, Hans-Georg, 4
Gatta, John, 27n, 29n, 49n, 63n, 66n, 69n
Gleckner, Robert, 131n, 134n, 153n
Gordon, E. V., 45, 48n, 51n, 53, 54

Halewood, William, 84n, 85, 100n
Hamlin, Cyrus, 153n
Handelman, Susan, 3–4, 25n, 146–47n, 179n
Happel, Stephen, 24n, 93n, 106n, 142n, 149–50, 185–86
Harman, Barbara, 78n, 79–80, 83n, 89n, 91n, 92, 99n, 100–101n
Harries, Karsten, 21
Harris, Victor, 173–74n
Hart, Ray, 133–34, 137, 138n, 172–74
Hawkins, Peter S., 28n
Heisenberg, Werner, 188–89
Herbert, George, 2, 21, 32, 73–122, 123–25, 126, 140, 145, 151, 156–57, 167, 175, 184–86, 202
  Topics: building, 78–80, 83–87, 89–90, 94, 99–100, 102, 104–6, 112–15, 121–22; eucharist, 15, 23, 75, 89, 119–20, 186; kingdom (of heaven), 80, 85, 88, 92, 119; labor, 84–89, 101–2, 115–19; reader in *The Temple*, 82, 84, 93–94, 104–6, 119; "rest" in *The Temple*, 87, 92, 102–3; sacrifice, 73, 75–77, 81, 83–84, 87, 102, 109, 112–14, 115, 119, 121; "sweetness" in *The Temple*, 102, 106–8, 113
  Works: "Affliction (I)," 73, 90–92,

Index 217

94, 97; "Affliction (IV)," 121–22; "The Altar," 81–85; "A Priest to the Temple," 77–78; "Artillerie," 80n; "The Banquet," 89; "Church Rents," 112; "The Collar," 87, 92, 94, 101; "Deniall," 87, 97–99, 104, 106; "Easter Wings," 104–7; "Employment (II)," 99; "Forerunners," 112–13; "Giddinesse," 86; "Grief," 104; "Heaven," 112, 113; "The Holdfast," 99–101; "Jordan (II)," 101–2, 111n; "Love (III)," 15–17, 81, 113–15; "Love Unknown," 83, 86, 114; "Mattens," 108–110; "Paradise," 103–4; "The Pearl," 94–97, 98; "The Pilgrimage," 80, 98–99; "Prayer (I)," 107, 119; "The Pulley," 112; "Quidditie," 110–11; "The Rose," 111–13; "Sion," 120–21; "Temper," 80n, 84
Herrstrom, David, 24n
Heschel, Abraham, 202
Hill, Christopher, 74n
Hill, John, 28n
Hillman, James, 156n, 192n, 195
Hilton, Nelson, 136, 159
Hugh of St. Victor, 66–67
Hutchinson, F. E., 76n, 110n

James, David E., 136n
Jerusalem, 9, 13–14, 24, 41, 48, 64, 178, 183, 191, 194. *See also* Blake, William; Kingdom; New earth
John, Saint, 123, 126, 133
Johnson, Mark, 4n
Jung, Carl, 63n, 168n
Jungmann, Joseph A., 34, 62n, 64n, 66n

Kandinsky, Wassily, 189, 191
Kant, Immanuel, 144n, 146
Kawin, Bruce, 25n
Kean, P. M., 38n
Keats, John, 22, 148
Kerrigan, William, 74–75
Kingdom (of heaven), 2, 6, 9–11, 13–15, 18, 26, 123, 180–86; *See also*

under Blake, Herbert, *Pearl*, kingdom. *See also* New earth, Jerusalem
Klauser, Theodore, 64n
Klee, Paul, 191

Krieger, Murray, 22, 26, 77, 142n, 147–48
Kristeva, Julia, 16n, 191, 195–96

Labor, 5–9, 12, 17–18, 125, 179, 194, 196–97, 199, 201. *See also under* Blake, Herbert, *Pearl*, labor
Lacan, Jacques, 17n
Lane, Beldan, 185n
Language, 4, 8, 14–15, 18–20, 42, 45, 75–77, 79, 81n, 87n, 115–18, 125–26, 177–79. *See also* Figurative language; Metaphor; "Visible language"
Larson, Kay, 19n
Last Supper. *See* Eucharist
Leahy, D. G., 5–6
Levertov, Denise, 177
Lewalski, Barbara, 87n, 90n, 94
Literal, 11, 30, 39, 69, 181. *See also* Figurative language
Lopez, Barry, 193–94
Lussier, Mark, 137n
Luttrell, C. A., 38–39n

Macrae-Gibson, O. D., 40n
Martin, F. David, 31n, 36n, 67n
Martz, Louis, 100n
Marx, Karl, 161n
Mass. *See* Eucharist
Mazzeo, Joseph A., 74, 92, 93, 121n
McCanles, Michael, 49n, 60n, 174n, 181n
McCloskey, Mark, 75n
McClung, William A., 9, 33n
McFague, Sallie, 180–83, 186n
Merton, Thomas, 8, 27
Metaphor. 1–2, 4–6, 11–13, 15, 17, 20–26, 74, 79, 82, 87, 106n, 123, 125, 180–89, 193, 195, 196, 202. *See also* Figurative language
Midrash, 25
Miller, Dan, 134–36
Miller, Perry, 183n
Milroy, James, 27n, 50n
Mitchell, Stephen, 198n

Mitchell, W. J. T., 127n, 137n
Mondrian, Piet, 189–91
Moskal, Jeanne, 130n
Mukarovsky, Jan, 16n
Munch, Edvard, 191
Murphy, Paul R., 75
Muscatine, Charles, 31n, 35

Nasr, Seyyed Hossein, 8
Nelson, Cary, 28n, 31n, 35–36, 58n, 59, 60, 63n, 67–68, 71
New earth, 6, 68, 84, 88, 103, 126, 183. *See also* Kingdom (of heaven), Jerusalem
Nolan, Barbara, 27n, 33, 35–36, 39, 42n
Nuttall, A. D., 87, 100n

Otto, Rudolf, 51–52n

Pahlka, William H., 75n, 76n, 87n, 88n, 107n, 116–17, 119n
Parable (New Testament), 2–3, 10–11, 28, 54–55, 62–64, 70, 77, 85–86, 106n, 123, 152, 180, 181–84, 192. *See also* under *Pearl,* parable
Patrick, J. Max, 105
Patrides, C. A. 96, 104n, 110n, 119n
Paul, Saint, 14, 32, 77–78, 124–25, 184
Paz, Octavio, 1
Pearl, 2, 16, 21, 27–72, 73–74, 81, 85, 89, 91, 97, 101–2, 107, 121, 123, 125, 140, 145, 151, 156–57, 167, 175, 184–86, 202
  Topics in: building, 76, 78; "courtesy" ("courtayse"), 52–53, 55, 57, 59; dreamer/narrator, 32–36; eucharist, 23, 35–37, 61–66, 69, 71; figurative language, 30, 45, 50–51, 58–61, 71; labor, 63, 65, 69–71; use of link words, 35, 40–41, 45, 50; "New Jerusalem" (or Kingdom of heaven), 31, 33–35, 42, 49, 54, 56–59, 63–65, 68–72; parables used, 54–55, 63–64, 70; the pearl, 46–48, 57–59, 64–65, 67, 70–71; the reader in, 33, 41–42, 68–69; sacrifice, 62–65, 71; "spot," 40–44
Perrin, Norman, 10n

Pettit, Norman, 84n
Petroff, Elizabeth, 39n
Philo, 3
Piers Plowman, 125, 131
Plato, 4, 15n, 199–200
Powers, David, 106n
Powers, Joseph M., 34n, 62n, 64n
Punter, David, 161
Pynchon, Thomas, 189n

Ragland-Sullivan, Ellie, 17n
Rahner, Karl, 2, 12n, 116n, 117n, 118–19n
Reich, Steve, 190
Richards, M. C., 200
Ricoeur, Paul, 2, 4, 10–11, 21–22, 26, 28, 74, 79–80, 106n, 124, 140–45, 149, 153n, 180, 184, 186n
Rilke, Rainier, 9–10, 197–98
Robinson, Crabb, 130
Rothko, Mark, 191
Roudiez, Leon, 16–17
Rubey, Daniel, 87
Rumi, Jalaluddin, 123

Sacrament, 13, 33, 35, 41, 66, 75, 113–16, 124, 167–68, 175, 181, 194. *See also* Eucharist
Sacrifice (of self), 5–6, 9, 12, 15, 18, 178, 196, 198. *See also* under Blake, Herbert, *Pearl,* sacrifice.
Schotter, Anne Howland, 28n
Schwartz, Rudolf, 69–72, 76, 79, 84, 107, 115, 121
Shakespeare, William, 114
Shaw, Robert B. 117
Shelley, Percy, 133, 139
Silence, 74, 92, 183–84, 190–91
Sir Gawain and the Green Knight, 27, 34n, 49, 55n, 69
Skillen, John E., 76n
Soskice, Janet Martin, 142n
Spearing, A. C., 31–32, 34–37, 52n
Staudt, Kathleen Henderson, 16n
Stein, Arnold, 78n
Stevens, Wallace, 139, 187
Summers, Joseph M., 83n

Tannenbaum, Leslie, 134n, 156
Taylor, Mark, 98, 100n, 111n
Temple, 12–14, 16, 21, 23, 102, 123,

124, 173, 178, 201–2; poem as, 78–79, 81
The Temple. *See* Herbert, George
Thomas, Lewis, 195
Thompson, E. P., 36n, 156n
Tillich, Paul, 36n, 182n, 186n
Todd, Richard, 76n
Todorov, Tzevetan, 2, 178–79n
Tolliver, Harold, 78–79
Tracy, David, 10–11
Turbayne, Colin, 146–47
Tuve, Rosamund, 83n

Vance, Eugene, 115–16, 118
Vendler, Helen, 78n

Via, Dan, 55
"Visible language," 15–18, 20–21, 74, 105, 127n, 133, 152, 173, 191–92
Vogler, Thomas, 194

Waldron, Ronald, 29n, 57, 62n
Watts, Ann Chalmers, 42n
Wilson, Edward, 38n, 39
Wordsworth, William, 139
Work. *See* Labor.

Yanagi, Soetsu, 7–8
Yeats, W. B., 104, 119, 174

Zukav, Gary, 19–20